The Book of the
HALL 4-6-0s
Part Two 5900-5999
By
Ian Sixsmith

5932 HAYDON HALL standing on Chargeman Stan Lewington's 'Finishing Off' Gang in Swindon's 'AE' Shop, 6 June 1962. Its overhaul nearing completion, it will shortly be re-painted before being traversed out of the Shop and moved down to the turntable area, to be coupled up to a tender. County 1019 has already been repainted and the Castle behind 5932 should be completed during the next couple of days. ColourRail

Irwell Press Ltd.

Copyright IRWELL PRESS LIMITED
ISBN 978-1-906919-89-4
First published in the United Kingdom in 2016
by Irwell Press Limited, 59A, High Street, Clophill,
Bedfordshire MK45 4BE
Printed by Akcent Media, UK

Acknowledgements

Thanks to Richard Derry who, as declared a number of times before, might well merit an Engine History Card incorporated into his family coat of arms. If he had one. Richard arranged the tables from the various GW/WR records as extracted from the National Archive by Dave Walker, marrying them to latter-day published records. Special thanks also to Eric Youldon, Nick Deacon, Brian Penney, Edward Chaplin, Tony Wright, Michael Back, Peter Coster and Brian Bailey.

Contents

Introduction Saintly Origins   Page 5
Engine Histories   Page 26

Lined black 5947 SAINT BENET'S HALL AT Oxford on 13 September 1956; Hawksworth tender. It has the first emblem and this will be pointed out occasionally through the book, even though the chronology of Hall livery developments meant that a Hall in lined black – as here – couldn't have the second emblem. M. Robertson, transporttreasury

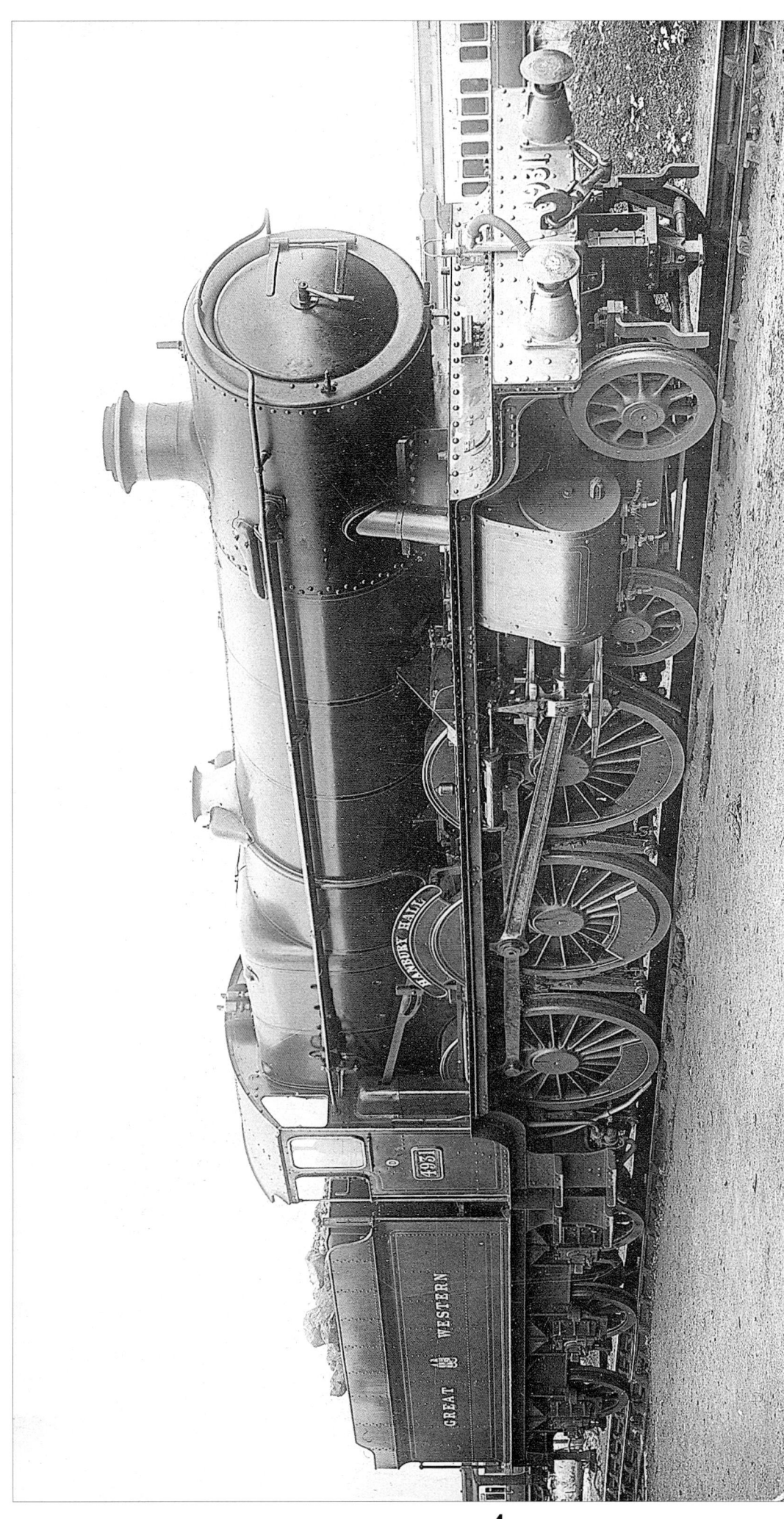

A new Hall, in original state; 4931 HANBURY HALL in lined dark green, with the 'intermediate' 3,500 gallon tender. The date is not known but 4931 had this tender from new in June 1929 until September 1932. The sharpness and clarity of an early glass plate effort such as this shows up well the four feed oil box on the curved section of the running plate. It fed oil to the tops of the bogie axleboxes from where it was channelled to lubricate the horn faces. As well as this oil 'pot' under the smokebox there were others, in the rocker shaft covers – by that plate projecting from the boiler to the running plate. The small upright object, like an oil bottle on the running plate in the middle of the forward splasher is the 'class B' vacuum pump lubricator. It supplied oil to the vacuum pump cylinder to lubricate the pump piston. The ATC shoe assembly is clearly seen, also the conduit for the ATC cable attached to the valence of the platform to the cab. Note the valve for the steam lance for cleaning the tubes, on the smokebox door rim. There is no lubricating oil pipe running down the smokebox from the oil lubricator cover above the hand rail on the smokebox; early on these seem to have been run inside the smokebox, where they would be vulnerable to damage and corrosion.

4

Introduction
SAINTLY ORIGINS

THE SERIES
There were well over three hundred Halls built and from 6959 in 1944 the last seventy or so were the much improved 'Modified Halls'. These (6959-6999, 7900-7929) will form the subject of the fourth and final part in this series. Part One was concerned with the first hundred original engines, 4900-4999 and this Part Two moves us on to the second hundred, 5900-5999. Part Three will cover 6900-6958. Much if not all the original notes concerning the origins and development of the Halls applies to all 330 engines and particularly to 4900-4999, 5900-5999 and 6900-6958. So, to repeat the introductory Part One notes in this Part Two or not? A sort of compromise has been arrived at with the notes (necessarily) in essence the same as in Part One but with added photographs, making them more relevant to 5900-5999 than to 4900-4999.

SAINTLY ORIGINS
Of all the vast fleet of British mixed traffic (almost entirely class 5 by BR days) 4-6-0s very few pre-dated the first Hall, 4900 SAINT MARTIN. The North Eastern B16 (before it was called a B16) was earlier but it wasn't quite a mixed traffic jack of all trades of the type that we came to know – like the Black 5s and B1s, say, of which there were well over a thousand. No, the lineage of the British 5MT goes back to that first Hall, a rebuild of an engine which first appeared in 1907. Almost exactly fifty years after this unlikely progenitor was built we had only lately *stopped* building the mixed traffic 4-6-0 – Doncaster's very different-looking but in essence the same 73171. (In an interesting quirk, these were the *only* 4-6-0s ever built at Doncaster). In that very year, 1958, Dr Tuplin in *Great Western Steam* (George Allen & Unwin) wrote: *with the trend in later years to make life gentler for locomotives, Collett introduced the Hall class which is (small details apart) just a Churchward Saint with 6ft wheels and these now do much of the work on which the 2-6-0s were first engaged.*

Dr Tuplin was drawing on his memories when the engines began appearing in numbers, back in 1929-30, *The Railway Gazette* announcing that: *In these days of heavy train loadings on British railways, and particularly where the 'going' is not easy, there is an increasing demand for engines of the 2-6-0 and 4-6-0 classes with coupled wheels so proportioned as to permit of the requisite average speeds, combined with better accelerative and grade-climbing propensities.* It was for just this purpose that Collett had Saint 4-6-0 2925 SAINT MARTIN rebuilt with 6ft wheels. Various minor changes were made to accommodate these but the only other 'new' feature was a side window cab. SAINT MARTIN retained its inside steam pipes. Four years were to pass before the first 'production' Hall – so, for the first years of its existence the class wasn't even called the Halls!

It was a canny way to proceed. The combination of the higher (225lb) boiler pressure of the Saints and smaller coupled wheels in an otherwise standardised engine produced the desired results without planning out an entirely new engine with all the attendant cost of new drawings, patterns, templates, and many other things. This was the practice now being followed on the Great Western Railway, records *The Railway Gazette*: *A new series of engines, to be known as the 'Hall' class has been put in hand at Swindon works, to the sum of 80. The new engines virtually constitute a repetition of the previous 'Saint' class, which, however, had larger coupled wheels and ranked as two-cylinder express locomotives, taking their turn with the four-cylinder classes, except perhaps for the heaviest trains. In the 'Hall' class, the combination of a boiler pressure of 225lb and a smaller diameter of coupled wheel provides those extra tractive and accelerative powers, and the ability to maintain average speeds on up grades, which are so necessary where heavy stopping passenger trains, or those in the intermediate or semi-fast category, have to be dealt with in difficult country, or, for the matter of that, on practically any section of the main and subsidiary line. Comparison of the 'Hall' and 'Saint' classes shows that in the first-named case the tractive effort at 85 per cent of the boiler pressure is 27,275lb as against 24,395lb in the second, and this to a large extent establishes the additional utility of the smaller wheeled engines for the purpose for which they have been designed. They further represent the solution of a problem created by the fact that the 4-4-0 type of engine is no longer able to deal with the traffic conditions mentioned.*

The 43XX and 53XX 2-6-0s played no part in the genesis of the Halls (as they did as 'donors' to the Granges and

A new 4923 EVENLEY HALL; lined dark green, low-sided tender with badge and serif GREAT WESTERN. There was nothing of any special importance in adopting 6ft wheels; it was just the biggest reduction from 6ft 8½in possible within the Saint framework. 5ft 8in (a standard size) would have done just as well – as it did admirably with the Granges some ten years later.

4912 BERRINGTON HALL in the 1930s, at Newton Abbot shed. Front lamp iron on top of smokebox, prominent weld line 18in or so above the running plate, no oil delivery pipes (they're inside the smokebox at this period) from the superheater lubricator cover, single cabside grab iron under the window, no lettering or emblem on tender, which is an 'intermediate' 3,500 gallon type: compare to 4,000 one opposite behind 5934. Tapered, rather than parallel, buffers typical of earlier Halls.

5934 KNELLER HALL at Didcot shed in the 1930s. The front lamp iron is now on the smokebox door, oil delivery pipes now external, and there is a second (vertical) grab iron ahead now of the window. The changes effected in the lamp and grab irons seems to have been effected from about 5921 – see picture of BINGLEY HALL. Later still, the two cabside grab irons were combined in a single iron, L-shaped to match the two separate ones. Strictly speaking, it was only an L shape on the fireman's side; on the driver's side it was a reversed L. 5934 also has a plug cock on the cylinder; it was last seen on 4933 HIMLEY HALL in *Part One*, page 14: *This would appear to be for the purpose of controlling the supply of steam or water with one quick movement of the handle through a 90 deg arc moving the valve from fully open to fully closed. It appears to be connected into the steam chest and may have been used in the recording of steam chest pressures. It is obviously only a temporary fitting and it is surprising that the loco is in normal service with it still fitted. The open end would have a sealing cap to prevent the cock being tampered with, allowing live steam to be discharged over adjacent personnel.* Note the little oil bottle again on the running plate in the middle of the forward splasher on both locos, feeding the 'class B' vacuum pump lubricator.

5986 ARBURY HALL on Hatton bank with a down express in the early post-war period, in a picture interesting for the low-sided tender. The Southern birdcage stock possibly indicates a Hastings-Birkenhead train. Michael Boakes Collection.

An entertaining picture, showing an original Hall being coupled to (or perhaps uncoupled from) a Siphon gangwayed van. The eyes of the lads of course are on the operation itself, but our eyes are on the lubricator feed valve cover (just below the chimney) which for once is OPEN. *transporttreasury*

Manors). Collett communicated to *The Railway Gazette* that SAINT MARTIN was a 'preliminary' to the Halls and 'generally similar' to the Saints with the standard No.1 boiler. SAINT MARTIN now 'virtually conformed to the new standard' and the Halls were 'being specially constructed to take the place of 4-4-0 type engines, which are not able to deal with the long and heavy trains called for under modern conditions.' This was particularly the case with heavy stopping passenger trains and semi-fast express trains over the difficult sections in the West of England.

The Halls went first to London and the West and must have been both a revelation and a revolution on any turns previously handled by 4-4-0s. They seem also to have particularly shone on the Weymouth trains and these serve as an illustration of the mark they made back then – they were not quite yet the sort of '5MT' maids of all work of BR days but rather they were passenger engines first, behind the Castles. Weymouth shed (it had no Castles) worked mile-a-minute trains (over 50-60 mile stretches at least) in the early 1930s using Halls. Other Halls were taking expresses at speeds well into the 80s on the Birmingham line and such performances were being matched all over the GWR. The 'Class 5' as we came to know it was beginning to emerge; a useful second rank express engine that could show a clean pair of heels, which the next day could be on a heavy fitted

The original, the Saint that was now a Hall (from page 25 of Part One). 4900 SAINT MARTIN with 4,000 gallon tender and first emblem, in lined black at Old Oak Common on 4 February 1956. It is from this angle that the most obvious detail difference in this former Saint, compared to the main run of Halls, is possible to see. This was the rather lower pitch of the boiler, for when the engine was rebuilt it was lowered by 4¼ inches – as someone pointed out this was half the difference in the diameters of the old and new wheels. 4900 was very much a hybrid and was, in its technical details, neither Saint nor Hall. When overhauled much of what it came in with it had to go out with. It caused some confusion in Worcester Factory, for instance; though officially a Hall it retained the reversing gear and motion of a Saint and its lower boiler meant that if standard Hall components were fitted the lifting arms of the weighbar shaft hit the boiler before full reverse was obtained; also the valve extension rods were of a different length. Conversely, 4900 parts caused similar trouble if fitting to a Hall was attempted. Those working on 4900 would have been glad to see the back of it and when it was withdrawn it was promptly cut up to make sure no change of mind could intervene, as had happened before. See also Page 20-21. Peter Groom.

5918 WALTON HALL at Oxford in the middle 1950s; the loco is lined black (traces are just visible on the cabside) though the unlined black tender might lately have been on a plain black engine, Grange or 4700, during the period around 1949 when markings were omitted. What makes livery identification difficult at times is when a shed makes a swap without a return to the original locomotive. This could mean that a tender could miss out on a works visit when it would have got a repaint. The result would mean the tender going perhaps five or six years before eventually getting repainted. Consequently that tender could have been observed in a superseded livery but paired with an engine in the latest style. Hence some of the photographs show a combination that defies simple analysis. M. Robertson, transporttreasury

5916 TRINITY HALL at Leebotwood, south of Shrewsbury, in March 1956; lined black with first emblem. D.K. Jones Collection.

5915 TRENTHAM HALL at Bristol Bath Road shed, 28 August 1948. It is on its way back from an Intermediate repair at Swindon, in an odd state; wheels, motion and smokebox have had attention while grimy all-black livery remains untouched, apart from the code PZ for its home shed Penzance, behind the buffer beam. H.C. Casserley, courtesy R.M. Casserley.

5913 RUSHTON HALL outside Swindon Works after overhaul and in lined black, 8 May 1955. The boiler lining famously showed up poorly in certain light in black and white photographs. B.K.B. Green Collection, Initial Photographics.

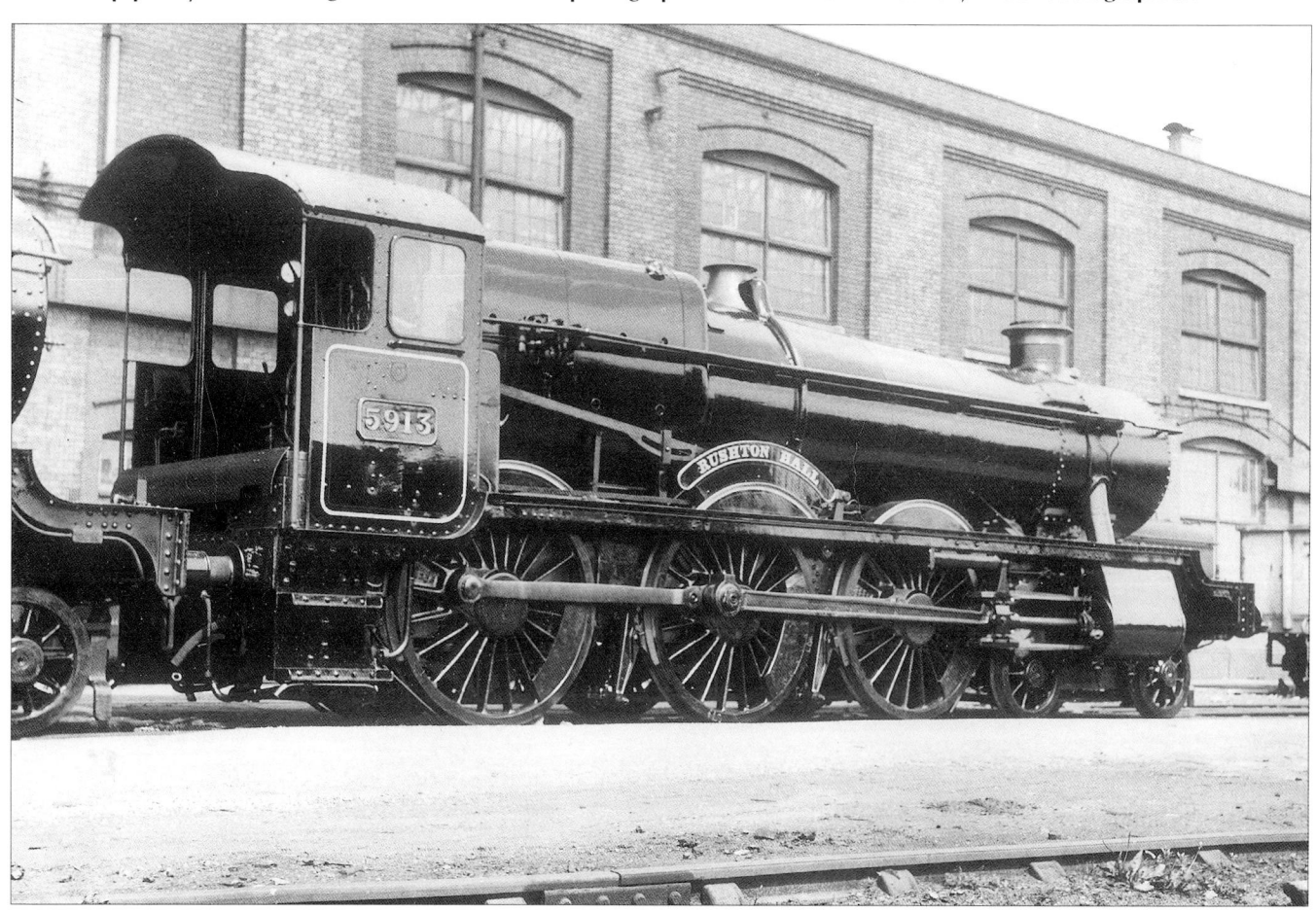

5987 BROCKET HALL, still in plain black with a typical of the period generous coating of grime, at Kingswear on 25 August 1945. It still has the wartime so-called 'anti-glare' blank cabside. H.C. Casserley, courtesy R.M. Casserley.

5989 CRANSLEY HALL with the blanked cab window; as detailed in Part One (repeated here) these were fitted early on; the Chargemens Log Book at Worcester Loco Factory for instance, has the following entries between 7 and 12 September 1939: *Drilling for Flack Screens Engines 6807, 5063, 4092, 5017, 5052, 5983, 4962, 4990, 4958, 4086, 6877.* The 'Flack Screens' were presumably the cab side window blanking plates so maybe they were first envisaged as protection from shrapnel! The work was a concentrated 'campaign' at Running Sheds and Factories during the early weeks of the war. See also 5999 for instance. ColourRail

5908 MORETON HALL finished and ready in typical ex-Factory condition at Swindon, 3 June 1962. It has either just completed its trial run or is about to go on it. It is carrying Class 'A' headlights which is a bit puzzling. RailOnline

5977 BECKFORD HALL during what the Record Card notes as a Heavy Casual overhaul at Wolverhampton Works, on 18 February 1962. It was withdrawn 18 months later. RailOnline

Serif BRITISH RAILWAYS on the tender of 4928 GATACRE HALL at Stourbridge Junction on 10 September 1949. The livery appears to be plain green still. H.C. Casserley, courtesy R.M. Casserley.

How to lift a Hall; 4984 ALBRIGHTON HALL at Chester shed in the late 1930s. The loco is undergoing a typical protracted lift, utilising a hoist, to enable the trailing coupled wheels to be removed. Presumably the loco had suffered a hot axlebox or some other problem with the wheelset. The first operation would have been to remove the bogie, either by lifting the front end with the hoist and running the bogie out, then moving the loco forward, or by positioning the cab end under the hoist and jacking up the front end to release the bogie. The bogie is standing clear, in front of the loco. The normal practice would then be to support the front buffer beam on a solid bed of wooden baulks and packing and then lift the cab end with the hoist, the whole loco pivoting on the front packing and giving sufficient height at the back end to allow the coupled wheels to be removed. What is unusual in this case is that the front packing appears to have been built up on a rail trolley, which would allow a certain amount of fore and aft movement when the back end was being lifted. Because the loco pivots about the front packing during the lift, the back end follows an arc during the lift which pulls the lifting cables away from the vertical position. The free movement allowed by the trolley will centralise the back end under the hoist, thus keeping the cables vertical. It was the same method used in rerailing operations where the wheels of the derailed loco that are on the track are allowed free movement to keep the crane cables vertical during the lift. If it is required to move 4984 off the hoist before the wheels can be refitted, it is probable that the dummy wheels alongside the loco will be placed in the trailing horn gap, suitably packed, to support the back end during the move.

everyone else, generally allocated new engines by the traditional 'half dozen') had twelve and six respectively which meant that there was something of a concentration of Halls in the London Division. Their greatest effect must have been felt in Devon and Cornwall, with twenty or more stationed at Newton Abbot, Laira, Truro and Penzance. A sure-footed 4-6-0 with modest wheels (the Granges coming later with 5ft 8in wheels were even more effective) must have radically improved the running of trains in Cornwall. Such an engine had to be capable of leaving in the morning with a fast passenger train and returning in the afternoon with fish vans for London or the West Midlands, putting a three coach local under its belt in between. The GWR, and the WR in turn, in steam days treated the section west of Plymouth more or less as a separate entity.

TENDERS
4900 SAINT MARTIN and the first production batch of eighty, 4901-4980 had the low-sided 3,500 gallon tenders; the first forty-odd mostly got older ones, the next half of the batch the later ones in the series spanning Churchward and Collett's time, from the 1900s to the early 1920s. They were thus not by any means so elderly as, say, the tenders fitted to the Granges a few years later. The twenty-six higher 3,500 gallon tenders built under Collett, 2242-2268 and familiar from the Granges, all ran with Halls at first. At first glance they look like the later familiar 4000 gallon (6 ton) type that ran behind nearly all the 4-6-0s (bar the Manors) in later years but they were only of 3,500 gallon and 5½ tons capacity. The clue to recognition is the same as for the Granges: what on the Southern, say, would be called the 'rave' ('fender' seems to have been in use with respect to GWR tenders) was lower and when coupled to a 'Grange', the rave top is in line with the middle of the cab windows, making it obvious.

The familiar high-sided Collett 4,000 gallon tenders became 'standard issue' with 5901 but a few Halls, almost all in the 4900 series, still had the low tenders even in 1948. The last of the 3,500 higher sided ones seem to have gone from the Halls by about 1947.

The new Hawksworth straight sided 4,000 gallon 6 ton capacity tenders made their appearance with 6971. All the 4,000 gallon tenders could appear on almost any engine. It is worth noting that only the thirty Hawksworth tenders for the Counties were 7 tons capacity; Hawksworth tenders built primarily for Castles and Halls were *six* tons and they were narrower than the County version.

HALL LIVERY
Going back to the 4900s, the Halls got the lined GW dark green as arrived at in the 1920s; this was officially 'middle chrome' and something akin to what in BR times we called 'Great Western Green' or, erroneously, 'Brunswick Green'. Lining was black and orange (black centre lining and two outer thin orange lines) with GREAT WESTERN on the tender, either side of the coat of arms. This was the 'garter' crest which changed from 1926 to the shields of London and Bristol. This is the livery the first 5900s would have had, but, as ever, a photograph with verified date is necessary for really rigorous modelling accuracy – this will not always be possible, you'd have to fear.

In 1934 the coat of arms and lettering gave way to the art deco roundel or 'shirt button' rather cleverly and pleasingly formed by 'GWR' within a circle.

In 1942 came unlined black – it was called 'wartime black' everywhere else – with a simple G/emblem/W in either block or serif on the tender.

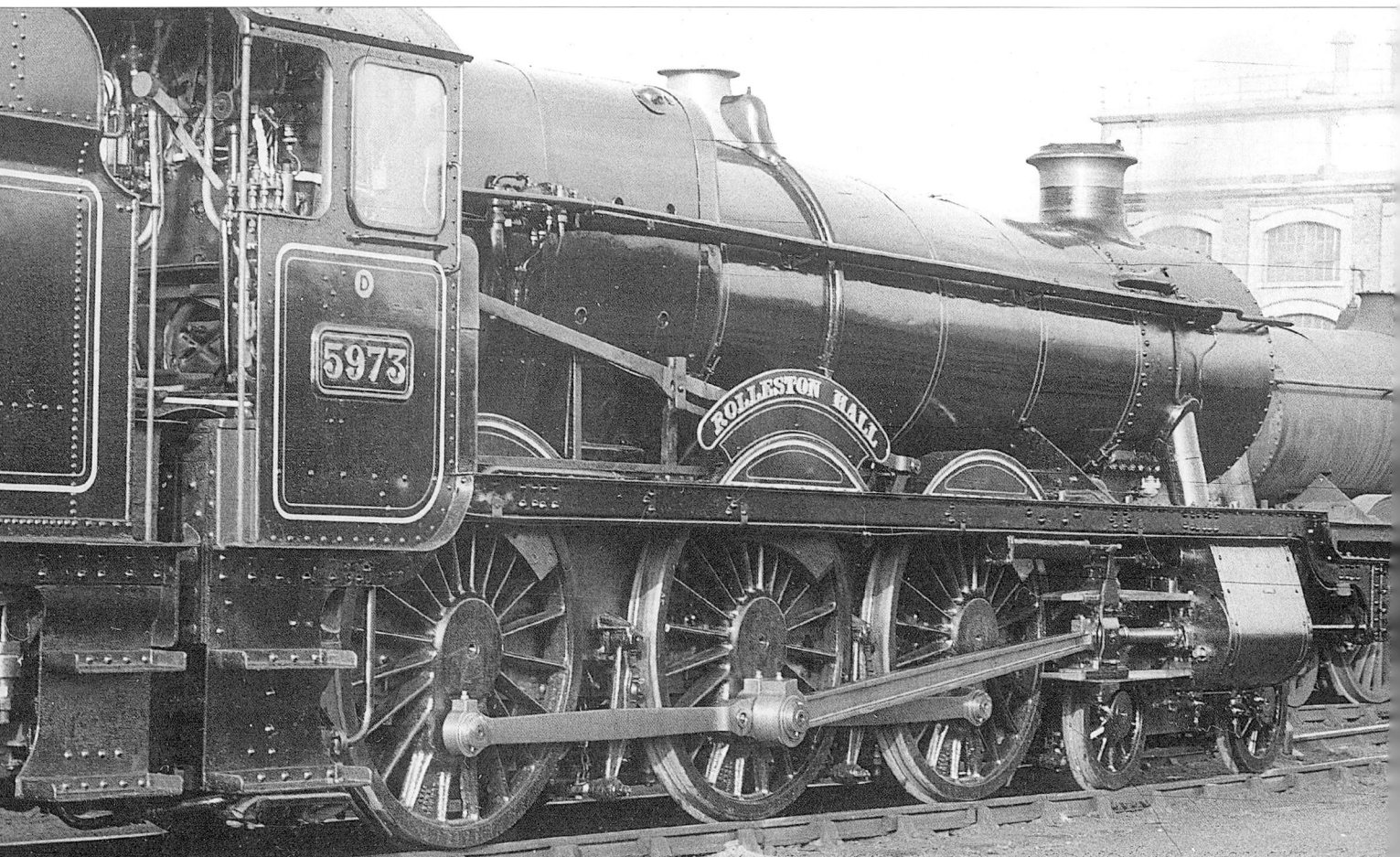

A lovely pristine lined black 5973 ROLLESTON HALL. On the right-hand side of most GWR 4-cylinder and 2-outside cylinder tender locomotives there was this long, prominent pipe behind the hand rail, the 4-cone ejector. As with all Great Western 4-6-0s, there was a lot more going on at the right-hand side than the left. As a matter of interest, the position of the reversing shaft indicates the engine is set for full forward gear.

A lined black 5931 HATHERLEY HALL at Worcester, 10 September 1949; blank tender, twin grab irons by the window by now standard. H.C. Casserley, courtesy R.M. Casserley.

A shabby 5921 BINGLEY HALL in the scruffy surrounds of Stafford Road shed, Wolverhampton, June 1938. With 5921 (see introductory notes) the lamp iron moved to the smokebox door and the extra grab iron appeared ahead of the window. Oil delivery pipe on smokebox still 'hidden'. The fire iron 'tunnel' also appeared – it is on the far side in this view and so not visible. Note tapered buffers. B.K.B. Green Collection, Initial Photographics.

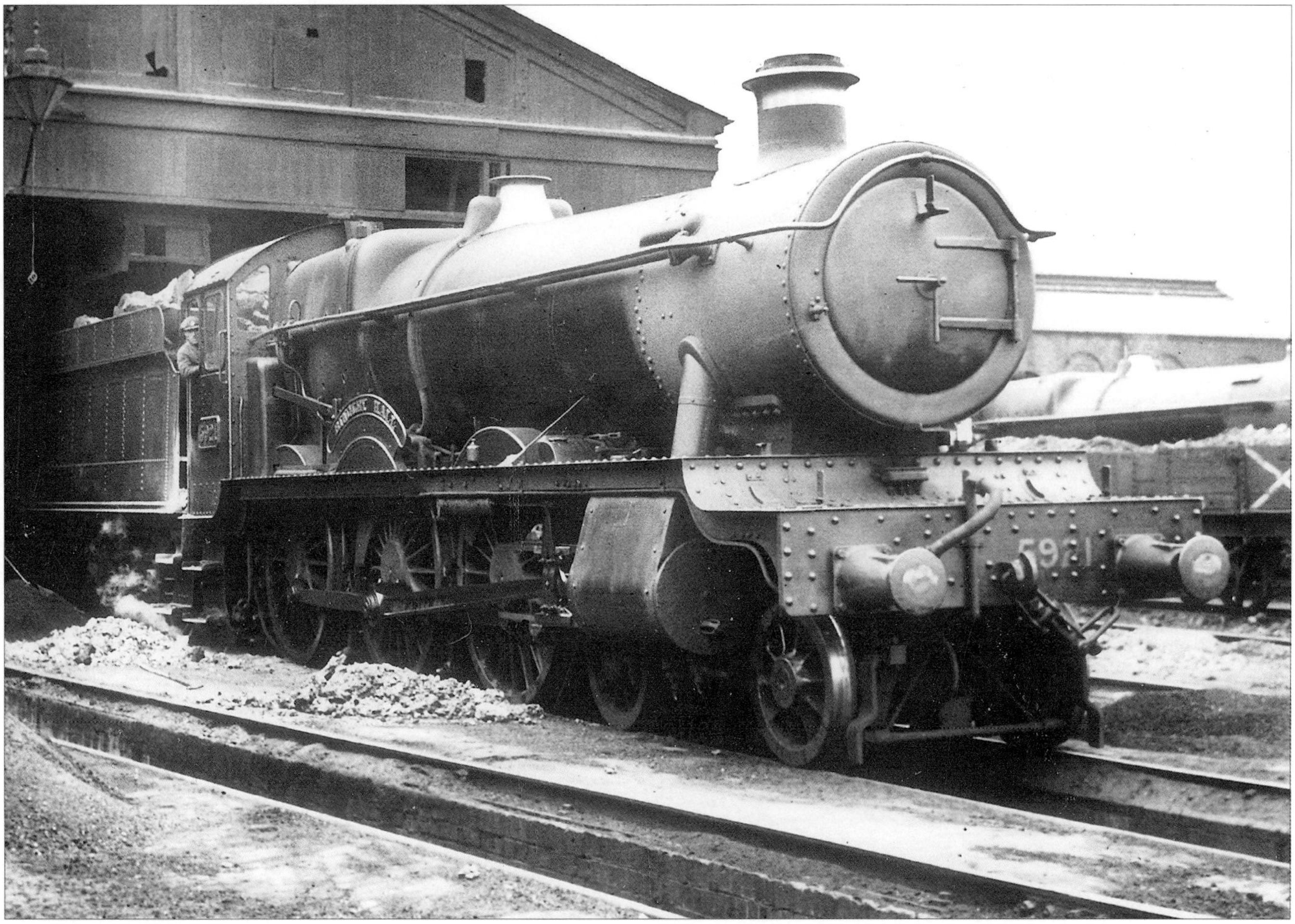

Green coal weighing tender 4127 at Swindon in 1957; similar tender 4128 was black. Both occasionally appeared with Halls. Brian Penney writes: *When the tender (4127) arrived at Worcester I was curious to see how it operated but found that the weighing equipment was in a compartment on top of the tank, securely padlocked. I expressed my disappointment to the fitter I was working with who promptly climbed up and gave the padlock a sharp tap with his hammer. It flew open and we were able to study the weighing mechanism, a not very impressive cantilever scaled with a moveable weight. A quick tap with the hammer and the padlock was closed. 4127 seemed to be the one that was used the most – sometimes appearing even when the loco was in black.*

5927 GUILD HALL with electrification warning-bedecked Hawksworth 4,000 gallon tender, at Tyseley on 18 February 1962. RailOnline

In 1945 plain green was applied with tender lettering unchanged. Modified Halls were lined out from 6974, new in October 1947. Original Halls were occasionally lined in 1948, the first being 4946 on 16 January.

In July 1948 5954 and 6910 were experimentally decked out in lined black with BRITISH RAILWAYS in plain lettering. In the case of 6910 this was soon replaced by the future lion-and-wheel emblem, hand painted. Transfers were not available until July 1949 by which time lined black without emblem (or lettering) had been applied for around nine months.

Lined black became standard for all Halls from about the time that 6991 was built in November 1948.

In 1956 lined black officially changed to lined green, with lining on the cylinder covers too, though 6997 was observed as early as 8 September 1955 'being painted green'. 'All 4-6-0s' were to have the lined dark green though some Halls apparently had managed to acquire it already. The second emblem came in 1957 after being exhibited in 1956 on Britannia 70016 ARIEL.

As an aside, 6990 NEVER received the lined black; it retained its 1948 lined green until the later period of lined green – seven years!

WAR

The most remarkable thing about wartime developments in the Halls was perhaps their continued construction. This went on uninterrupted through 1939 to the end of 1944, only to pause (for the Counties and new Castles) before resuming in 1947. In the meantime, the Modified Halls were introduced – see Part Four – with seamless continuity. The only difference was that most of the wartime engines were turned out with blank cab sides as a blackout precaution; the last would have been 6970. All side window classes were altered thus (or were supposed to have been) and the process appears to have been fairly rapid. In the first weeks of 1940 numbers of earlier Halls were noted so dealt with (the work was presumably done at sheds) while 5989 for instance (new in December 1939) was noted as 'built without side windows'. Most if not all of the other Halls had the window blanked out at some time and all were put back in order over the years from the end of the war to 1947-48. In fact the only engines *built* without side windows were 2251 0-6-0s and 6900 series Halls; a number of the former were still to be seen in this condition in the very early 1950s but the 69XXs seem to have been dealt with more expeditiously.

The wartime-built Halls, from 6916, did not carry names (it would have appeared wasteful to the public, it was felt) at first but instead had HALL CLASS painted on the splasher. The name plates were fixed as and when convenient from 1946 through to 1948. Most momentously, one Hall, 4911, was destroyed by enemy action. This was statistically unusual, and locos in this country had to be all but destroyed to warrant scrapping rather than repair/replacement. The unfortunate BOWDEN HALL received a direct hit at Keyham, Plymouth, in April 1941. This was perhaps the worst month for Plymouth when at least five intense night attacks took place. The mortal remains were moved to Swindon and eventually scrapped

CHIMNEYS

Later engines (and the Granges) had a shorter chimney though it needs the eye

The Great Western built two eight wheel tenders, one for THE GREAT BEAR and this conventional one, No.2586, here attached to 5957 HUTTON HALL, at Didcot (with red-backed plates) on 22 August 1951. The wheels were smaller than standard. It had been behind a Castle for a while but so far as Halls were concerned in ran in succession behind 5919, 6951, 4918, 5957, 6912 and 6905 before being withdrawn with 5904 in November 1963.

19

31 August 1950

5900 Westbury	5934 Swindon	5968 Weymouth
5901 Reading	5935 Didcot	5969 Penzance
5902 Exeter	5936 Old Oak	5970 Canton
5903 Didcot	5937 Old Oak	5971 Westbury
5904 Oxford	5938 Old Oak	5972 Carmarthen
5905 Goodwick	5939 Old Oak	5973 Reading
5906 Ebbw Junction	5940 Old Oak	5974 Westbury
5907 Tyseley	5941 Old Oak	5975 Pontypool Road
5908 Goodwick	5942 Stafford Road	5976 Exeter
5909 Tyseley	5943 Oxford	5977 Canton
5910 Canton	5944 Stafford Road	5978 Weymouth
5911 Ebbw Junction	5945 Oxley	5979 Reading
5912 Chester	5946 Canton	5980 Gloucester
5913 Landore	5947 Old Oak	5981 Shrewsbury
5914 Worcester	5948 Reading	5982 St Philips Marsh
5915 Penzance	5949 St Philips Marsh	5983 Southall
5916 Tyseley	5950 Tyseley	5984 Carmarthen
5917 Worcester	5951 Gloucester	5985 Westbury
5918 Old Oak	5952 Old Oak	5986 Old Oak
5919 St Philips Marsh	5953 Canton	5987 Old Oak
5920 Newton Abbot	5954 Leamington	5988 Gloucester
5921 Oxley	5955 Llanelly	5989 Southall
5922 Swindon	5956 Reading	5990 Gloucester
5923 Chester	5957 Reading	5991 Oxley
5924 Westbury	5958 Canton	5992 St Philips Marsh
5925 Westbury	5959 Reading	5993 Tyseley
5926 St Blazey	5960 Oxford	5994 Shrewsbury
5927 Tyseley	5961 Westbury	5995 Stafford Road
5928 Goodwick	5962 Old Oak	5996 Old Oak
5929 Landore	5963 Carmarthen	5997 Tyseley
5930 Banbury	5964 Laira	5998 Carmarthen
5931 Old Oak	5965 Oxford	5999 Taunton
5932 Old Oak	5966 Chester	
5933 Reading	5967 Banbury	

21 March 1959

5900 Stafford Road	5934 Penzance	5968 Shrewsbury
5901 Reading	5935 St Philips Marsh	5969 St Philips Marsh
5902 Llanelly	5936 Old Oak	5970 Canton
5903 Neyland	5937 Carmarthen	5971 Worcester
5904 St Philips Marsh	5938 Carmarthen	5972 Laira
5905 Goodwick	5939 Old Oak	5973 Reading
5906 Reading	5940 Old Oak	5974 Westbury
5907 Reading	5941 Old Oak	5975 Westbury
5908 Goodwick	5942 Reading	5976 Old Oak
5909 Llanelly	5943 Didcot	5977 Reading
5910 Canton	5944 Oxley	5978 Swindon
5911 Canton	5945 Westbury	5979 Reading
5912 Tyseley	5946 Canton	5980 Worcester
5913 Landore	5947 Banbury	5981 Swindon
5914 Gloucester	5948 Pontypool Road	5982 Reading
5915 Reading	5949 Bath Road	5983 Swindon
5916 Oxley	5950 Bath Road	5984 Worcester
5917 Worcester	5951 Gloucester	5985 Oxley
5918 Southall	5952 Worcester	5986 Swindon
5919 Oxley	5953 Llanelly	5987 Old Oak
5920 Newton Abbot	5954 Old Oak	5988 Landore
5921 Banbury	5955 Landore	5989 Banbury
5922 Swindon	5956 Worcester	5990 Landore
5923 Old Oak	5957 Reading	5991 Oxley
5924 St Philips Marsh	5958 Old Oak	5992 Taunton
5925 Southall	5959 Exeter	5993 Reading
5926 Stafford Road	5960 Oxford	5994 Worcester
5927 Tyseley	5961 Llanelly	5995 Oxley
5928 Goodwick	5962 Oxley	5996 Southall
5929 Old Oak	5963 Westbury	5997 Swindon
5930 Banbury	5964 Swindon	5998 Hereford
5931 Old Oak	5965 Oxley	5999 Taunton
5932 Old Oak	5966 Oxford	
5933 Southall	5967 Newton Abbot	

9 February 1963

5900 St Philips Marsh	5934 St Philips Marsh	5968
5901 Reading	5935	5969
5902	5936 Reading	5970 Hereford
5903 Llanelly	5937 Cardiff East Dock	5971 Southall
5904 St Philips Marsh	5938 Ebbw Junction	5972 Old Oak
5905 Goodwick	5939 Swindon	5973
5906	5940	5974 Westbury
5907	5941	5975 St Philips Marsh
5908 St Philips Marsh	5942 Shrewsbury	5976 Llanelly
5909	5943 Swindon	5977 Reading
5910	5944 Gloucester	5978 Swindon
5911	5945 Oxford	5979 Reading
5912	5946	5980
5913	5947	5981
5914 Reading	5948 Pontypool Road	5982
5915	5949	5983 Tyseley
5916	5950	5984 Old Oak
5917	5951 Gloucester	5985 Southall
5918	5952 Hereford	5986 Westbury
5919 Old Oak	5953	5987 Didcot
5920	5954 St Philips Marsh	5988 Old Oak
5921	5955 Oxford	5989
5922 Oxford	5956 Oxford	5990 Banbury
5923 Oxford	5957 Oxford	5991 Shrewsbury
5924 St Philips Marsh	5958 St Philips Marsh	5992 Taunton
5925	5959	5993 Reading
5926	5960	5994 Shrewsbury
5927 Tyseley	5961 Neath	5995 Oxley
5928	5962 Cardiff East Dock	5996
5929 Southall	5963 St Philips Marsh	5997
5930	5964	5998 Hereford
5931	5965	5999
5932 Southall	5966	
5933 Oxford	5967 Old Oak	

2 November 1963

5900 St Philips Marsh	5934 St Philips Marsh	5968
5901 Reading	5935	5969
5902	5936 Gloucester	5970
5903	5937 Cardiff East Dock	5971 Old Oak
5904 St Philips Marsh	5938	5972 Cardiff East Dock
5905	5939 Ebbw Junction	5973
5906	5940	5974 Westbury
5907	5941	5975 St Philips Marsh
5908	5942 Shrewsbury (LM)	5976 Pontypool Road
5909	5943	5977
5910	5944	5978
5911	5945	5979 Gloucester
5912	5946	5980
5913	5947	5981
5914 Gloucester	5948	5982
5915	5949	5983 Tyseley (LM)
5916	5950	5984 Cardiff East Dock
5917	5951 Gloucester	5985
5918	5952 Hereford	5986
5919	5953	5987 Oxford
5920	5954	5988 Tyseley (LM)
5921	5955 Oxford	5989
5922 Oxford	5956	5990 Banbury (LM)
5923 Oxford	5957 Oxford	5991 Shrewsbury (LM)
5924 St Philips Marsh	5958 St Philips Marsh	5992 Taunton
5925	5959	5993
5926	5960	5994
5927 Tyseley (LM)	5961 Neath	5995
5928	5962 Pontypool Road	5996
5929	5963 St Philips Marsh	5997
5930	5964	5998 Hereford
5931	5965	5999
5932 Reading	5966	
5933 Oxford	5967 Westbury	

12 October 1964

5900	5934	5968
5901	5935	5969
5902	5936 Gloucester	5970
5903	5937	5971 Reading
5904	5938	5972
5905	5939 Ebbw Junction	5973
5906	5940	5974 Severn Tunnel Jct
5907	5941	5975
5908	5942	5976
5909	5943	5977
5910	5944	5978
5911	5945	5979 Worcester
5912	5946	5980
5913	5947	5981
5914	5948	5982
5915	5949	5983 Tyseley (LM)
5916	5950	5984 Cardiff East Dock
5917	5951	5985
5918	5952	5986
5919	5953	5987
5920	5954	5988 Tyseley (LM)
5921	5955 Barrow Road	5989 Banbury (LM)
5922	5956	5990
5923	5957	5991
5924	5958	5992 Westbury
5925	5959	5993
5926	5960	5994
5927 Tyseley (LM)	5961 Neath	5995
5928	5962 Worcester	5996
5929	5963	5997
5930	5964	5998
5931	5965	5999
5932 Severn Tun. Jct	5966	
5933 Oxford	5967	

The converted Saint in service with its original number 2925. See Additional Notes opposite. Note 'reversed' coupling rods (see pages 12-13).

20

of faith to differentiate them; some of us find it impossible. Inevitably shorter chimneys appeared on engines that previously had taller ones and so on. As early as 1939 4963 was observed 'fitted with a short chimney similar to those fitted to later engines of this class.'

A capuchon was the order of the day with the main body of the Halls 4900s through to the 5900s but not so with the later series though it is unwise to try to pronounce upon any thing for a given engine at a given time without photographs. An edition of *The Railway Observer* late in 1953 noted that *Halls 7919, 7924 and 7927 have chimneys without capuchons and of narrower external diameter than others of their series; 7924 and possibly the others, carries a plate to the effect that the chimney and blast pipe have been modified to increase the steaming capacity of the boiler.* This plate was presumably in the cab or by the steps, where other companies put their 'mod plates'.

By 1958 7912 had an 'ID' stencilled on the framing to denote 'Improved Draughting' though it is unclear if this was related to the narrower chimneys on 7919, 7924 and 7927; 6917, 6934 and 6957 were noted at the same time carrying Hawksworth AK boilers 'with narrow (improved draughting) chimneys' which rather suggests it did. What happened with these chimneys is unclear, though one at least, turned up on 6979. They certainly weren't replicated on any scale.

LIGHTS
In 1947 oil burner 3904 (4972) was noted at Swindon works being fitted up with electric headlamps and cab lights, the power obtained from a small generator bolted on the right-hand side of the smokebox. A photograph in the RCTS *Locos of the Great Western Railway* shows cables draped untidily over the smokebox in a way that suggests Swindon was not exactly serious about it. In October 1949 5922 was noted similarly fitted 'with electric headlamps' at Swindon though how long the fitments lasted (not long presumably) is unclear.

Front Lamp Iron
Was originally on the smokebox top but moved to smokebox door on engines constructed from 1933. The existing, earlier locos were so altered over the next few years.

ATC
For years the Automatic Train Control apparatus and its shoe was mounted behind the buffer beam. From the first of the 1933 batch, 5921, it was mounted instead inside the bogie. This meant it moved with the bogie so the final connection had to be by flexible hose, which is visible in plenty of photographs in various looping configurations; seemingly it got out of position as time went by. The Modified Halls that followed had a similar arrangement but it was more obscured, behind the plate front of the new design of bogie. The new ATC arrangement does not seem to have been retrospectively applied to the earlier engines – so the bogies were not interchangeable. Any categorical statement as to this, however, is always risky in the world of engine picking! To accommodate the new ATC arrangement there was also a slight change in the way the ATC conduit was clipped along the valence of the running plate, from the top edge of to the bottom edge.

Fire Iron Tunnel
Appeared on the first of the 1933 batch, 5921.

Cab Windows
It requires the eye of faith somewhat but the front windows appear distinctly narrower after 5975; that is, from 5976 onwards. What other dimensional changes (if any) this might have involved and why is not clear. Once again, if a particular loco is being modelled, then dated photographs are *de rigueur...*

Lubricators
The Halls had sight feed lubricators in the cab, presumably 3-glass at first; from the early 1930s 5-glass would have been used. The oil pipes passed under the boiler lagging on the right-hand side, emerging under the cover on the smokebox.

From 7910 on, a mechanical lubricator was provided on the running plate, right-hand side behind the steam pipe. There was further lubrication at the front; on the original locos a small reservoir sat on the sloping plate under the smokebox. Four pipes led from this to (presumably) lubricate the bogie bearing surfaces and side bearers. On the Modified Halls this was moved aside (to the right, looking at the locomotive front) to the new framing emerging at the front.

Additional Notes – The Reformed Saint
The conversion of Saint 2925 took place in 1924 – see Part One. At the time the Hall class was around five years in the future and so SAINT MARTIN continued carrying its Saint number, 2925. When the decision was taken in 1928 to build eighty locomotives based on 2925, their numbering was planned to commence at 4900 and the first example actually carried 4900 plates in Swindon Works briefly. Before it emerged revised ideas prevailed and ADDERLEY HALL came out as 4901, vacating the number 4900 for the hybrid SAINT MARTIN.

OIL

In September 1945, as the first of the (lined green!) 1000 class County 4-6-0s were coming off Swindon works and a new batch of Castles was about to be embarked upon, it was announced that six 28XX class 2-8-0s would be converted for oil burning. This was afterwards characterised as the GWR's own, independent scheme with the Government 'intervening' in 1946 to make it a national, state-directed project. This seems unlikely, given the state of GWR finances, Government control of exports/imports, direction of resources and so on. It would have been Government-prompted from the first and was of course the first stirrings of yet another famous national debacle, the Great Post-War Oil Burning Fiasco, a close rival to the Great Ground Nut Scheme. At least those given the task of implementing the oil disaster did not have to contend with lions, crocodiles and killer bees. The oil burning scheme was misunderstood in enthusiast circles, at least so far as the GW was concerned, for it is was thought that the 2-8-0s were 'an experiment' that, if successful, would mean that a 'new type of passenger locomotive' would be built.

About October 1945 Llanelly's 2872 was found to be the first of the 2-8-0s to be equipped for oil burning. Oil fuel was fed by gravity from an 1800 gallon tank on the tender to a burner fitted in the front of the firebox; there the fuel oil was atomised by a steam jet incorporated in the burner. The fuel was heavy, viscous stuff and steam heating coils were fitted to ensure that it 'flowed'. Huge 36,000 gallon storage were installed at Llanelly, from where the 2-8-0s would work and soon they would appear at sheds across the country, let alone the GWR; by the end of 1945 more and more locos were being converted. There were to be 84 Halls converted as the scheme acquired an early dizzying impetus of its own; the actual numbers were eleven (see end).

The first Hall converted was 5955 GARTH HALL, in June 1946 whereupon it worked from Swindon where it was presumably under the close eye of the works. Tentatively at first, it worked Swindon-Gloucester locals. It could hardly have performed better, the authorities said; by September it was managing nearly 1500 miles a week, 9.0a.m. Swindon to Paddington, 1.18 p.m. Paddington to Bristol and 825 p.m. Bristol to Swindon. All went well enough till economic reality set in. Despite coal shortages and its soaring expense, the country's limping economy could not afford precious dollars for oil – the same reason BR decided on steam rather than American diesels shortly afterwards. It all quietly faded away. The Irish had also got caught up in the oil burning fever and after converting some ninety engines in 1947 Coras Iompair Eireann announced early in 1948 that an improvement in the coal supply had prompted a reconversion at the rate of six engines per week – that is, as quick as possible. 'It is understood that no oil burning locomotives will be running after 26th September 1948' was the terse sentence marking the abandonment of oil burning on the Western.

Above. **5955 GARTH HALL newly equipped for oil burning; it was the first converted, in June 1946 and unlike the others was not renumbered straight away, getting the plates 3950 a few months later. There is a fascinating short film (accessible by typing some combination of 'GW oil burning' and 'YouTube' on line which shows the operation of the oil burners in some considerable detail). The Churchward tender 2141 was soon changed to Collett standard 2764 (see page 136).**

**OIL BURNING HALLS
From the RCTS *Locos of the Great Western Railway*:**

Old	New	To Oil	To Coal
4968	3900	5/47	3/49
4971	3901	5/47	4/49
4948	3902	5/47	9/48
4907	3903	5/47	4/50
4972	3904	5/47	10/48
5955	3950	6/46	10/48
5976	3951	4/47	11/48
6957	3952	4/47	3/50
6953	3953	4/47	9/48
5986	3954	5/47	2/50
6949	3955	5/47	4/49

5955 renumbered 10/46; the others when converted.

3950 (5955) GARTH HALL did not retain the low sided tender (it presumably went to a 2-8-0) with its prominent tank and piping; here it is at Bristol St Philips Marsh on 28 August 1948. It would be reconverted a few weeks later. H.C. Casserley, courtesy R.M. Casserley.

3951, ex-5976 ASHWICKE HALL, newly converted at Swindon in April 1947. It was reconverted about a year and a half later, which involved, it should be remembered, twice lifting the boiler; firstly to fit the jets, then to remove them. That sliding shutter (and the roof ventilator) was fitted to all the oil burners.

Two Halls, a combination that was not all that usual, emerging from Dainton tunnel with a down train on 29 June 1957. Leading is 5920 WYCLIFFE HALL followed by 4908 BROOME HALL. Are those chimneys different? You decide! Note too that the two whistles with the shield tucked behind are different – one is bigger than the other. One was the whistle normally heard and the other (a different tone) was an emergency alarm. R.C. Riley, transporttreasury

Engine Histories

These Engine Histories follow more or less those of previous 'Book Of' volumes, derived from the Swindon Registers and other sources at The National Archive. The codes are as follows:

G General
H Heavy
I Intermediate
L Light
R Thought to be 'Running'

The relative frequencies of **L** and **R** indicate they were not recorded with consistency. Also 'Swindon Works' is often noted with no indication as to the level of work done.

WR/BR equivalents after 1948 were:
HC Heavy Casual
HG Heavy General
HI Heavy Intermediate
LC Light Casual
LI Light Intermediate
U Unclassified
C Casual

X/S is thought to stands for 'ex-store'
Cont 'Continuation' – often called 'Rectification' elsewhere. It is a brief recall to works to attend to some minor (or sometimes not so minor) fault showing up after running in following works attention.

Works Dates Compilation of the record from several sources means that dates given of works/outstation shops visits can indicate completion OR beginning of the work. **They thus indicate a period rather than a specific date in or out.**
In some cases not all the information is to hand and 'Mileages and Boilers' might not be represented, say.

In some tables with restricted details available, the second column of mileage figures indicates the total since the previous main overhaul.

Tenders. For a number of the locos, the sequence of tenders is missing.

As pointed out in other volumes of this series, railway company Engine History Cards, while containing much useful and even fascinating information, are an *indication of* what happened to the engines. A very good and complex indication – the best we will have – but not something that is 100% reliable and accurate in every instance (though it is in many). In the end they were, after all, for Accountants rather than Engineers!

A note on Disposals. The disposal dates and buyers; that is, sale dates to buyers, are normally hand written entries on the GWR/WR engine history sheets and these have been used in the book.

Since the first part of the Halls went to press, a few further details/differences have come to light, *Richard Derry writes:*
4903 sold to Steel Supply (Western Ltd co) Jersey Marine, Swansea 19/11/64
4904 sold to Birds Morriston 28/2/64
4916 sold to G Cohen Morriston 29/9/64
4919 sold to Steel Supply (Western Ltd co) Jersey Marine Swansea 19/11/64
4923 mileage 1,353,155 as at 28/12/63
4928 sold to J Cashmore Newport 27/10/64
4929 sold to J Cashmore Newport 4/5/65
4932 sold to R S Hayes Bridgend 12/1/65
4933 mileage 1,259,049 at 28/12/63
4949 sold to Birds Morriston 14/10/64
4951 sold to J Cashmore Newport 4/9/64
4954 mileage 1,341,161 at 28/12/63
4956 sold to J Cashmore Newport 18/9/63
4958 sold to J Cashmore Newport 27/10/64
4959 sold to J Buttigieg Newport 11/1/65
4962 sold to Birds Risca 9/11/65
4978 sold to R S Hayes Bridgend 27/10/61
4980 sold to J Cashmore Newport 18/9/63
4985 sold to J Cashmore Newport 27/10/64
4989 sold to R S Hayes Bridgend 12/1 65
4992 sold to Birds Risca 2/6/65
4993 sold to R S Hayes Bridgend 5/3/65

Concerning Part One...

Page 9: The second emblem of course came in 1957 not 1956 (March to be precise); there was however a demonstration of it in 1956 – hand painted on 70016.
Page 18: 4985, on closer examination, turns out to have the much modified Dean tender of 1901, no.1513. So, a hidden rarity – gem even. It also enables the date of the photograph to be narrowed down, to 8/36-9/39.
Page 24: Works p/e 23/12/38 should of course read 23/12/28.
Page 131: The Hawksworth tender on 4953 is a temporary match.
Page 171: 'late in the 1950s' should really read 'early 1960s'.
Page 85: 4930 is at Magor on a Bristol express on 26 June 1956 not as described.
Page 192: Date 16/1/31 Westbury is incorrect. We're working on it!

How they ended up. 5961, TOYNBEE HALL that was, on one of its last jobs, at Snow Hill on 3 August 1965. It was withdrawn three days later. ColourRail

5900 HINDERTON HALL

Built in 1931 to Lot no.268 at Swindon Works
To traffic 2/1931

Mileages and Boilers
Date	Mileage/Boiler
From new	4490
11/7/33	98,947 C4490
10/1/35	173,372 C2871
26/5/36	247,766 C2871
15/3/38	329,502 C4480
15/12/39	407,244 C4480
15/6/42	507,652 C4480
1/6/44	572,185 C2955
25/11/46	659,719 C4911
28/5/48	707,506 C4005
23/1/50	757,491 C7268
9/7/52	841,525 C4962
14/1/55	941,303 C4962
27/6/56	980,063 C7265
25/11/57	1,029,190 C7234
3/9/59	1,091,697 C7267
16/3/61	1,129,359 C8246

Sheds and works history
Date	Location
11/4/31	Old Oak
9/5/31	Worcester
6/6/31	Hereford
28/9/31	Shrewsbury shops **R**
11/7/33	Swindon Works **I**
1933	Carmarthen
3/8/33	Danygraig shops **L**
10/1/35	Swindon Works **G**
12/1/35	Swindon
18/2/36	Swindon Works **R**
26/5/36	Swindon Works **I**
19/9/36	Bristol Bath Road
22/1/37	Bristol Bath Road shops **R**
16/2/37	Swindon Works **L**
29/5/37	St Philips Marsh
23/9/37	Swindon Works **L**
17/11/37	St Philips Marsh shops **R**
15/3/38	Swindon Works **G**
29/9/39	Old Oak shops **R**
15/12/39	Swindon Works **I**
6/1/40	Swindon
19/2/42	Newton Abbot Works **R**
15/6/42	Swindon Works **I**
29/6/42	Swindon Works **R**
1/6/44	Swindon Works **G**
7/1944	St Philips Marsh
21/5/45	Bristol Bath Road Shops **R**
5/12/45	Bristol Bath Road shops **R**
25/11/46	Swindon Works **I**
30/11/46	Westbury
28/5/48	Swindon Works **L**
9/3/49	Westbury shops **U**
22/9/49	Westbury shops **U**
23/1/50	Swindon Works **HG**
9/7/52	Swindon Works **HG**
21/2/53	Tyseley
2/4/54	Worcester shops **U**
11/9/54	Tyseley shops **U**
14/1/55	Wolverhampton Works **HI**
31/12/55	Oxley
24/1/56	Tyseley shops **U**
27/6/56	Swindon Works **HC**
9/9/57	Oxley shops **U**
25/11/57	Swindon Works **HG**
3/3/59	Oxley shops **U**
7/5/59	Oxley shops **U**
3/9/59	Wolverhampton Works **HC**
5/10/59	Oxford shops **U**
16/2/60	Oxley shops **U**
9/11/60	Oxley shops **U**
3/1/61	Oxley shops **U**
16/3/61	Swindon Works **HI**
13/2/62	Tyseley shops **U**
3/11/62	Old Oak
17/11/62	St Philips Marsh
16/2/63	Worcester shops **U**

Tenders
From new	1852
10/1/35	2652
26/5/36	2400
22/1/37	2319
16/2/37	2635
15/3/38	2669
15/12/39	2744
15/6/42	2681
29/6/42	2732
1/6/44	2259
20/11/46	2907
28/5/45	2826
22/9/49	2531
16/2/52	4079
9/7/52	2594
6/11/54	2538
27/6/56	2550
25/11/57	2673
7/5/59	4054

Mileage 1,200,282

Withdrawn 2/12/63 Engine preserved

5900 HINDERTON HALL; there are no details as to date or location but a brave soul has proffered 'approaching Danzey after Henley-in-Arden heading towards Tyseley and so on on the Birmingham & North Warwick Line' which certainly seems likely enough. The shed plate carries 84; it's impossible to make out the letter but it would indicate either Tyseley or Oxley where 5900 was employed through most of the 1950s. HINDERTON HALL possibly plain black; with no emblem present then 1953, the year it went to Tyseley, seems a good estimate as to the period.

5901 HAZEL HALL

Built in 1931 to Lot no.275 at Swindon Works
To traffic 5/1931

Mileages and boilers
From new	4415
17/1/33	66,775 C4415
5/7/34	139,204 C4415
21/12/35	200,132 C4934
29/11/37	288,268 C4934
6/3/39	343,117 C4441
19/2/40	383,054 C4441
8/1/43	475,952 C4441
29/12/43	502,710 C2973
21/8/45	551,077 C7226
9/4/48	637,912 C4065
18/8/50	718,231 C2865
3/12/52	791,495 C4947
16/5/55	882,735 C4947
20/9/57	966,046 C8221
30/9/60	1,071,879 C8221
13/4/62	1,114,476 C8285

Sheds and Works history
3/6/31	Old Oak shops **R**
4/7/31	Truro
14/4/32	Truro shops **R**
17/1/33	Swindon Works **I**
1933	Old Oak
5/7/34	Swindon Works **I**
28/7/34	Reading
19/6/35	Reading shops **R**
2/8/35	Old Oak shops **R**
21/12/35	Swindon Works **G**
16/2/37	Oxford shops **R**
18/6/37	Old Oak shops **R**
26/6/37	Old Oak
24/7/37	Reading
29/11/37	Swindon Works **I**
6/3/39	Swindon Works **L**
19/2/40	Swindon Works **I**
24/11/40	Reading shops **R**
27/2/42	Reading shops **R**
17/10/42	Taunton shops **R**
8/1/43	Reading shops **I**
29/12/43	Swindon Works **L**
17/10/44	Reading shops **R**
11/5/45	Reading shops **L**
21/8/45	Swindon Works **G**
25/1/46	Swindon Works **L**
16/8/46	Reading shops **L**
11/1/47	Old Oak shops **R**
22/2/47	Reading shops **R**
12/9/47	Old Oak shops **R**
4/10/47	Reading shops **R**
19/11/47	Reading shops **L**
	Tender work only
9/4/48	Swindon Works **I**
1/9/49	Reading shops **U**
10/1/50	Swindon Works **U**
18/8/50	Swindon Works **HG**
20/3/52	Newton Abbot Works **LC**
3/12/52	Swindon Works **HG**
16/5/55	Swindon Works **HI**
13/11/56	Reading shops **U**
20/9/57	Swindon Works **HG**
3/2/58	Old Oak shops **U**
6/2/59	Wolverhampton Works **LC**
30/9/60	Caerphilly Works **HI**
7/10/61	Southall
8/11/61	Reading shops **U**
13/4/62	Wolverhampton Works **HC**
21/4/62	Reading

Tenders
From new	2567
9/11/35	2653
30/1/39	2634
19/2/40	2684
21/11/42	2589
20/8/43	2625
21/8/45	2787
25/1/46	2531
12/9/47	2427
9/4/48	2320
10/1/50	2824
9/7/50	2603
20/3/52	4011
1/11/52	2416
3/12/52	2660
16/5/55	2621
20/9/57	2684
11/61	2845

Mileage 1,159,566 as at 28/12/63

Withdrawn 25/6/64. Sold to J. Cashmore, Newport 4/9/64

5901 HAZEL HALL at Southall shed, 28 April 1963.

5901 HAZEL HALL now distinctly down at heel (front number plate gone) at Reading shed, 24 April 1964. It was withdrawn a few weeks later. D.K. Jones Collection.

29

5902 HOWICK HALL
Built in 1931 to Lot no.275 at Swindon Works
To traffic 5/1931

Mileages and Boilers
From new	4414
1/2/34	114,140 C4414
6/2/35	160,633 C4080
20/2/36	203,643 C4080
31/3/38	298,096 C4960
1/12/39	381,067 C4960
11/4/42	476,308 C2847
22/6/44	557,853 C2847
30/11/45	605,732 C4415
8/1/48	675,564 C8268
15/6/50	764,730 C4968
13/5/53	877,604 C4968
11/11/55	961,264 C7201
19/3/58	1,049,834 C7201
10/1/61	1,150,415 C7270

Sheds and Works history
4/7/31	Truro
17/6/31	Worcester shops **R**
6/10/31	Truro shops **R**
5/9/32	Swindon Works **L**
4/5/33	Newton Abbot shed **R**
1/2/34	Swindon Works **I**
10/2/34	Penzance
6/4/34	Swindon Works **L**
21/11/34	Swindon Works **L**
6/2/35	Swindon Works **L**
6/6/35	Swindon Works **L**
20/2/36	Swindon Works **L**
7/3/36	Laira
4/2/37	Swindon Works **L**
22/9/37	Newton Abbot Works **L**
31/3/38	Swindon Works **G**
15/10/38	Truro
7/3/39	Truro Shops **R**
29/4/39	Penzance
1/12/39	Swindon Works **I**
9/1940	Laira
12/1940	Penzance
5/1941	Taunton
17/5/41	Newton Abbot Works **L**
19/12/41	Taunton shops **R**
11/4/42	Swindon Works **G**
26/6/43	Taunton shops **R**
11/3/44	Taunton shops **R**
4/1944	Penzance
22/6/44	Swindon Works **I**
18/11/44	Swindon Works **R**
14/4/45	Penzance shops **R**
10/8/45	Penzance shops **R**
8/1945	Taunton
30/11/45	Swindon Works **G**
18/4/46	Taunton shops **R**
5/2/47	Taunton shops **R**
24/4/47	Taunton shops **R**
2/6/47	Taunton shops **R**
1/11/47	Exeter
8/1/48	Swindon Works **I**
6/5/48	Newton Abbot Works **R**
10/2/49	Newton Abbot Works **LC**
6/4/50	Old Oak shops **U**
15/6/50	Swindon Works **HG**
2/3/51	Swindon Works **LC**
6/7/52	Taunton shops **U**
12/7/52	Severn Tunnel Jct
13/5/53	Caerphilly Works **HI**
15/3/54	Southall shops **U**
14/8/54	Llanelly
11/11/55	Swindon Works **HG**
14/6/57	Caerphilly Works **LC**
30/12/57	Llanelly shops **U**
19/3/58	Swindon Works **HI**
18/6/60	Carmarthen
10/1/61	Swindon Works **HG**
20/5/61	Carmarthen shops **U**
29/11/61	Carmarthen shops **U**
24/2/62	St Philips Marsh
29/5/62	Taunton shops **U**
10/8/62	Worcester shops **U**

Tenders
From new	2569
21/10/33	2618
21/11/34	2602
8/6/35	2591
6/1/36	2406
22/1/37	2618
18/2/38	2739
30/10/39	2538
28/2/42	2717
22/6/44	2444
19/10/45	2912
8/1/48	2493
5/4/48	2594
6/5/48	2567
10/11/50	2562
21/1/51	2810
11/11/55	2667
19/3/58	2581
10/1/62	2620

Mileage 1,211,388

Withdrawn 13/11/62 Cut up 26/163

5902 HOWICK HALL at Shrewsbury shed, about 1958; second emblem and lined green somewhere under that grime. D.K. Jones Collection.

5902 HOWICK HALL with the 1.20pm Paddington-Swindon approaching Southall station; MPD to the right, 21 February 1960. B. Wadey, transporttreasury

5903 KEELE HALL

Built in 1931 to Lot no.275 at Swindon Works
To traffic 5/1931

Mileages and Boilers
From new   4415
11/4/33   86,008 C4415
16/1/35   156,267 C4965
27/8/36   219,229 C4944
19/5/38   311,428 C4910
22/12/39   395,283 C4910
18/12/41   474,433 C4910
17/2/44   551,262 C2830
28/11/46   638,185 C7239
1/10/48   691,934 C8273
25/11/49   733,474 C8273
9/5/52   815,844 C2953
15/7/54   899,274 C2953
9/10/56   991,784 C4915
2/1/59   1,085,055 C4915
10/8/61   1,166,049 C4423

Sheds and Works history
4/7/31   Chester
24/9/32   Penzance
11/4/33   Swindon Works I
1933   Oxley
27/1/34   Wolverhampton Works L
10/2/34   Stafford Road
10/3/34   Oxley
28/7/34   Neath
22/9/34   Chester
10/11/34   Oxley shops R
17/11/34   Oxley
16/1/35   Swindon Works G
27/8/36   Swindon Works G
19/5/38   Swindon Works G
28/5/38   Old Oak
22/12/39   Swindon Works I
18/12/41   Swindon Works I
24/7/43   Old Oak shops R
10/1943   Didcot
17/2/44   Swindon Works G
14/9/45   Didcot shops R
13/7/46   Didcot shops L
28/11/46   Swindon Works I
18/3/47   Didcot shops R
31/3/48   Didcot shops R
1/10/48   Swindon Works L
26/8/49   Reading shops U
25/11/49   Swindon Works HI
24/7/51   Old Oak shops LC
9/5/52   Swindon Works HG
8/4/53   Didcot shops U
15/7/54   Swindon Works HI
14/8/54   Neyland
11/9/54   Swindon
6/11/54   Carmarthen
5/11/55   Neyland
9/10/56   Swindon Works HG
30/4/58   Neyland shops U
3/6/58   Neyland shops LC
2/1/59   Caerphilly Works HI
3/4/59   Neyland shops LC
11/7/59   Llanelly
21/5/60   Canton
5/12/60   Canton shops U
10/8/61   Swindon Works HI
9/4/62   Caerphilly Works LC
19/9/62   Danygraig shops U
18/11/62   Llanelly shops U
12/2/63   Newport Ebbw Jct shops U

Tenders
From new   2571
31/12/32   2613
11/7/33   2268
16/1/35   2634
17/6/36   2540
5/4/38   2744
22/12/39   2601
6/11/41   2410
10/12/43   2803
9/10/46   2561
21/10/49   2625
22/5/54   2791
11/7/54   2418
24/1/59   2437
10/8/61   2524
11/1962   4068

Mileage 1,232,460

Withdrawn 10/9/63 Sold to Messrs Coopers Ltd Swindon 31/12/63

32

5903 KEELE HALL in fresh paint, at Salisbury SR shed on 27 August 1961; the low horizontal row of rivets shows to good effect. J.B. Hall, ColourRail

5903 KEELE HALL in lined black passing through Oxford on 15 January 1954. M. Robertson, transporttreasury

5904 KELHAM HALL

Built in 1931 to Lot no.275 at Swindon Works
To traffic 5/1931

Mileages and Boilers
From new	4416
18/5/33	90,684 C4416
16/12/33	116,644 C2892
4/1/35	170,772 C2892
21/5/36	237,983 C2821
26/2/38	327,596 C2821
6/11/39	412,722 C2821
6/6/42	507,893 C4965
3/9/45	601,458 C4965
20/8/48	684,143 C4027
5/6/50	750,645 C8242
30/4/52	824,766 C4475
19/8/54	921,989 C2928
4/10/56	1,014,977 C4957
27/1/59	1,106,058 C8276
24/8/61	1,202,075 C7275

Sheds and Works history
6/6/31	Chester
10/9/32	Chester shops **R**
18/5/33	Swindon Works **I**
1933	Banbury
16/12/33	Swindon Works **L**
13/1/34	Stafford Road
2/6/34	Oxley
4/1/35	Oxley shops **I**
12/1/35	Stafford Road
2/4/36	Banbury shops **R**
21/5/36	Swindon Works **G**
30/5/36	Oxford
15/6/37	Oxford shops **R**
14/8/37	Swindon Works **L**
26/2/38	Swindon Works **I**
13/3/39	Tyseley shops **R**
6/11/39	Swindon Works **I**
13/5/41	Swindon Works **L**
6/6/42	Swindon Works **G**
29/8/44	Tyseley shops **L**
3/9/45	Swindon Works **I**
29/10/46	Swindon Works **L**
20/8/48	Swindon Works **I**
23/8/49	Swindon Works **LC**
5/6/50	Swindon Works **HG**
12/12/50	Oxford shops **U**
29/12/51	Bristol Bath Road
30/4/52	Swindon Works **HI**
2/5/54	St Philips Marsh
19/8/54	Swindon Works **HG**
11/9/54	Bristol Bath Road
1/7/55	Swindon Works **U**
11/3/56	Canton shops **U**
16/6/56	St Philips Marsh
4/10/56	Swindon Works **HI**
11/10/57	Newton Abbot Works U
27/1/59	Swindon Works **HG**
16/5/59	Westbury
15/6/59	Bristol Bath Road shops **LC**
3/12/60	St Philips Marsh
12/2/60	Newton Abbot Works **LC**
14/7/60	Caerphilly Works **LC**
24/8/61	Swindon Works **HI**
2/8/63	St Philips Marsh shops **U**

Tenders
From new	2568
14/11/33	2610
14/4/36	2625
15/7/37	2553
12/1/38	2427
3/4/38	2255
27/9/39	1831
6/11/39	2577
13/5/41	2566
6/6/42	2601
3/9/45	2558
20/8/46	2821
1/7/48	2558
16/7/48	2767
23/8/49	2579
5/6/50	2404
12/7/54	2448
4/10/56	2592
27/1/59	2560
4/5/59	2876
24/8/61	2586

Mileage 1,261,250

Withdrawn 13/11/63 Sold to R S Hayes Bridgend 29/1/64

5904 KELHAM HALL at Didcot, 29 March 1947. The livery is plain black and though the tender side looks bare, on the original the faintest outline of GW in serif with the badge in between can just be discerned. The little 'class B' vacuum pump lubricator is still present, by the leading splasher but would soon be removed. H.C. Casserley, courtesy R.M. Casserley.

The 5.20pm to Bristol train at Weymouth Town, in the charge of 5904 KELHAM HALL on 29 August 1963. By now it is coupled to the eight wheel tender; the last loco in fact, to be paired with it. RailOnline

5905 KNOWSLEY HALL
Built in 1931 to Lot no.275 at Swindon Works
To traffic 5/1931

Mileages and Boilers
From new	4417
24/8/33	87,998 C4417
18/3/35	166,190 R2836
15/9/36	245,525 R2836
31/5/38	324,454 R2836
18/7/40	403,915 R2836
22/1/43	493,546 C7222
20/12/45	576,915 C4033
3/11/47	645,619 C8204
27/5/52	819,756 C8202
29/12/54	928,027 C2831
15/2/57	1,105,677 C2831
22/4/59	1,113,310 C9203
14/2/62	1,210,074 C9248

Sheds and Works history
6/6/31	Swindon
4/7/31	Westbury
20/12/31	St Philips Marsh
8/6/32	Shrewsbury shops R
30/6/32	St Philips Marsh shops R
1933	Fishguard Goodwick
24/8/33	Swindon Works I
18/3/35	Swindon Works G
15/9/36	Swindon Works I
31/5/38	Swindon Works I
10/11/38	Swindon Works L
12/9/39	Swindon Works L
18/7/40	Swindon Works I
22/1/43	Swindon Works G
13/9/44	Carmarthen shops R
20/12/45	Swindon Works L
18/9/47	Fishguard Goodwick shops R
3/11/47	Swindon Works I
5/5/49	Llanelly shops U
14/4/52	Carmarthen shops U
27/5/52	Swindon Works HI
29/12/54	Swindon Works HG
15/2/57	Swindon Works HI
22/4/59	Swindon Works HG
31/8/59	Newport Ebbw Jct shops U
27/2/60	Llanelly shops U
14/2/62	Swindon Works HI

Tenders
From new	2570
22/5/33	2413
22/1/35	2615
15/9/36	2574
11/4/38	2701
9/8/39	2698
14/6/40	2841
14/12/42	2778
20/9/45	2824
3/11/47	2746
23/11/49	2434
18/4/52	2417
3/8/53	2558
18/7/53	2554
26/12/53	2604
19/6/54	2731
6/1/54	2583
29/10/54	4009
15/2/57	2014
22/4/59	4016

Mileage 1,262,580

Withdrawn 29/7/63 Sold to G Cohen Ltd Morriston 1/1/64

Above. 5905 KNOWSLEY HALL is gilded by the late sun at Whitland station; date unrecorded but with 4,000 gallon tender, second emblem, lined green. J. Davenport, Initial Photographics.

Bottom right. 5905 KNOWSLEY HALL spent almost the entirety of its life working from Goodwick (Fishguard) shed, shuttling the length of South Wales and here it is at St Fagans near Cardiff with a freight, 1 June 1954. S. Rickard/ J&J Collection.

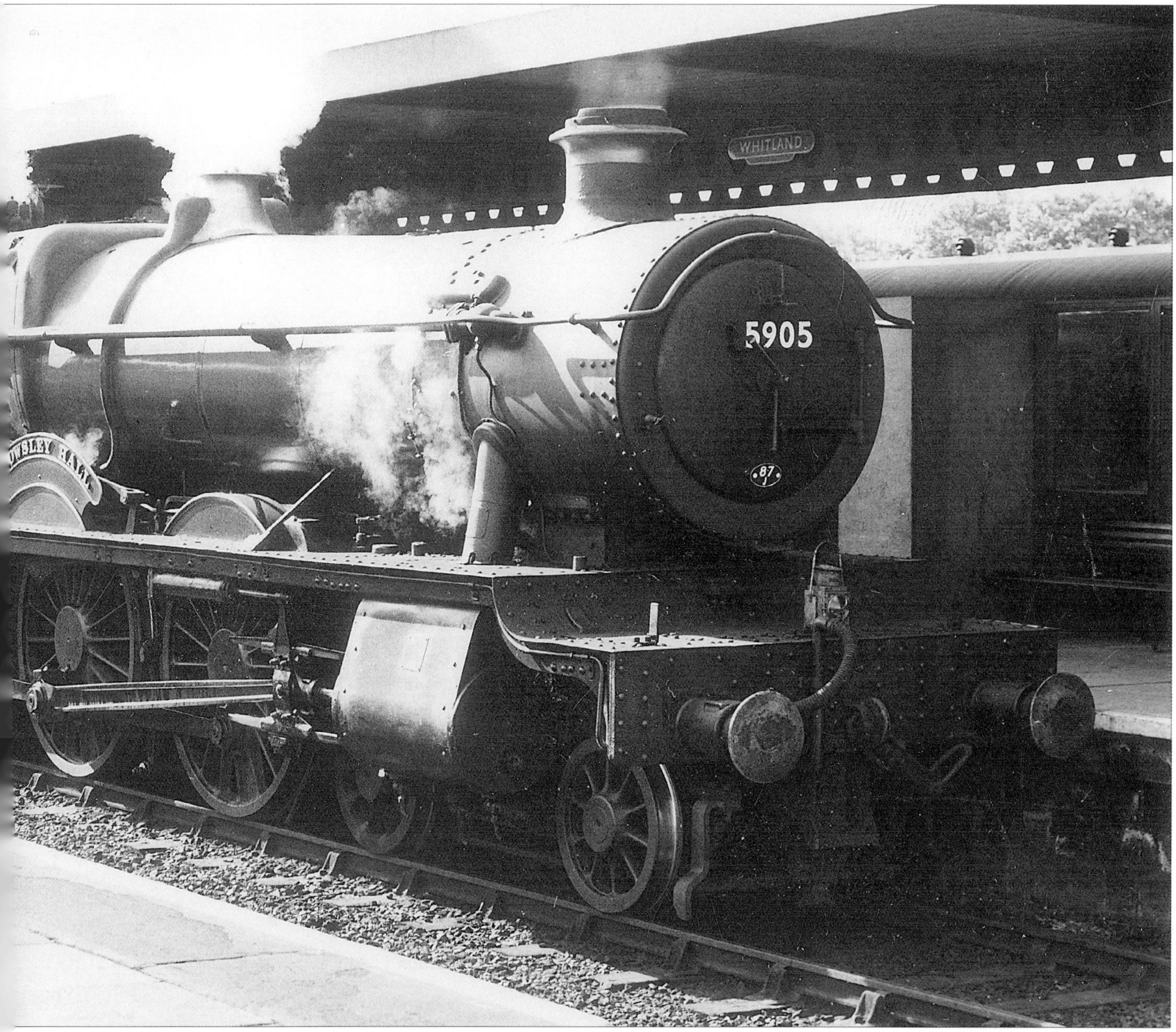

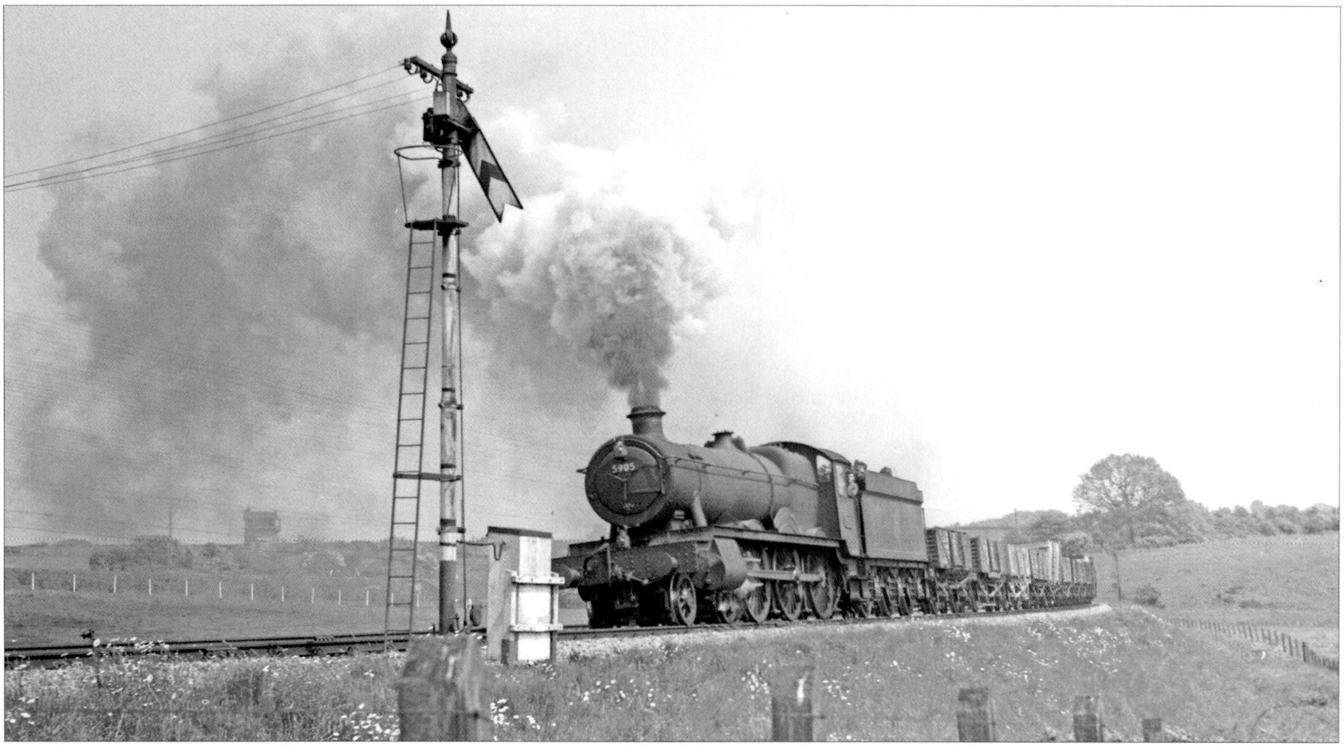

5906 LAWTON HALL

Built in 1931 to Lot no.275 at Swindon Works
To traffic 6/1931

Mileages and Boilers

From new	2839
6/9/33	81,181 C2839
24/8/35	150,981 C4425
17/9/37	240,319 C4425
9/11/39	315,019 C4425
14/7/42	406,210 C2820
15/2/46	521,320 C4913
19/5/48	601,965 C4952
3/11/50	701,038 C8255
3/6/53	807,121 C8255
28/4/55	883,482 C2907
4/9/57	966,559 C2907
1/7/60	1,058,280 C9289

Sheds and Works history

6/6/31	St Philips Marsh
6/7/31	Old Oak shops R
11/7/32	St Philips Marsh shops R
21/8/32	Bristol Bath Road shops R
31/10/32	St Philips Marsh shops R
24/1/33	Reading shops R
6/9/33	Swindon Works I
12/10/33	Tyseley shops R
29/3/34	St Philips Marsh shops R
22/11/34	St Philips Marsh shops R
8/3/35	St Philips Marsh shops R
31/5/35	Newport Ebbw Jct shops R
24/8/35	Swindon Works G
6/10/36	Swindon Works L
19/11/36	Banbury shops R
15/12/36	St Philips Marsh shops R
17/9/37	Swindon Works I
13/11/37	Newport Ebbw Jct
9/11/39	Swindon Works I
14/7/42	Swindon Works G
17/4/43	Newport Ebbw Jct shops L
15/12/43	Swindon Works L
25/6/44	Canton shops R
8/2/45	Newport Ebbw Jct shops R
18/7/45	Tyseley shops R
15/2/46	Swindon Works I
31/7/47	Swindon Works L
19/5/48	Swindon Works I
6/10/48	Newport Ebbw Jct shops L
	Tender work only
10/2/50	Newport Ebbw Jct shed U
20/6/50	Taunton shops U
3/11/50	Swindon Works HG
22/1/52	Swindon Works LC
23/3/52	Old Oak
8/8/52	Gloucester shops U
7/11/52	Taunton shops U
26/1/53	Taunton shops U
3/6/53	Swindon Works HI
24/4/54	Reading
19/2/55	Reading shops LC
28/4/55	Swindon Works HG
22/6/55	Swindon Works LC
25/7/56	Canton shops U
31/10/56	Old Oak shops U
4/9/57	Swindon Works HI
9/4/58	Swindon Works HC
6/6/59	Reading shops U
1/7/60	Swindon Works HG
12/3/61	Reading shops U
18/4/62	Tyseley shops U

Tenders

From new	2572
12/6/33	2560
26/6/35	2539
29/9/39	2545
15/5/42	2448
15/8/43	2841
15/2/46	2856
9/6/47	2580
25/3/48	2405
26/9/50	2753
7/12/51	2545
21/4/53	2555
27/5/54	2392
17/3/55	4109
4/9/57	2729
9/4/58	2612
21/1/60	2801
1/5/60	2763
16/4/62	2684

Mileage 1,124,590

Withdrawn 25/5/62 Cut up 1/12/62

5906 LAWTON HALL finding itself at Fratton shed in 1956; Hawksworth tender, lined black livery with the first emblem. Michael Boakes Collection.

Reading's 5906 LAWTON HALL, resplendent after the completion of its Heavy General at Swindon a few days before, at Temple Meads in July 1960. Glorious dark green, lining, second emblem. Rail Photoprints.

5907 MARBLE HALL

Built in 1932 to Lot no.275 at Swindon Works
To traffic 6/1931

Mileages and Boilers
From new	2840
25/4/33	76,057 C2840
18/12/34	155,646 C4487
17/6/36	234,936 C4424
28/4/38	324,929 C4424
19/1/40	397,110 C4438
30/4/42	479,130 C4438
9/2/44	529,201 C4405
29/3/46	589,510 C4405
9/4/48	643,677 C2838
28/12/49	699,607 C2838
11/2/52	781,853 C2831
15/6/54	882,506 C4921
25/6/56	965,608 C9297
19/6/58	1,049 216 C9297

Sheds and Works history
16/7/31	Swindon Works **L**
1/8/31	Truro
16/11/31	Truro shops **R**
21/11/31	Oxley
1933	Chester
25/4/33	Swindon Works **I**
26/2/34	Chester shops **R**
18/12/34	Swindon Works **G**
19/2/36	Chester shops **R**
17/6/36	Swindon Works **G**
18/1/37	Chester shops **R**
20/9/37	Chester shops **R**
28/4/38	Swindon Works **I**
29/4/39	Wolverhampton Works **L**
19/1/40	Swindon Works **G**
4/1940	Tyseley
7/1940	Leamington Spa
9/1940	Tyseley
9/5/41	Tyseley shops **R**
6/7/41	Tyseley shops **R**
30/4/42	Swindon Works **I**
26/5/42	Swindon Works **L**
16/11/42	Stourbridge shops **R**
19/12/42	Tyseley shops **R**
18/4/43	Tyseley shed **R**
9/2/44	Swindon Works **L**
29/4/44	Tyseley shops **R**
5/7/44	Tyseley shops **R**
3/9/45	Old Oak shops **L**
5/10/45	Tyseley shops **R**
1/12/45	Leamington Spa
29/3/46	Wolverhampton Works **I**
20/4/46	Tyseley
18/5/46	Leamington Spa
15/6/46	Tyseley
6/11/46	Newton Abbot Works **R**
14/12/46	Tyseley shops **R**
4/7/47	Newton Abbot Works **L**
9/4/48	Swindon Works **L**
30/8/49	Tyseley shops **U**
28/12/49	Swindon Works **HI**
20/1/51	Canton shops **U**
22/6/51	Shrewsbury shops **U**
23/8/51	Swindon Works **LC**
11/2/52	Swindon Works **HG**
31/10/52	Gloucester
15/6/54	Swindon Works **HI**
25/6/56	Swindon Works **HG**
30/4/57	Newton Abbot Works **LC**
19/6/58	Wolverhampton Works **HI**
4/9/58	Wolverhampton Works **LC**
27/12/58	Reading
28/11/59	Oxford
26/12/59	Didcot
2/2/60	Old Oak shops **U**
26/3/60	Reading
11/5/60	Newton Abbot Works **LC**

Tenders
From new	2573
14/5/36	2568
27/3/38	2430
3/12/39	2613
30/4/42	2626
26/5/42	2744
7/11/43	2752
2/1/52	2826
1/5/54	2396
28/10/56	4124

Mileage 1,148,244

Withdrawn 3/11/61 Cut up 2/12/61

5907 MARBLE HALL near Denham with a freight on 11 April 1953. Amid several Hall names for which the term 'barrel scraping' seems apt, this perhaps was one of the most startling – 'probably' some gardens in London erased in redevelopment well over a century before! Rail Photoprints.

MARBLE HALL looking a bit disreputable at St Philips Marsh shed. Underneath that coating of 'BR Grey' lined green (probably, rather than lined black) is struggling to get out. 5907 has acquired the larger lubricator cover below the chimney but retains the little 'class B' vacuum pump lubricator in front of the leading splasher. The photograph is not dated but the shed plate is 81D Reading, where 5907 was allocated 1958-59 and briefly again in 1960. So it's late on for the lubricator and getting late on for the livery/emblem. Its last Heavy General had been in 1956 at which it acquired this Hawksworth tender 4124, and it's had plenty of time to get filthy since then. A good view of the conduit on the running plate, linking the ATC shoe with the cab. J. Davenport, Initial Photographics.

41

5908 MORETON HALL

Built in 1931 to Lot no.275 at Swindon Works
To traffic 6/1931

Mileages and Boilers
From new   2843
13/1/33   81,719 C2843
16/5/34   150,736 C2843
7/11/35   222,198 C4969
4/5/37   311,133 C4969
6/4/39   392,872 C4969
17/3/41   469,583 C4969
26/2/43   530,924 C4413
25/1/46   630,396 C4053
5/8/48   710,731 C4997
9/2/51   799,385 C4455
24/3/53   878,677 C4955
30/6/55   973,884 C4476
13/11/57   1,063,320 C4476
23/2/60   1,149,353 C7224
12/6/62   1,233,519 C9222

Sheds and Works history
4/7/31   Swindon
13/1/33   Swindon Works **I**
1933   Fishguard Goodwick
16/5/34   Swindon Works **I**
13/6/34   Newport Ebbw Jct shops **R**
7/11/35   Swindon Works **G**
14/12/35   Landore
7/3/36   Carmarthen
4/5/37   Swindon Works **I**
29/5/37   Fishguard Goodwick
28/9/37   Newport Ebbw Jct shops **L**
7/7/38   Swindon Works **L**
14/1/39   Carmarthen shops **L**
6/4/39   Swindon Works **I**
17/3/41   Swindon Works **I**
26/2/43   Swindon Works **G**
3/1/45   Swindon Works **L**
25/1/46   Swindon Works **I**
1/5/47   Newton Abbot Works **L**
1/11/47   Llanelly
17/4/48   Landore
5/8/48   Swindon Works **I**
2/10/48   Fishguard Goodwick
23/3/50   Newton Abbot Works **U**
12/9/50   Llanelly shops **U**
9/2/51   Swindon Works **HG**
24/3/53   Swindon Works **HI**
30/6/55   Swindon Works **HG**
24/3/57   Carmarthen shops **U**
11/4/57   Newport Ebbw Jct shops **U**
13/11/57   Swindon Works **HI**
26/6/58   Caerphilly Works **LC**
17/10/59   Fishguard Goodwick shops **U**
23/2/60   Swindon Works **HG**
8/4/61   Newport Ebbw Jct shops **LC**
27/1/62   St Philips Marsh
12/6/62   Swindon Works **HG**

Tenders
From new   2574
3/4/34   2545
19/3/37   2657
21/9/37   2413
4/6/38   2589
24/2/39   2643
30/1/41   2401
17/5/41   2683
26/2/43   2808
3/1/45   2825
25/1/46   2838
9/6/48   2445
26/2/49   2652
9/1/51   2705
13/2/53   2891
10/5/55   2248
31/12/55   2573
13/11/57   4121
23/2/60   2624
12/6/62   2821

Mileage 1,273,198

Withdrawn 29/7/63 Sold to Messrs Coopers Ltd Swindon 31/12/63

42

5908 MORETON HALL at Goodwick (Fishguard) shed in 1955; it spent the great part of its working life in South Wales, only going late on to Bristol. D.K. Jones Collection.

5908 MORETON HALL with a class C parcels train at Gowerton, in August 1960. Michael Boakes Collection.

5910 PARK HALL

Built to Lot no.275 at Swindon Works
To traffic 7/1931

Mileages and Boilers
From new	4429
6/6/33	82,152 C4429
8/3/35	164,892 C2809
3/10/36	249,700 C2809
9/7/38	331,840 C2809
17/6/40	409,731 C4415
27/1/43	502,070 C4415
23/3/45	574,290 C8278
11/2/47	659,130 C2843
9/8/49	753,101 C2841
22/2/52	857,592 C8226
12/4/54	950,028 C8226
29/6/56	1,039,407 C7253
23/5/58	1,135,144 C7253
3/4/60	1,235,126 C6202

Sheds and Works history
14/8/31	Old Oak shops **R**
28/9/31	Old Oak shops **R**
24/10/31	Oxford
13/2/32	Old Oak
30/8/32	Swindon Works **R**
21/9/32	Swindon Works **R**
6/6/33	Swindon Works **I**
28/7/34	Worcester
22/9/34	Old Oak
3/11/34	Old Oak shops **R**
8/3/35	Swindon Works **G**
21/11/35	Old Oak shops **R**
3/10/36	Swindon Works **I**
17/10/36	Canton
9/7/38	Swindon Works **I**
21/9/39	Swindon Works **L**
17/6/40	Swindon Works **G**
3/1941	Weymouth
27/6/42	Canton shops **L**
27/1/43	Swindon Works **I**
2/8/44	Canton shops **R**
12/9/44	Newton Abbot Works **R**
4/1/45	Westbury shops **R**
23/3/45	Swindon Works **G**
11/2/47	Swindon Works **I**
15/9/48	Newton Abbot Works **L**
9/8/49	Swindon Works **HG**
22/2/52	Swindon Works **HG**
13/10/53	Canton shops **U**
12/4/54	Swindon Works **HI**
7/10/54	Newport Ebbw Jct shops **U**
21/5/55	Westbury
17/7/55	Taunton shops **U**
10/9/55	Bristol Bath Road
29/6/56	Swindon Works **HG**
7/2/57	Bristol Bath Road shops **LC**
23/5/58	Swindon Works **HI**
21/2/59	Canton
3/4/60	Swindon Works **HG**
3/12/60	Oxley
8/8/61	Didcot shops **U**
11/4/62	Oxley shops **U**

Tenders
From new	2579
23/2/53	2536
28/1/35	2569
24/8/36	2613
2/5/38	2620
7/5/40	2794
27/1/43	2785
1/2/45	2884
11/2/47	2389
4/7/48	2248
9/8/49	2706
8/1/52	4111
12/4/54	2554
7/10/54	2442
21/5/56	2779
23/5/58	2568
3/4/60	4011

Mileage 1,295,056

Withdrawn 21/9/62 Sold to John Cashmore, Great Bridge 17/10/63

5910 PARK HALL with a freight at Gerrards Cross, June 1962. ColourRail

PARK HALL passing Gobowen station, 12 April 1960. B.W.L. Brooksbank, Initial Photographics

47

5911 PRESTON HALL

Built in 1931 to Lot no.275 at Swindon Works
To traffic 7/1931

Mileages and Boilers
From new	4418
20/9/33	112,316 C4418
3/5/35	190,274 C4418
10/2/37	267,132 C4980
12/12/38	354,730 C4980
23/10/39	390,693 C4435
28/1/41	437,997 C4435
14/5/43	525,044 C4435
3/11/45	588,616 C4412
7/8/47	678,941 C4412
14/4/50	770,746 C2951
23/10/52	864,744 C8225
4/2/55	960,378 C8225
12/6/57	1,051,892 C8204
18/1/60	1,145,306 C2877

Sheds and Works history
4/7/31	Carmarthen
1/8/31	Fishguard Goodwick
10/5/32	Fishguard Goodwick shops **R**
5/7/32	Carmarthen shops **R**
27/8/32	Landore
24/9/32	Carmarthen
1933	Swindon
20/9/33	Swindon Works **I**
29/3/34	Swindon Works **L**
30/6/34	Bristol Bath Road
4/10/34	Bristol Bath Road shops **R**
15/12/34	St Philips Marsh
3/5/35	Swindon Works **I**
5/2/36	St Philips Marsh shops **R**
2/7/36	Chester shops **R**
10/2/37	Swindon Works **G**
18/3/38	St Philips Marsh shops **R**
12/12/38	Swindon Works **I**
17/5/39	St Philips Marsh shops **R**
23/10/39	Swindon Works **L**
28/1/41	Swindon Works **I**
3/1942	Westbury
5/1942	Newport Ebbw Jct
14/5/43	Swindon Works **I**
3/11/45	Swindon Works **G**
15/11/46	Newport Ebbw Jct shed **R**
7/8/47	Wolverhampton Works **I**
22/4/48	Taunton shops **R**
14/4/50	Swindon Works **HG**
2/12/50	Canton
16/2/51	Canton shops **LC**
24/3/51	Newport Ebbw Jct
14/7/51	Canton
7/9/51	Southall shops **U**
2/4/52	Leamington Spa shops **U**
23/10/52	Swindon Works **HG**
13/2/53	Swindon Works **LC**
7/5/54	Newport Ebbw Jct shops **LC**
4/2/55	Newton Abbot Works **HI**
27/6/55	Swindon Works **LC**
10/11/55	Swindon Works **HC**
16/3/56	Newport Ebbw Jct shops **LC**
12/6/57	Swindon Works **HG**
10/11/58	Canton shops **U**
19/6/59	Bristol Bath Road shops **U**
18/1/60	Swindon Works **HI**
26/3/61	Oxford shops **U**
12/10/61	Hereford shops **U**
2/3/62	Aberdare shops **U**

Tenders
From new	2576
7/3/35	2075
2/7/36	2629
19/7/36	2253
10/2/37	2431
7/11/38	2572
23/10/39	2637
28/1/41	2796
27/3/43	2663
3/4/48	1696
30/10/46	2008
21/1/47	2926
10/3/50	2560
8/9/51	2559
22/9/52	4093
3/1/53	2764
10/11/55	2590
21/6/57	2807
18/1/60	4047

Mileage 1,239,075

Withdrawn 21/9/62 Sold to R S Hayes Ltd Bridgend 26/8/63

5911 PRESTON HALL climbing out of Patchway Tunnel towards Patchway station in September 1961. This is the Up line, on an easier gradient of 1 in 100 through the Up tunnel than the Down line running above. See for instance 4999 and 4977 in Part One. The bracket signal would be (right-hand) for Bristol Temple Meads and (left-hand) for the Badminton route. Rail Photoprint.

PRESTON HALL at an unrecorded date and a year or more overdue for a clean, at Salisbury ready to head west from platform 3 with a train for Bristol. J. Davenport, Initial Photographics.

5912 QUEEN'S HALL

Built in 1931 to Lot no.275 at Swindon Works
To traffic 6/1931

Mileages and Boilers

From new	4419
14/8/33	93,084 C4419
18/4/35	154,253 C4415
25/10/35	174,496 C4415
8/6/37	256,845 C4415
20/3/39	353,371 C4981
1/10/40	401,068 C4981
27/4/42	463,505 C3005
9/2/44	517,274 C3005
12/3/46	580,563 C2990
5/11/47	642,878 C2922
2/9/49	698,678 C7250
1/11/51	776,812 C8246
3/6/54	878,334 C8246
18/1/56	949,881 C7238
18/3/58	1,035,408 C4058
17/11/60	1,106,323 C2851

Sheds and works history

4/7/31	Oxford
13/7/31	Stafford Road shed **R**
19/1/32	Worcester shops **R**
13/2/32	Reading
1/4/32	Reading shops **R**
14/8/33	Swindon Works **I**
21/4/34	Swindon Works **R**
14/12/34	Old Oak shops **L**
18/4/35	Swindon Works **L**
25/10/35	Swindon Works **I**
16/11/35	Fishguard Goodwick
7/3/36	Carmarthen
30/5/36	Fishguard Goodwick
8/6/37	Swindon Works **I**
24/7/37	Stafford Road
20/3/39	Swindon works **G**
6/1/40	Chester
1/10/40	Swindon Works **I**
27/4/42	Swindon Works **L**
24/4/43	Swindon Works **R**
9/2/44	Swindon Works **I**
14/3/46	Swindon Works **G**
14/2/47	Swindon Works **R**
5/11/47	Swindon Works **I**
23/4/48	Tyseley shops **R**
14/1/49	Chester shops **U**
1/3/49	Stourbridge shops **U**
2/4/49	Worcester shops **LC**
3/6/49	Gloucester shops **U**
2/9/49	Swindon Works **HG**
18/5/50	Chester shops **U**
1/11/51	Swindon Works **HG**
19/4/52	Croes Newydd
14/6/52	Tyseley
22/9/53	Tyseley shops **U**
3/6/54	Swindon Works **HI**
18/1/56	Swindon Works **HG**
24/7/56	Old Oak shops **U**
18/3/58	Swindon Works **HG**
17/6/58	Caerphilly Works **U**
29/5/58	Tyseley shops **U**
22/4/59	Wolverhampton Works **LC**
10/12/59	Tyseley shops **U**
20/4/60	Tyseley shops **U**
23/4/60	Stourbridge
17/11/60	Stafford Road shed **U**
7/10/61	Banbury

Tenders

From new	2577
17/5/33	2634
17/11/34	2410
19/9/35	2581
13/7/36	2634
8/6/37	2444
20/3/39	2600
1/10/40	2844
16/4/43	2631
9/2/44	2699
21/12/45	2431
30/3/47	2438
5/11/47	2624
25/7/49	2647
3/10/51	4084
24/1/53	2593
27/2/53	4084
27/4/54	2409
3/6/54	2539
18/1/56	4011
17/11/60	2930

Mileage 1,168,821

Withdrawn 18/12/62 Cut up 7/9/63

5812 QUEEN'S HALL rests among the weeds in a corner of the yard at Stourbridge Junction shed. At Tyseley throughout the 1950s, the loco had been sent to Stourbridge to work out its last in April 1960, and was withdrawn at the end of 1962. A 'Hall' in the sense of concert hall, not stately home, it had originally appeared as QUEENS HALL until gaining a corrective apostrophe in 1934. J. Davenport, Initial Photographics.

5914 RIPON HALL

Built in 1931 to Lot no.275 at Swindon Works
To traffic 7/1931

Mileages and Boilers
Only Engine Record Cards available

Sheds and Works history

1/8/31	Old Oak		
24/10/31	Oxford		
13/2/32	Old Oak		
1933	Reading		
25/8/34	Worcester		
3/1/43	Swindon Works **I**		
24/12/44	Swindon Works **I**	86,857	
16/11/46	Swindon Works **G**	66,473	397,311
4/7/48	Swindon Works **I**	62,942	
28/1/50	Swindon Works **G**	64,281	127,222
1/3/52	Swindon Works **G**	78,798	78,798
28/10/54	Swindon Works **HI**		
19/6/56	Worcester shops **LC**		
22/11/56	Swindon Works **HG**		
25/1/58	Gloucester		
9/1/59	Swindon Works **HI**		
21/3/59	Oxley		
1/3/60	Swindon Works **LC**		
20/6/61	Swindon Works **HG**		
25/3/61	Southall		
14/7/62	Reading		
6/4/63	Gloucester		

Tenders (no dates)
BR days

2888
4112
2625
2920
2443
2749
2587

Mileage 1,209,922

Withdrawn 22/1/64. Sold to J Cashmore, Newport 24/3/64

5914 RIPON HALL at Swindon shed, 2 March 1952. A General overhaul had been officially 'booked off' the day before and 5914 would soon be back off to Worcester, its home since 1934. Red-backed cab number and nameplate and new lined black livery. T. Owen, ColourRail

5914 at Shrewsbury in the early 1950s; Fowler 2-6-2T 40005 at left. RailOnline

5914 RIPON HALL at Oxford, 13 July 1963; livery impossible to discern under the grime, though a Heavy General in 1961 would have resulted in lined green. Much larger lubricator cover on smokebox compared to previous illustration.

5915 TRENTHAM HALL
Built in 1931 to Lot no.275 at Swindon Works
To traffic 7/1931

Mileages and Boilers
From new	4421
15/2/33	92,916 C4940
27/3/35	163,013 C4940
5/3/37	243,878 C4016
8/11/38	326,552 C4016
17/1/41	404,503 C4016
2/1/43	471,404 C2827
16/1/46	561,037 C2942
25/8/48	656,562 C2961
6/11/50	754,722 C7204
21/11/52	845,449 C4978
20/4/55	950,699 C4980
30/7/57	1,039,915 C4980

Sheds and Works history
13/8/31	Banbury shops **R**
29/8/31	Shrewsbury
24/10/31	Oxley
1/2/32	Canton shops **R**
1933	Landore
15/12/33	Swindon Works **G**
17/11/34	Carmarthen
27/3/35	Swindon Works **I**
6/4/35	Llanelly
27/11/35	Llanelly shops **R**
14/12/35	Landore
5/3/37	Swindon Works **G**
15/10/38	Carmarthen
8/11/38	Swindon Works **I**
10/12/38	Penzance
14/7/39	Penzance shops **R**
11/4/40	Newton Abbot Works **L**
1/8/40	Newton Abbot Works **L**
20/8/40	*Damaged in air raid on Newton Abbot*
24/9/40	Newton Abbot Works **R**
23/10/40	Newton Abbot Works **R**
17/1/41	Swindon Works **I**
20/9/41	Penzance shops **R**
14/1/42	Penzance shops **R**
4/3/42	Penzance shops **R**
15/6/42	Swindon Works **L**
7/10/42	Penzance shops R
10/1942	Newton Abbot
1/1943	Penzance
2/1/43	Swindon Works **G**
25/3/44	Newton Abbot Works **L**
12/12/44	Penzance shops **R**
11/5/45	Penzance shops **R**
4/7/45	Newton Abbot Works **L**
16/1/46	Swindon Works **I**
27/9/46	Penzance shops **R**
23/6/47	Penzance shops **L**
25/2/48	Penzance shops **R**
25/8/48	Swindon Works **I**
16/9/49	Newton Abbot Works **U**
5/8/50	Penzance shops **U**
6/11/50	Swindon Works **HG**
16/4/51	Penzance shops **U**
17/9/51	Newton Abbot Works **LC**
21/11/52	Swindon Works **HI**
7/5/53	Penzance shops **U**
28/12/53	Newton Abbot Works **LC**
6/8/54	Penzance shops **U**
20/4/55	Swindon Works **HG**
11/5/56	Penzance shops **U**
15/8/56	Newton Abbot Works **LC**
8/9/56	Reading
30/7/57	Swindon Works **HI**
12/9/57	Swindon Works **LC**
13/12/57	Wolverhampton Works **LC**
17/6/58	Wolverhampton Works **LC**
12/7/58	Didcot
6/9/58	Reading

Tenders
From new	2581
1/7/33	1755
15/12/33	2608
5/1/37	2602
23/10/40	2812
20/11/40	2397
11/4/42	2795
9/11/42	2794
25/3/44	1459
19/10/45	2620
1/7/48	2413
25/8/48	2890
8/9/51	2423
8/10/52	4109
17/3/55	2708
15/8/56	2770
30/7/57	2701

Mileage 1,126,453

Withdrawn 13/1/60 Cut up 27/2/60

Lined green 5915 **TRENTHAM HALL** at Newton Abbot (where it had been damaged in the raid of August 1940, famously losing its chimney) on 12 August 1957. A Penzance engine for almost the entirety of its working life, it had recently gone to Reading. J. Robertson, transporttreasury

5915 at Stafford Road a few weeks later, on 10 November 1957; almost certainly it has arrived for the Light Casual recorded in the Engine History. Ken Fairey, ColourRail

57

5916 TRINITY HALL

Built in 1931 to Lot no.275 at Swindon Works
To traffic 7/1931

Mileages and Boilers
From new	4422
3/3/33	84,430 C4422
26/11/34	161,670 C4408
18/5/36	240,054 C4408
16/12/37	319,679 R7248
27/9/39	405,393 R7248
9/1/42	489,780 C4028
20/6/44	568,903 C4028
19/12/45	608,764 C4980
8/1/48	686,224 C2898
2/8/50	782,660 C4432
6/2/53	869,509 C8261
5/9/55	954,424 C6208
1/11/57	1,040,528 C6211
18/8/59	1,108,265 C9298
13/2/61	1,161,225 C7265

Sheds and Works history
1/8/31	Shrewsbury
3/3/33	Swindon Works I
1933	Leamington Spa
10/2/34	Chester
12/5/34	Chester shops R
26/11/34	Swindon Works G
15/12/34	Landore
17/6/35	Newton Abbot shed R
29/6/35	Laira
10/9/35	Newton Abbot shed L
21/12/35	Swindon Works L
18/5/36	Swindon Works I
30/5/36	Shrewsbury
16/12/37	Swindon Works G
22/1/38	Tyseley shops R
5/3/38	Tyseley
22/10/38	Tyseley shops R
27/9/39	Swindon Works I
11/11/39	Oxley
9/1/42	Swindon Works G
3/6/42	Swindon Works L
2/9/43	Swindon Works R
30/10/43	Wolverhampton Works L
20/6/44	Swindon Works I
19/12/45	Swindon Works L
4/6/47	Oxley shops R
19/7/47	Taunton shops R
8/1/48	Swindon Works I
26/2/49	Tyseley
9/11/49	Tyseley shed U
30/1/50	Tyseley shed U
2/8/50	Swindon Works HG
9/8/51	Tyseley shops U
14/6/52	Canton
12/7/52	Pontypool Road
6/2/52	Swindon Works HG
26/9/53	Shrewsbury shops U
28/10/53	Severn Tunnel Jct shops U
5/9/55	Swindon Works HI
1/12/56	Newport Ebbw Jct
23/2/57	Oxley
1/11/57	Swindon Works HG
18/8/59	Swindon Works HI
13/2/61	Swindon Works HC
30/10/61	Oxley shops U
9/1/62	Gloucester shops U

Tenders
From new	2397
1/4/36	2646
6/11/37	2684
27/9/39	2604
12/11/41	2822
3/6/42	2816
12/4/44	2647
4/12/45	2587
19/12/45	2861
8/1/48	2616
21/6/50	2628
12/7/51	2418
8/1/53	2655
1/11/57	2547
18/8/59	2600
13/2/61	2914

Mileage 1,200,731

Withdrawn 13/7/62 Sold to John Cashmore Ltd Great Bridge 4/9/62

5916 TRINITY HALL, running light between the tunnels beyond the western end of Chester General station. Tony Wright comments: *It's impossible to know the aspect of the banner repeater (controlled by the elevated No.6 'box the other side of the tunnel the loco is about to enter) but it could be that 5916 will come to a stand here, before passing through the single bore eastern tunnel to either reverse on the triangle or go straight into the General Station (probably the former). Judging by the presence of electric warning flashes, I'd say the period is the early 1960s, and summer; note the light and the evidence on the smokebox of the loco having recently worked 1C48, a general service train. Specials usually had an X or Z in their descriptions, but to aid train identification for signalmen at busy times, ordinary trains often were described as well. The loco is on the Down line from the Western Region, but it also served as the Up slow off the LMR North Wales coast route. The road to the left is the Up WR track to Shrewsbury and, eventually, Paddington, and also the Down slow LMR route. Saltney Junction, a couple of miles further west was where the respective routes diverged. The tracks to the right are the LMR Down and Up mains respectively. The 50 mph speed restriction will be for where the WR lines curve through the tunnel, go beneath Canal Street, cross the Shropshire Union Canal and go through the two bridges carrying the city walls footpath, and the loco could well have come from Mold Junction MPD (Chester's WR depot having by this time become a DMU servicing site).*
RailOnline

5918 WALTON HALL

Built in 1931 to Lot no.275 at Swindon Works
To traffic 8/1931

Mileages and Boilers

Date	Mileage
From new	4424
17/8/33	92,874 C4424
7/3/35	163,696 C4424
29/2/36	210,822 C4932
4/2/37	247,067 C4932
6/1/39	328,392 C4937
8/5/41	429,673 C4937
11/5/43	497,880 C4979
25/9/45	576,446 C2944
30/7/47	644,550 C8205
29/8/49	717,085 C2924
13/10/52	803,375 C4964
23/6/55	889,985 C2902
16/8/57	972,387 C8271
30/8/60	1,063,745 C2992

Sheds and Works history

1/8/31	Bristol Bath Road
4/6/32	St Philips Marsh
6/4/33	St Philips Marsh shops **R**
17/8/33	Swindon Works **I**
20/3/34	St Philips Marsh shops **R**
28/9/34	St Philips Marsh shops **R**
7/3/35	Swindon Works **I**
19/11/35	Newton Abbot shed **L**
29/2/36	Swindon Works **L**
1/8/36	Newton Abbot Works **L**
4/2/37	Swindon Works **I**
9/4/38	Newton Abbot Works **L**
6/1/39	Swindon Works **G**
4/3/39	Stafford Road
24/6/39	Shrewsbury
22/7/39	Stafford Road
5/1940	Oxley
8/5/41	Swindon Works **I**
16/12/41	Oxley shops **R**
24/10/42	Didcot shops **R**
11/5/43	Swindon Works **G**
28/6/45	Old Oak shops **R**
25/9/45	Swindon Works **I**
30/7/47	Swindon Works **I**
9/8/47	Stafford Road
6/9/47	Oxley
26/5/48	Oxley shops **L**
	Tender work only
25/12/48	Old Oak
27/2/49	Old Oak shed **U**
29/8/49	Swindon Works **HG**
15/9/49-29/6/50	Stored at Swindon
2/12/50	Southall
13/4/51	Newton Abbot Works **LC**
13/7/51	Shrewsbury shops **U**
1/4/52	Southall shops **U**
13/10/52	Swindon Works **HG**
1/12/52	Swindon Works **LC**
18/7/53	Worcester shops **U**
8/11/54	Southall shops **U**
23/6/55	Swindon Works **HI**
1/6/56	Old Oak shops **U**
16/8/57	Swindon Works **HG**
6/2/58	Wolverhampton Works **U**
11/9/59	Old Oak shops **U**
31/10/59	Didcot
30/8/60	Swindon Works **HI**
7/10/61	Oxford
25/4/62	Oxford shops **LC**
27/7/62	St Philips Marsh shops **U**

Tender

From new	2582
29/5/33	2385
14/1/35	2624
2/1/37	2643
25/11/38	2721
22/3/41	2427
15/3/43	2697
16/7/45	2770
30/7/47	2568
16/7/49	2442
11/2/51	2768
4/9/52	4054
9/10/54	2424
6/11/54	2417
14/1/55	2912
23/6/55	2630
16/8/57	2548
9/8/58	2588
27/12/58	2419
10/1959	2625
18/6/60	4031
30/8/62	2562

Mileage 1,123,847

Withdrawn 21/9/62 Sold to A King and Sons Horford Norwich 28/10/63

5918 WALTON HALL at Southall, its home shed since 1950, on 18 January 1959. Ken Fairey, ColourRail

5918 WALTON HALL with an up freight in March 1959 has left Patchway Tunnel behind and is nearing the point near the Tunnel signal box where the up and down lines come together again. The exhaust of the 2-6-2T banker, attached at Pilning, blossoms in the cutting in the background. Rail Photoprint.

5920 WYCLIFFE HALL

Built in 1931 to Lot no.275 at Swindon Works
To traffic 8/1931

Mileages and Boilers

Date	Mileage	Boiler
From new		4428
13/6/33	66,485	C4969
20/3/35	149,610	C4490
19/12/36	230,578	C4490
18/9/37	261,901	C4988
27/2/39	317,839	C4988
16/4/41	405,641	C4926
10/11/43	499,039	C4926
7/9/45	566,462	C4991
16/8/47	636,994	C8265
24/10/49	722,591	C9219
26/1/53	824,959	C2922
15/6/55	917,872	C4914
27/9/57	1,022,532	C2833
30/3/60	1,132,892	C8224
27/4/61	1,161,456	C4941

Sheds and Works history

29/8/31	Leamington Spa
10/12/31	Swindon Works **L**
13/6/33	Swindon Works **G**
1933	Chester
28/9/33	Chester shops **R**
24/11/33	Swindon Works **L**
20/3/35	Swindon Works **G**
19/12/36	Swindon Works **I**
12/2/37	Wolverhampton Works **R**
18/9/37	Swindon Works **L**
16/10/37	Oxley
17/2/38	Oxford shops **R**
27/4/38	Reading shops **R**
27/2/39	Swindon Works **I**
16/4/41	Swindon Works **G**
9/1/43	Westbury shops **R**
10/11/43	Swindon Works **I**
7/9/45	Swindon Works **G**
17/9/46	Bristol Bath Road shops **R**
16/8/47	Swindon Works **I**
20/6/48	Oxley shops **R**
20/9/48	Oxley shops **R**
27/11/48	Old Oak
7/4/49	Old Oak shops **U**
24/10/49	Swindon Works **HG**
12/11/49-6/7/50	Stored at Swindon
17/6/50	Newton Abbot
2/4/51	Newton Abbot shed **U**
8/4/52	Newton Abbot Works **LC**
26/1/53	Swindon Works **HI**
21/8/53	Swindon Works **LC**
15/6/55	Swindon Works **HG**
27/9/57	Swindon Works **HG**
13/12/59	Laira shops **U**
30/3/60	Swindon Works **HI**
27/4/61	Swindon Works **HC**
20/5/61	Taunton
31/7/61	Taunton shops **U**
7/10/61	Westbury

Tenders

From new	2583
26/3/33	2426
16/10/33	2409
31/3/35	2388
21/10/36	2594
21/1/39	2713
29/7/40	2727
16/4/41	2423
4/9/43	2700
30/12/44	2703
7/9/45	2611
16/8/47	2604
24/6/52	2753
26/1/53	2431
21/8/53	2435
15/6/55	2770
11/6/56	2708
27/9/57	2810
20/3/60	2573
2/1962	2557

Mileage 1,181,312

Withdrawn 18/1/62 Cut up 24/3/62

5920 WYCLIFFE HALL heads a Castle on Dainton, 5 August 1960. ATC buffer beam-mounted, conduit clipped to top of running plate valence. Ken Fairey, ColourRail

5920 WYCLIFFE HALL at old Oak Common, 24 April 1960. It was an Old Oak loco back in 1948 but had been at Newton Abbot since 1950; with dieselisation in the West it spent time at Taunton and Westbury in the last year or two before withdrawal. Ken Fairey, ColourRail

5921 BINGLEY HALL

Built in 1933 to Lot no.281 at Swindon Works
To traffic 5/1933

Mileages and Boilers
From new	4433
29/5/35	92,710 R4986
21/1/37	185,702 R4986
22/9/38	264,441 C2919
11/7/40	344,642 C2919
21/9/42	424,577 C2987
25/11/44	498,566 C2987
12/11/45	534,185 C8208
31/12/47	600,361 C4986
26/9/49	659,324 C4454
28/12/51	741,269 C7247
8/10/54	847,077 C4953
11/1/57	939,695 C4953
26/3/59	1,018,300 C7242

Sheds and Works history
5/1933	Reading
2/5/34	Reading shops R
28/7/34	Stafford Road
11/9/34	Newport Ebbw Jct shops R
20/10/34	Oxley
29/6/35	Stafford Road
29/5/35	Swindon Works G
21/1/37	Swindon Works I
5/3/37	Oxley
29/9/37	Wolverhampton Works L
16/10/37	Stafford Road
22/9/38	Swindon Works G
15/10/38	Oxley
11/7/40	Swindon Works I
21/9/42	Swindon Works G
7/7/44	Oxford shops R
25/11/44	Swindon Works I
12/11/45	Swindon Works L
2/2/47	Oxley shops L
2/4/47	St Blazey shops R
20/11/47	Oxley shops I
	Tender repair only
31/12/47	Swindon Works I
9/4/48	Oxley shops R
19/7/49	Oxley shops U
26/9/49	Swindon Works HG
4/12/50	Leamington Spa shops U
24/3/51	Newport Ebbw Jct
8/5/51	Newport Ebbw Jct shops U
19/10/51	Newport Ebbw Jct shops U
28/12/51	Swindon Works HI
8/5/52	Newport Ebbw Jct shops U
1/11/52	Neyland
1/5/53	Carmarthen shops LC
31/10/53	Newport Ebbw Jct
8/10/54	Swindon Works HG
11/1/57	Caerphilly Works HI
25/1/58	Banbury
17/1/59	Banbury shops U
26/3/59	Swindon Works HG
9/9/59	Banbury shops LC
3/6/60	Old Oak shops LC
18/6/60	Tyseley
8/10/60	Westbury
10/9/61	Westbury shops U

Tenders
From new	2423
23/6/33	2436
12/1/35	2251
9/2/35	2436
29/1/37	2405
10/8/38	2603
6/6/40	2837
31/10/42	2880
24/9/44	2587
6/6/43	2818
12/11/45	2425
29/11/47	2677
31/12/47	2633
25/8/49	2384
18/11/51	2442
7/9/54	2911
11/2/56	2907
26/3/59	2700

Mileage 1,124,884

Withdrawn 8/1/62   Cut up 24/3/62

5921 BINGLEY HALL in lined black, at Exeter St David's, 6 August 1955. The second, vertical, grab iron ahead of the window has now appeared, and will be standard until the 'all in one' iron is introduced. ATC now mounted inside bogie, conduit clipped to bottom of running plate valence. J. Robertson, transporttreasury

5921 BINGLEY HALL entering Churston with the rear portion of the down Cornishman on 25 August 1952; Brixham branch to the right. R.J. Buckley, Initial Photographics.

5922 CAXTON HALL

Built in 1933 to Lot no.281 at Swindon Works
To traffic 5/33

Mileages and Boilers
From new	4434
19/2/35	87,178 C4434
15/10/36	165,743 C4447
6/9/38	247,387 C4447
22/8/40	329,787 C4429
13/4/43	428,802 C4429
23/4/45	504,455 C8268
15/9/47	600,545 C8213
10/10/49	684,003 C8257
14/5/51	747,076 C2999
1/10/53	863,806 C7204
23/12/55	951,244 C7204
20/2/58	1,030,034 C7265
16/12/60	1,132,447 C2934

Sheds and Works history
1933	Old Oak
20/10/34	Reading
7/12/34	Reading shops **R**
19/2/35	Swindon Works **I**
9/3/35	Fishguard Goodwick
5/9/35	Carmarthen shops **R**
25/2/36	Fishguard Goodwick shops **R**
15/10/36	Swindon Works **G**
14/11/36	Penzance
36/5/37	Penzance shops **R**
25/11/37	Penzance shops **R**
6/9/38	Swindon Works **I**
12/11/38	Old Oak
16/6/39	Old Oak shops **L**
25/7/39	Old Oak shops **R**
22/8/40	Swindon Works **G**
17/4/42	Old Oak shops **L**
9/10/42	Banbury shops **R**
13/4/43	Swindon Works **I**
18/5/44	Old Oak shed **R**
23/2/45	Old Oak shed **R**
23/4/45	Swindon Works **G**
11/4/47	Old Oak shops **L**
15/9/47	Swindon Works **I**
13/5/48	Old Oak shops **L**
	Tender work only
10/10/49	Swindon Works **HG**
3/12/49	Swindon
9/3/50	Swindon Works **U**
	RD hot box
14/5/51	Swindon Works **HI**
1/10/53	Swindon Works **HG**
23/12/55	Swindon Works **HI**
11/1/56	Swindon Works **U**
30/4/57	Swindon Works **LC**
20/2/58	Swindon Works **HG**
23/9/59	Laira shops **U**
16/12/60	Swindon Works **HI**
1/8/61	Bristol Barrow Road shops **U**
4/11/61	Oxford
12/1/62	Old Oak shops **U**
6/3/62	Shrewsbury shops **U**

Tenders
From new	2431
27/12/34	2632
10/9/36	2587
6/7/39	2578
15/7/40	2842
9/3/43	2830
7/3/45	2419
4/6/46	2554
15/9/47	2931
26/8/49	2737
2/4/51	2829
31/5/53	2813
23/12/55	2602
30/4/57	2641
20/2/58	2927
5/6/59	2698
8/10/59	2651
16/12/60	2680
24/9/63	2881
No date	2724
No date	2680

Mileage 1,203,947 as at 28/12/63

Withdrawn 6/1/64 Cut up 21/3/64

5922 CAXTON HALL (the only British locomotive linked to one of Elizabeth Taylor's weddings?) at Oxford in June 1962. ColourRail

5926 GROTRIAN HALL

Built in 1933 to Lot no.281 at Swindon Works
To traffic 6/1933

Mileages and Boilers
From new	4438
13/5/35	96,133 C4438
17/3/37	177,992 C4438
27/10/38	263,240 C4428
4/3/41	361,214 C4428
18/11/42	446,370 C4440
12/2/45	557,699 C2963
16/1/47	648,040 C2888
8/12/48	729,200 C9218
29/1/51	813,223 C4969
13/10/53	926,538 C4461
4/6/56	1,038,116 C4461
27/6/58	1,123,020 C8249
26/9/60	1,197,740 C8203

Sheds and Works history
1933	Fishguard Goodwick
10/7/34	Fishguard Goodwick shops **R**
13/5/35	Swindon Works **I**
1/6/35	Penzance
18/1/36	Penzance shops **R**
12/8/36	Newton Abbot shed **L**
17/3/37	Swindon Works **I**
1/5/37	Laira
16/3/38	Laira shops **R**
24/6/38	Newton Abbot shed **L**
27/10/38	Swindon Works **G**
12/11/38	Penzance
2/6/39	Penzance shops **R**
7/10/39	Penzance shops **R**
10/5/40	Newton Abbot shed **L**
4/3/41	Swindon Works **I**
9/1941	St Blazey
18/11/42	Swindon Works **G**
6/4/44	Newton Abbot Works **L**
12/2/45	Swindon Works **I**
10/8/45	Newton Abbot Works **L**
16/1/47	Swindon Works **I**
9/4/48	Newton Abbot Works **L**
	Tender work only
8/12/48	Swindon Works **G**
5/4/50	St Blazey shops **U**
21/7/50	St Blazey shops **LC**
25/9/50	Newton Abbot Works **LC**
29/1/51	Swindon Works **HI**
10/8/51	Newton Abbot Works **U**
23/2/52	Laira
19/5/52	Laira shops **U**
1/11/52	St Blazey
13/10/53	Swindon Works **HG**
1/2/55	St Blazey shops **U**
4/6/56	Swindon Works **HI**
18/5/57	Stafford Road
27/6/58	Swindon Works **HG**
22/12/58	Tyseley shops **U**
26/9/60	Swindon Works **HI**
6/10/61	Wolverhampton Works **LC**
7/10/61	Tyseley
21/4/62	Banbury

Tenders
From new	2619
26/3/35	2685
20/7/36	2420
3/2/37	2449
8/6/38	2724
22/1/41	2709
18/11/42	2401
12/2/45	2860
16/1/47	2549
23/11/48	1518
8/12/48	2545
2/1/51	2652
10/9/53	2765
4/5/56	2429
27/6/58	2538
26/9/60	2422

Mileage 1,263,834

Withdrawn 21/9/62 Sold to J Cashmore, Great Bridge 17/10/63

5926 GROTRIAN HALL at Shrewsbury shed; the 84A shed plate indicates the period is May 1957-October 1961. B.K.B. Green Collection, Initial Photographics.

5926 GROTRIAN HALL in lined black at speed approaching Widney Manor station with the 8.8pm Birmingham Snow Hill-Paddington train, 27 June 1957. Michael Mensing.

5927 GUILD HALL
Built in 1933 to Lot no.281 at Swindon Works
To traffic 6/1933

Only Engine Record Cards available

Mileage and Boilers

Sheds and Works history
1933	Old Oak		
6/4/35	Oxley		
6/2/37	Banbury		
17/9/38	Shrewsbury		
9/1941	Stafford Road		
31/8/42	Swindon Works **HG**		
4/11/44	Swindon Works **I**	83,948	
21/9/46	Swindon Works **I**	47,570	
20/3/48	Swindon Works **L**		
26/3/49	Tyseley		
17/9/49	Swindon Works **HG**	106,994	248,512
25/8/51	Worcester shops **LC**	91,795	
8/12/51	Swindon Works **HI**		
16/12/53	Swindon Works **HG**	79,763	171,558
19/4/56	Swindon Works **HI**		
17/5/60	Wolverhampton Works **U**		
19/5/61	Swindon Works **HI**	95033	Boiler 7215
11/10/63	Wolverhampton Works **HC**	68065	Boiler 2872

Withdrawn 10/1964

Mileage 1,180,726

5927 GUILD HALL at Kidderminster, 13 April 1964. It was withdrawn later in the year. ColourRail

5927 GUILD HALL with an up train near Bishopton, 9 September 1962. John Jennings, transporttreasury

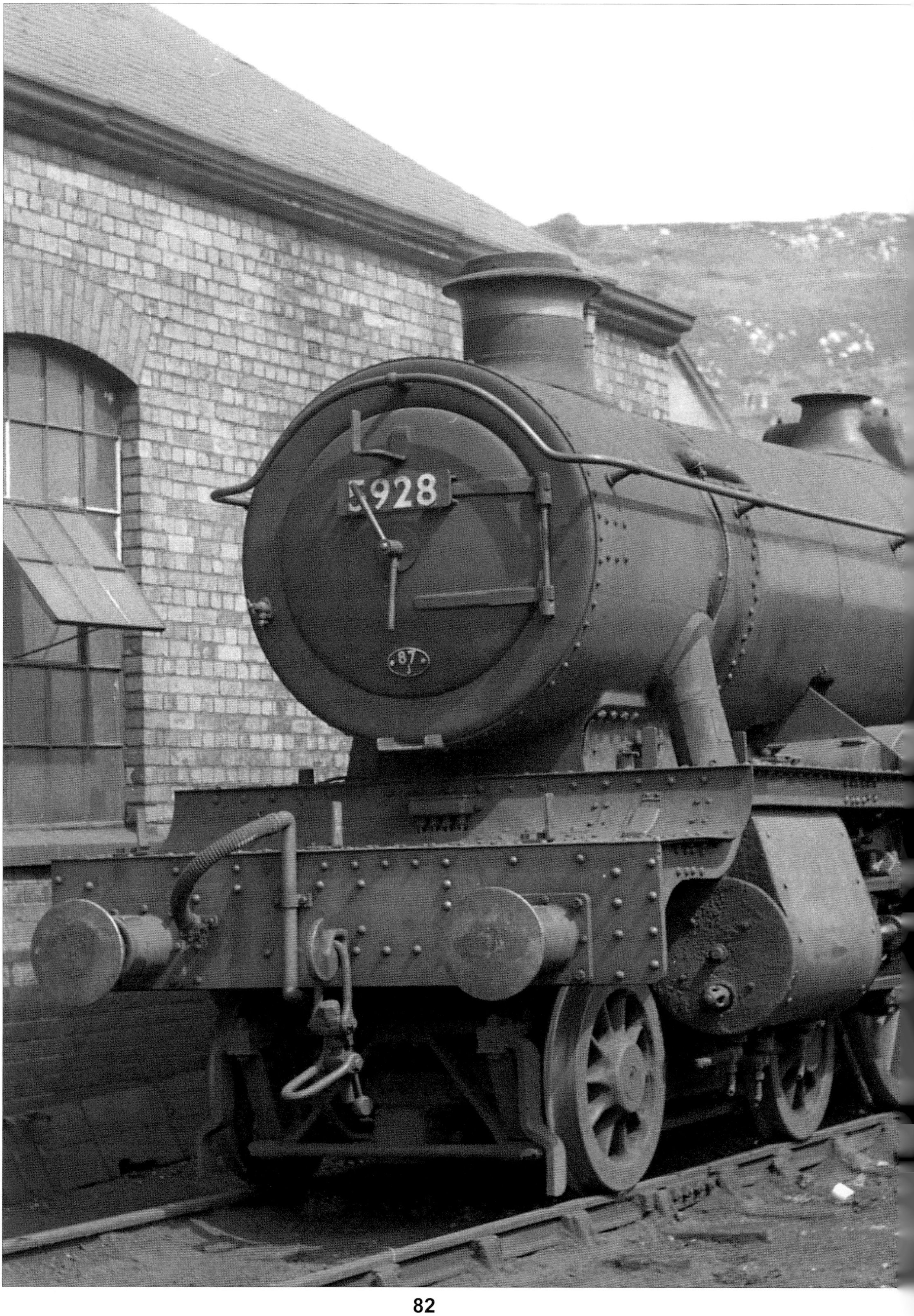
5928

5928 HADDON HALL at home at Goodwick (Fishguard) shed, 6 July 1961. It spent almost its entire life allocated here and must have made for a blank in many an English spotter's *abc*. L.W. Rowe, ColourRail

5928 HADDON HALL

Built in 1933 to Lot no.281 at Swindon Works
To traffic 6/1933

Mileages and Boilers

From new	4440
2/5/35	91,850 C4440
26/11/36	178,037 C4440
2/9/38	258,753 C2812
17/5/40	332,319 C2812
23/9/43	423,798 C2812
21/11/45	485,826 C2973
27/2/48	570,023 C7270
28/2/50	643,367 C8240
11/8/52	728,693 C7269
30/3/55	843,023 C7269
26/6/57	932,395 C8263
1/1/60	1,030,390 C6217

Sheds and Works history

1933	Fishguard Goodwick
11/2/35	Swindon Works **R**
2/5/35	Swindon Works **I**
4/5/35	Landore
21/9/35	Fishguard Goodwick
21/9/36	Carmarthen shops **R**
26/11/36	Swindon Works **I**
29/6/37	Fishguard Goodwick shops **R**
2/9/38	Swindon Works **G**
17/5/40	Swindon Works **I**
8/12/42	Carmarthen shops **L**
23/9/43	Swindon Works **I**
24/11/44	Landore shops **R**
21/11/45	Swindon Works **G**
30/10/47	Carmarthen shops **L**
27/2/48	Swindon Works **I**
13/10/49	Swindon Works **LC**
28/2/50	Swindon Works **HG**
11/8/52	Swindon Works **HG**
10/9/52	Swindon Works **LC**
30/3/55	Swindon Works **HI**
26/6/57	Swindon Works **HG**
23/9/57	Fishguard Goodwick shops **U**
27/2/58	Carmarthen shops **U**
17/10/58	Carmarthen shops **U**
1/1/60	Swindon Works **HG**
19/1/61	Fishguard Goodwick shops **U**

Tenders

From new	2622
12/3/35	2620
13/10/36	2531
14/6/37	2662
25/7/38	2676
17/5/40	2714
23/9/43	2810
21/11/45	2444
19/1/48	2437
2/10/48	2797
13/10/49	2919
28/2/50	2607
11/8/52	2564
26/12/53	2553
24/4/54	2532
19/6/54	2746
30/3/55	2687
26/6/57	2715
1/1/60	2412

Mileage 1,180,889

Withdrawn 11/5/62 Cut up 11/8/62

5929 HANHAM HALL

Built in 1933 to Lot no.281 at Swindon Works
To traffic 6/1933

Mileages and Boilers
From new	4441
17/5/35	88,688 C4441
10/12/36	176,082 C4441
2/12/38	261,317 C4944
4/11/40	338,711 C4944
22/2/44	437,625 C4944
24/11/45	501,453 C8214
13/10/47	576,030 C4468
2/6/50	671,702 C4468
7/4/53	754,810 C7219
18/10/55	847,193 C7219
25/2/58	929,421 C7217
13/10/60	1,028,338 C7217

Sheds and Works history
1933	St Philips Marsh
25/8/34	Llanelly
21/9/34	Llanelly shops **R**
22/9/34	St Philips Marsh
23/1/35	Swindon Works **L**
17/5/35	Swindon Works **I**
1/6/35	Bristol Bath Road
29/7/36	St Philips Marsh shops **R**
10/12/36	Swindon Works **I**
9/1/37	Landore
7/5/38	Swindon Works **L**
26/6/38	Fishguard Goodwick
2/12/38	Swindon Works **G**
9/2/40	Fishguard Goodwick shops **R**
4/11/40	Swindon Works **I**
21/10/42	Swindon Works **L**
22/2/44	Swindon Works **I**
25/4/44	Swindon Works **R**
5/1944	Neyland
23/5/45	Neyland shops **R**
24/11/45	Swindon Works **G**
24/2/46	Neyland shops **R**
9/9/46	Danygraig shops **L**
13/10/47	Swindon Works **I**
8/9/48	Old Oak shops **L**
	Tender work only
2/10/48	Landore
28/10/49	Taunton shops **U**
2/6/50	Wolverhampton Works **HI**
24/2/51	Newport Ebbw Jct
24/3/51	Landore
31/7/51	Old Oak shops **U**
21/4/52	Old Oak shops **U**
30/7/52	Old Oak shops **U**
23/1/53	Old Oak shops **U**
7/4/53	Swindon Works **HG**
12/11/53	Landore shops **U**
18/10/55	Swindon Works **HI**
23/2/57	Danygraig shops **U**
20/7/57	Carmarthen shops **U**
25/2/58	Swindon Works **HG**
1/11/58	Old Oak
20/11/59	Newport Ebbw Jct shops **LC**
13/10/60	Wolverhampton Works **HI**
20/10/61	Wolverhampton Works **LC**
2/12/61	Old Oak shops **U**
24/2/62	St Philips Marsh
28/2/62	Shrewsbury shops **U**
14/7/62	Westbury
7/9/62	Caerphilly Works **LC**
17/11/62	Southall
29/6/63	Pontypool Road

Tenders
From new	2620
27/3/35	2629
7/7/36	2575
3/1/36	2660
21/3/38	2534
31/10/38	2591
23/9/40	2553
12/11/44	2662
23/12/44	2441
24/11/45	2587
13/10/47	2543
5/11/49	2886
11/7/51	2407
23/2/52	2752
16/2/53	2449
16/7/55	2565
18/10/55	2399
25/2/58	2695
16/5/59	2799
No date	2823

Mileage 1,096,640

Withdrawn 28/10/63 Sold to R S Hayes Bridgend 1/1/64

5929 HANHAM HALL finds itself on down empty stock at Birmingham Snow Hill, standing at platform 5/6 on 7 November 1957. Pannier 9680 to left. Michael Mensing.

Landore's 5929 HANHAM HALL at Carmarthen shed on 16 August 1954. The Pembroke Coast Express called in at Swansea High Street, a terminus, and the train would reverse there. It would therefore require an engine change on both the Up and Down workings. The train would also reverse at Carmarthen where another engine change would take place. 5929 would only work the train over the Carmarthen to Swansea section. R. Broughton, ColourRail

Still a Landore engine (though it would soon move to Old Oak) 5929 HANHAM HALL at Carmarthen again (the Repair Shop stands behind) on 7 July 1958. H.C. Casserley, courtesy R.M. Casserley.

5930 HANNINGTON HALL

Built in 1933 to Lot no.281 at Swindon Works
To traffic 6/1933

Mileages and Boilers
From new	4442
3/6/35	95,329 C4442
13/3/37	182,775 R2947
9/2/39	269,524 R2947
20/6/41	349,295 R2947
30/3/44	432,428 C7239
13/11/46	525,999 C4989
2/6/48	562,645 C4074
21/12/49	619,605 C4986
20/2/52	696,711 C2887
10/6/54	773,397 C4985
29/8/56	854,729 C4985
28/11/58	937,733 C8260

Sheds and Works history
1933	Oxley
3/6/35	Swindon Works I
29/6/35	Banbury
13/3/37	Swindon Works G
19/4/38	Swindon Works R
9/2/39	Swindon Works I
20/6/41	Swindon Works I
20/10/42	Banbury shops R
2/10/43	Tyseley shops L
30/3/44	Swindon Works G
13/11/46	Swindon Works I
25/3/47	Tyseley shops R
2/6/48	Swindon Works L
21/12/49	Swindon Works HG
20/2/52	Swindon Works HI
6/6/53	Banbury shops U
10/6/54	Swindon Works HG
28/4/56	Banbury shops U
29/8/56	Wolverhampton Works HI
28/11/58	Wolverhampton Works HG
28/1/59	Tyseley
20/4/59	Banbury shops U
23/4/60	Stourbridge
24/3/61	Wolverhampton Works HC
7/10/61	Worcester
30/12/61	Wolverhampton Works LC

Tenders
From new	2626
10/4/35	2602
5/2/37	2703
3/1/39	2708
16/4/41	2839
2/2/44	2681
17/11/49	2390
18/1/52	2858
10/5/54	2609

Mileage 1,037,428

Withdrawn 21/9/62 Sold to John Cashmore Ltd Great Bridge 23/9/63

Right. 5930 HANNINGTON HALL after attention in the works at Swindon; lined dark green, GREAT WESTERN with badge on tender, 2 June 1935. It would be 5930's Intermediate repair of that year. Part work apparent on smokebox; a full repaint would have seen the monogram on the tender. RailOnline

Bottom right. 5930 HANNINGTON HALL at Bristol Temple Meads in very different state... There is no date to be had and the shed plate is not visible but the survival of the vacuum pump lubricator in front of the leading splasher suggests the earlier part of the 1950s, before its Heavy General of 1954 perhaps. B.K.B. Green Collection, Initial Photographics.

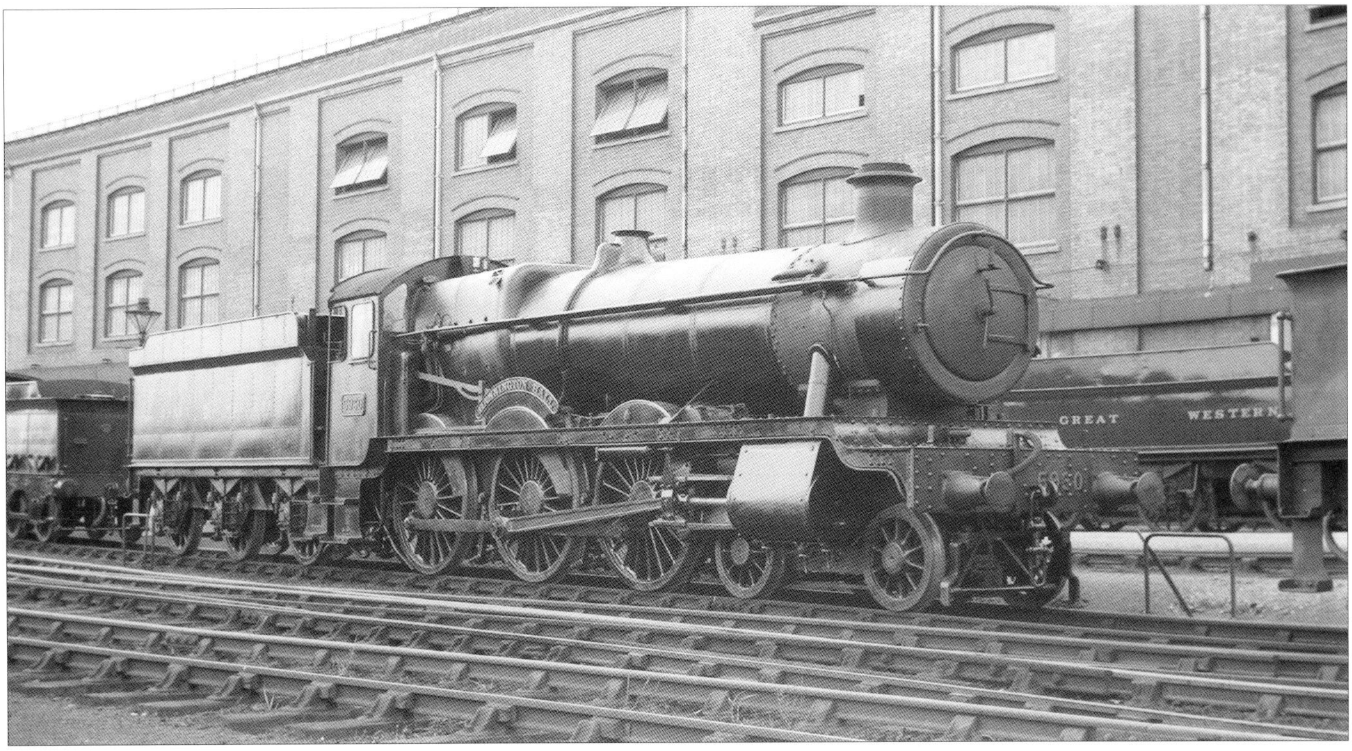
5930
GREAT
WESTERN

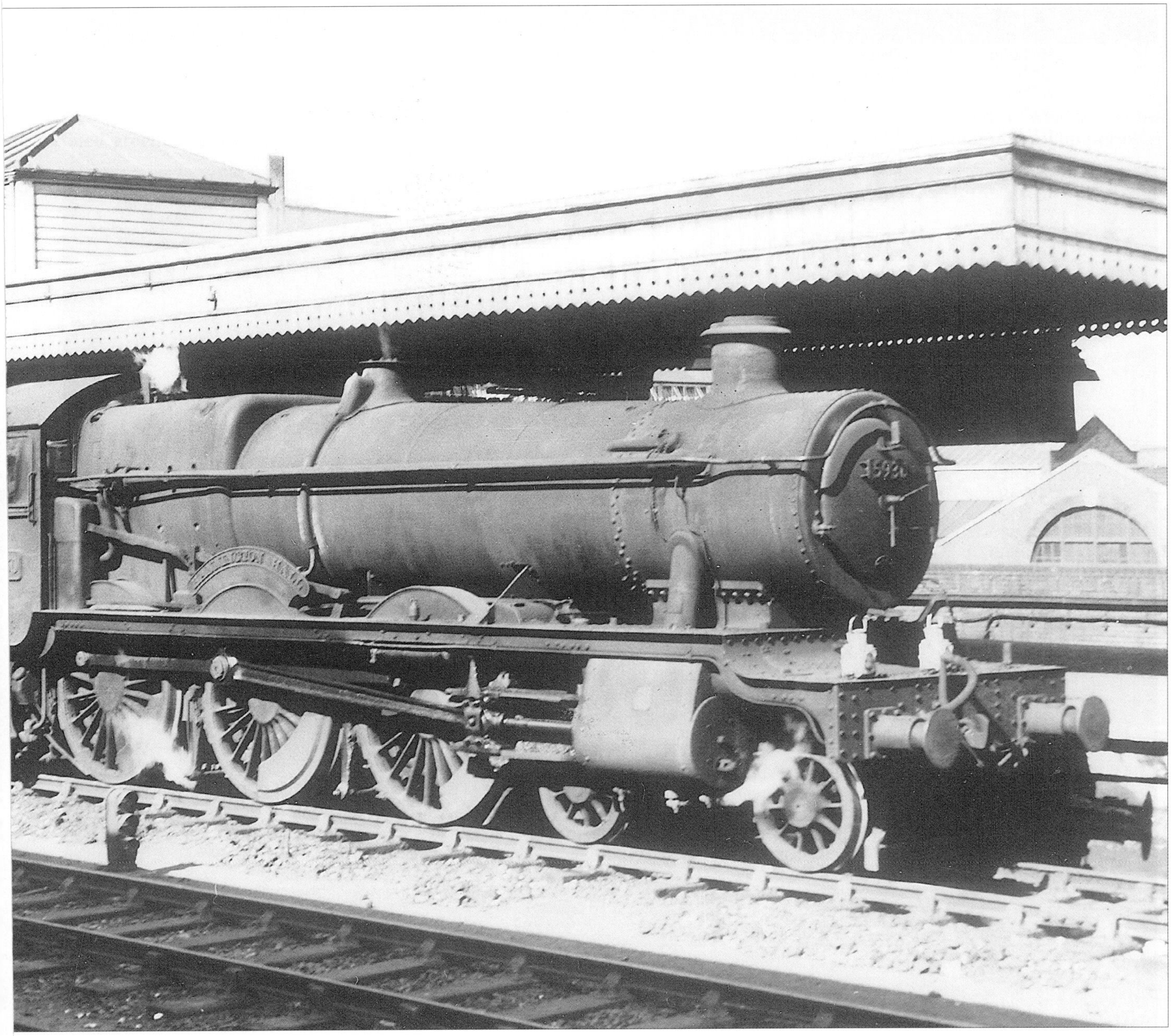
5930

5932 HAYDON HALL

Built to in 1933 to Lot no.281 at Swindon Works
To traffic 6/1933

Mileages and Boilers
From new	4444
1/2/35	84,773 C4444
30/6/36	154,977 C4444
5/2/38	230,046 C4490
14/9/39	315,043 C4490
5/11/41	406,038 C4490
6/2/44	467,379 C2842
1/1/46	544,432 C8285
29/8/46	570,791 C4005
8/9/48	645,538 C2918
27/9/50	734,786 C4479
28/11/52	835,133 C4944
29/12/54	946,853 C4967
19/3/57	1,043,302 C4967
8/1/60	1,146,628 C2934
14/5/62	1,235,216 C8209

Sheds and Works history
1933	Bristol Bath Road
27/6/34	Bristol Bath Road shops **R**
30/6/34	Swindon Works
	ATC clip up
1/2/35	Swindon Works **I**
9/3/35	Swindon
30/6/36	Swindon Works **I**
5/2/38	Swindon Works **G**
10/8/38	Swindon Works **L**
14/9/39	Swindon Works **I**
13/10/39	Oxley
3/2/40	Swindon
5/11/41	Swindon Works **I**
14/3/42	Westbury shops **R**
20/9/42	Swindon Works **L**
6/2/44	Swindon Works **G**
10/1944	Bristol Bath Road
1/1/46	Swindon Works **I**
20/4/46	Swindon
29/8/46	Swindon Works **L**
5/10/46	Old Oak
19/11/47	Gloucester shops **L**
13/2/48	Old Oak shed **R**
8/9/48	Swindon Works **I**
15/12/48	Old Oak shops **I**
	Tender work only
27/9/50	Swindon Works **HG**
22/10/50-4/11/50	Stored at Swindon
28/11/52	Swindon Works **HI**
29/12/54	Swindon Works **HG**
30/6/55	Banbury shops **U**
20/6/56	Old Oak shops **U**
19/3/57	Swindon Works **HI**
15/10/58	Old Oak shops **U**
30/1/59	Old Oak shops **U**
9/2/59-11/5/59	Stored at Didcot shed
8/1/60	Swindon Works **HI**
27/1/61	Old Oak shed **U**
27/6/61	Old Oak shed **U**
14/11/61	Old Oak shops **LC**
14/5/62	Swindon Works **HG**
4/5/63	Reading
12/7/63	Reading shops **LC**
31/12/63	Oxford
13/4/64	Cardiff East Dock
4/5/64	Westbury
24/8/64	Severn Tunnel Jct
27/8/64	Worcester shops **U**
10/4/65	Bristol Barrow Road

Tenders
From new	2631
16/5/36	2619
31/12/37	2398
10/8/38	2601
3/8/39	2740
22/9/41	2700
8/8/42	2258
21/10/43	2398
17/10/45	2389
27/4/46	2243
29/8/46	2601
14/7/48	2859
29/8/50	2927
27/10/52	2696
19/2/57	2644
10/1959	4065
8/1/60	2794
3/1962	2563
14/5/62	2595

Mileage 1,284,369 at 28/12/63

Withdrawn 26/10/65 Sold to J Cashmore Newport 7/12/65

Old Oak Common's 5932 HAYDON HALL on Teignmouth sea wall; date not recorded, though the second emblem indicates the later part of the 1950s. J. Davenport, Initial Photographics.

5932 HAYDON HALL looking very tired at Shrewsbury shed in 1959. D.K. Jones Collection.

At Banbury in 1959 but clean enough to suggest that this might be *post* its Heavy Intermediate at Caerphilly that year; it would be in lined green.

5933 KINGSWAY HALL

Built in 1933 to Lot no.281 at Swindon Works
To traffic 6/1933

Mileages and Boilers
Only ERCs Available

Sheds and Works history

1933	Bristol Bath Road		
28/7/34	Reading		
7/8/42	Swindon Works **G**		
15/12/45	Swindon Works **I**	112,727	
6/12/47	Swindon Works **I**	77,221	
20/5/50	Swindon Works **HG**	89,477	219,425
6/9/52	Swindon Works **HG**	89,001	89,001
9/4/54	Reading shops **LC**		
2/5/55	Swindon Works **HI**		
24/5/57	Swindon Works **HG**		
22/2/58	Southall		
12/5/59	Caerphilly Works **HI**	79,752	
27/2/60	Oxford		
21/5/60	Banbury		
3/12/60	Oxford		
23/8/61	Wolverhampton Works **HI** 154,032 boiler 7207		
9/11/61	Continuation of **HI**		
11/10/63	Swindon Works **HC** 44,535 boiler 8265		

Tenders
No dates
2807
2600
2442
2798
2568
2774
2812

Mileage 1,131,460

Withdrawn 6/8/65 Sold to Birds Bynea 6/9/65

Left. 5933 KINGSWAY HALL newly outshopped in lined black, at Bath Road shed. It was possibly Reading's longest serving Hall so the 81D plate does little to help determine the period; 1950, after its Heavy General that year is a good bet. Note taper buffers. J. Davenport, Initial Photographics.

At Pontypool Road, late in the day; after years spent at Reading it had moved around the London Division from 1958, to Southall, then to Oxford with a short stay at Banbury in between. It was still at Oxford when withdrawn in 1965. The buildings in the left background were the other side of the main Hereford - Newport line and were part of the local gas works. Most views of Pontypool Road were taken at the south end, showing the 1860s straight shed with the hipped slated roof. This is the north end, showing the 1880s roundhouse which was the same style as Swindon and Reading. ColourRail

5934 KNELLER HALL

Built in 1933 to Lot no.281 at Swindon Works
To traffic 6/1933

Mileages and Boilers

From new	4446
2/5/35	90,000 C4446
9/11/36	174,794 C4930
21/6/39	257,545 C4930
1/8/40	339,979 C4930
25/4/43	423,975 R9221
17/10/45	515,723 C8233
21/11/46	551,171 C7244
2/11/48	621,879 C7244
25/10/50	703,856 C4488
28/7/52	776,919 C8292
4/2/55	877,377 C4076
12/12/56	965,292 C4076
4/3/59	1,066,367 C7243
30/10/61	1,163,761 C7238

Sheds and Works history

1933	Stafford Road
4/7/34	Swindon Works ATC clip up
28/7/34	Didcot
2/9/34	Didcot shops **R**
2/5/35	Swindon Works **I**
1/6/35	Old Oak
22/5/36	Old Oak shops **R**
9/11/36	Swindon Works **G**
14/11/36	Didcot
1/9/37	Swindon Works ATC repair
26/1/39	Swindon Works **I**
4/3/39	Old Oak
1/8/40	Swindon Works **I**
11/9/40	Reading shops **R**
27/7/41	Reading shops **R**
31/10/41	Westbury shops **R**
11/1941	Westbury
11/4/42	Westbury shops **R**
30/12/42	Westbury shops **R**
25/4/43	Swindon Works **G**
17/3/44	Weymouth shops **R**
10/1944	Bristol Bath Road
17/10/45	Swindon Works **I**
11/2/46	Bristol Bath Road shops **L**
15/6/46	Swindon
21/11/46	Swindon Works **G**
6/8/47	Swindon Works **L**
2/11/48	Swindon Works **I**
27/5/49	Swindon Works **LC**
25/10/50	Swindon Works **HG**
8/12/50	Swindon Works **I**
28/7/52	Swindon Works **HI**
28/11/53	Bristol Bath Road
26/1/54	Bristol Bath Road shops **U**
27/2/54	Laira
19/11/54	Laira shops **U**
4/2/55	Swindon Works **HG**
17/7/55	Laira shops **U**
2/2/56	Laira shops **U**
22/5/56	Laira shops **U**
8/10/56	Lairs shops **U**
12/12/56	Swindon Works **HI**
22/2/58	Penzance
4/3/59	Swindon Works **HG**
27/10/59	Swindon Works **LC**
28/11/59	Bristol Bath Road
10/9/60	St Philips Marsh
30/10/61	Swindon Works **HI**
9/2/62	Banbury shops **U**
22/8/63	Wolverhampton Works **LC**
27/2/64	St Philips Marsh shops **U**

Tenders

From new	2623
7/3/35	2578
5/10/36	2561
23/12/38	2703
29/6/40	2754
4/3/43	2590
8/8/45	2757
21/11/46	2787
6/8/47	2696
2/11/48	2711
27/5/49	2578
16/11/50	2844
8/12/50	2851
28/7/52	2848
5/1/55	2610
24/3/56	4039
12/12/56	2589
4/3/59	2869
27/10/59	2768
6/1961	2304
30/10/61	2849

Mileage 1,223,568 as at 28/12/63

Withdrawn 6/5/64 Sold to R S Hayes Bridgend 22/6/64

A filthy 5934 KNELLER HALL is without the least hint of livery so thick are the layers of grime at Oxford in 1950... RailOnline

KNELLER HALL a little cleaner, enough to reveal a trace of lined black at least, at Newton Abbot in 1957. D.K. Jones Collection.

5935 NORTON HALL
Built in 1933 to Lot no.281 at Swindon Works
To traffic 7/1933

Mileages and Boilers
From new	4447
18/5/35	100,681 C4447
23/6/36	157,661 C4450
27/2/37	187,738 C4450
11/11/38	271,882 C4450
19/7/42	382,782 C4972
28/9/45	476,577 C4972
27/3/47	529,919 C8259
28/7/49	608,346 C4427
14/1/52	697,672 C2904
4/11/53	773,090 C2904
6/9/55	841,366 C2981
20/9/57	920,150 C2981
27/11/59	996,715 C7247

Sheds and Works history
1933	Stafford Road
10/3/34	Chester
25/7/34	Swindon Works
	ATC clip up
28/7/34	Reading
18/5/35	Swindon Works **I**
23/6/36	Swindon Works **L**
27/2/37	Swindon Works **I**
11/11/38	Swindon Works **I**
16/12/38	Oxford shops **R**
4/2/39	Didcot
7/10/40	Didcot shops **R**
6/12/41	Didcot shops **R**
29/4/42	Didcot shops **R**
19/7/42	Swindon Works **G**
10/4/43	Didcot shops **R**
19/11/43	Old Oak shops **L**
18/10/44	Didcot shops **R**
30/3/45	Gloucester shops **R**
22/5/45	Old Oak shops **L**
28/9/45	Swindon Works **I**
27/3/47	Swindon Works **L**
19/8/48	Old Oak shops **R**
16/11/48	Old Oak shops **R**
28/7/49	Swindon Works **HG**
14/1/52	Swindon Works **HG**
27/1/53	Didcot shops **U**
21/8/53	Didcot shops **U**
4/11/53	Swindon Works **HI**
26/3/54	Didcot shops **LC**
6/9/55	Swindon Works **HG**
20/9/57	Swindon Works **HI**
10/1/58	Swindon Works **U**
3/6/58	Swindon Works **U**
14/6/58	St Philips Marsh
4/5/59	Didcot shops **U**
16/5/59	Westbury
27/11/59	Swindon Works **HG**
18/1/61	Wolverhampton Works **LC**
2/12/61	Canton

Tenders
From new	2627
2/4/35	2618
25/1/37	2397
10/10/38	2448
30/5/42	2724
12/7/45	2768
26/3/49	2833
10/12/51	2765
4/11/53	2902
6/11/55	4040
20/9/57	2597
3/6/58	2731
27/11/59	2704

Mileage 1,097,229

Withdrawn 15/5/62 Cut up 11/8/62

5935 NORTON HALL at Didcot, 12 October 1949; tender, as so often in this period, is bare of any lettering or emblem. H.C. Casserley, courtesy R.M. Casserley.

5935 NORTON HALL at Shrewsbury at an unrecorded date, in lined black with a barely visible first emblem. ColourRail

5936 OAKLEY HALL, new, at Old Oak Common in 1933. Rail Photoprint.

Main photograph. Taking water at the shed; it was at Reading for a year or two until 1961, when it had a Heavy General and was sent on to Gloucester. Peter Groom

5936 OAKLEY HALL, now in lined green with the second emblem, serving as station pilot at Reading about 1960-61. Michael Boakes Collection.

The End. In the crumbling environs of its last shed, Gloucester Horton Road on 4 January 1965. It was withdrawn that very month. RailOnline

5936 OAKLEY HALL

Built in 1933 to Lot no.281 at Swindon Works
To traffic 7/1933

Mileages and Boilers
Date	Mileage/Boiler
From new	4448
18/4/35	91,957 C4448
3/2/37	192,165 C2932
5/9/38	276,682 C2932
11/6/40	366,443 C2932
18/2/43	469,569 C4434
10/7/45	563,226 C2945
21/8/47	652,415 C4950
25/11/49	750,584 C4023
15/11/51	842,814 C4921
28/4/54	960,215 C8217
25/5/56	1,048,151 C8217
13/6/58	1,129,078 C7259
2/8/61	1,219,960 C9202

Sheds and Works history
1933	Old Oak
29/6/34	Swindon Works ATC clip up
18/4/35	Swindon Works I
3/2/37	Swindon Works G
5/9/38	Swindon Works I
22/11/39	Old Oak shops R
11/6/40	Swindon Works I
11/3/41	Old Oak shops R
18/7/41	Old Oak shops L
15/9/41	Old Oak shops R
30/8/42	Old Oak shops R
18/2/43	Swindon Works G
31/7/44	Swindon Works L
10/7/45	Swindon Works I
2/8/46	Old Oak shops L
25/2/47	Taunton shops R
21/8/47	Swindon Works I
7/7/49	Old Oak shops U
25/11/49	Swindon Works HG
15/11/51	Swindon Works HG
30/11/53	Old Oak shops U
28/4/54	Swindon Works HG
25/5/56	Wolverhampton Works HI
5/11/57	Old Oak shops U
30/1/58	Old Oak shops U
13/6/58	Caerphilly Works HI
29/8/58	Old Oak shops U
11/2/59-23/3/59	Stored at Didcot shed
16/5/59	Reading
2/8/61	Swindon Works HG
6/4/63	Gloucester

Tenders
Date	Tender
From new	2607
9/3/35	2622
31/12/36	2567
2/8/38	2663
11/6/40	2699
11/5/41	2708
5/1/43	2914
15/5/44	2563
21/8/49	2625
21/10/49	2390
18/10/51	2820
25/3/54	2424
9/10/54	4054
18/6/56	2845
4/1961	2848
2/8/61	2899

Mileage 1,294,179 as at 28/12/63

Withdrawn 1/65

5938 STANLEY HALL

Built in 1933 to Lot no.281 at Swindon Works
To traffic 7/1933

Mileages and Boilers
From new	4450
7/12/34	71,164 C4450
8/4/36	146,681 C4413
11/2/38	285,109 C4413
13/11/39	323,096 C4413
6/11/42	417,427 C2907
30/6/45	525,409 C4943
26/11/47	613,795 C4076
12/5/50	710,207 C7264
20/11/52	817,818 C8238
30/12/54	924,241 C7275
13/3/57	1,014,675 C8269
20/8/58	1,105,252 C4036
14/11/61	1,185,888 C8242

Sheds and Works history
1933	Stafford Road
10/2/34	Oxley
7/12/34	Swindon Works **I**
15/12/34	Old Oak
8/4/36	Swindon Works **G**
24/8/36	Swindon Works **L**
18/9/37	Swindon Works **L**
1/11/37	Old Oak shops **R**
11/2/38	Swindon Works **I**
13/11/39	Swindon Works **I**
20/3/40	Gloucester shops **R**
8/4/41	Bristol Bath Road shops **R**
29/5/41	Old Oak shops **R**
27/3/42	Old Oak shops **R**
6/11/42	Swindon Works **G**
12/8/43	Old Oak shops **L**
7/2/44	Old Oak shops **I**
30/6/45	Swindon Works **I**
26/7/45	Bristol Bath Road shops **R**
29/3/47	Old Oak shops **R**
19/6/47	Old Oak shops **L**
26/11/47	Swindon Works **I**
18/2/48	Old Oak shops **L**
	Tender work only
20/3/48	Reading
17/4/48	Old Oak
22/12/48	Old Oak shops **R**
12/5/50	Swindon Works **HG**
1/12/50	Swindon Works **U**
21/2/52	Old Oak shops **U**
20/10/52	Old Oak shops **U**
20/11/52	Swindon Works **HI**
8/8/53	Carmarthen
30/12/54	Swindon Works **HG**
27/1/55	Swindon Works **U**
	ATC
13/3/57	Swindon Works **HG**
23/5/58	Neyland shops **U**
26/6/58	Carmarthen shops **U**
20/8/58	Swindon Works **HI**
10/9/59	Swindon Works **U**
14/11/61	Swindon Works **HG**
9/2/63	Newport Ebbw Jc**t**
28/3/63	Hereford shops **U**

Tenders
From new	2530
6/10/34	2420
22/8/36	2635
20/4/37	2625
11/2/38	2445
25/9/42	2679
30/6/45	2438
26/11/47	2391
14/4/50	2558
11/2/50	2812
22/10/52	4116
25/11/54	2443
13/3/57	2943
20/8/59	2790
18/11/61	2782

Mileage 1,239,861

Withdrawn 3/5/63 Cut up at Wolverhampton Works 10/8/63

Carmarthen's own 5938 STANLEY HALL ready for the next up Pembroke Coast Express, on 7 February 1962. M.J. Reade, ColourRail

5938 STANLEY HALL at Neyland shed, date unknown. ColourRail

5940 WHITBOURNE HALL

Built in 1933 to Lot no.281 at Swindon Works
To traffic 8/1933

Mileages and Boilers
From new	4492
1/3/35	82,710 C2978
2/1/37	165,760 C2978
13/8/38	242,804 C4030
29/11/39	316,602 C4030
6/4/42	412,652 C4030
3/6/44	494,660 C4030
26/10/45	550,229 C4048
16/9/47	629,866 C4048
21/7/49	700,600 C4985
26/4/51	784,215 C2988
24/2/53	873,072 R6207
25/5/55	996,064 C2995
8/8/57	1,081,140 C2995
15/6/60	1,189,967 C7257

Sheds and Works history
1933	Stafford Road
10/2/34	Tyseley
7/4/34	Stafford Road
22/9/34	Oxley
1/3/35	Swindon Works **G**
9/3/35	Old Oak
2/5/35	Wolverhampton Works **L**
4/5/35	Didcot
28/10/35	Weymouth shops **R**
6/12/35	Old Oak shops **R**
8/2/36	Old Oak
2/1/37	Swindon Works **I**
9/5/38	Swindon Works **L**
13/8/38	Swindon Works **G**
29/11/39	Swindon Works **I**
21/5/40	Swindon Works **L**
15/11/40	Old Oak shops **R**
6/4/42	Swindon Works **I**
4/3/44	Bristol Bath Road shops **R**
15/4/44	Bristol Bath Road shops **R**
3/6/44	Swindon Works **I**
26/10/45	Swindon Works **G**
4/2/47	Old Oak shed R
16/9/47	Swindon Works **I**
1/6/48	Newton Abbot shed **L**
5/8/48	Old Oak shops **L**
21/7/49	Swindon Works **HG**
26/4/51	Swindon Works **HI**
21/9/52	Old Oak shed **U**
24/2/53	Swindon Works **HG**
25/5/55	Swindon Works **HG**
21/10/55	Old Oak shops **LC**
3/4/57	Old Oak shops **U**
8/8/57	Swindon Works **HI**
4/12/58	Old Oak shops **U**
26/2/59-13/6/59	Stored at Didcot
11/7/59	Bristol Bath Road
15/6/60	Swindon Works **HG**
10/9/60	St Philips Marsh
11/11/61	St Philips Marsh shops **U**

Tenders
From new	2633
28/10/39	2386
19/4/40	2384
17/2/42	2773
4/3/44	2683
14/4/44	2662
5/9/45	2393
16/9/47	2445
15/5/48	2720
12/6/48	2751
21/7/49	2606
12/8/50	2596
2/11/50	2391
23/4/55	2560
25/5/55	2549
5/11/55	2440
16/6/56	2593
11/8/56	2535
6/10/56	2536
12/2/57	2573
8/8/57	2630
29/4/58	2722
27/11/58	2563
1/9/59	2754
15/6/60	2785

Mileage 1,265,086

Withdrawn 21/9/62 Sold to Messrs John Cashmore Ltd Newport 23/8/63

5940 WHITBOURNE HALL in 1935 bound for Old Oak Common sidings, taking out empty stock after working in on a train. 'Shirt button' on the tender. Rail Photoprint.

5940 WHITBOURNE HALL at what looks like Bournemouth SR shed; lined black, first emblem. It had been an Old Oak engine more or less since it was built. ColourRail

5940 WHITBOURNE HALL at Paddington awaiting departure in July 1954. B.H. Fletcher, transporttreasury

5941 CAMPION HALL

Built in 1935 to Lot no.290 at Swindon Works
To traffic 2/1935

Mileages and Boilers
From new	2845
1/3/37	107,612 C2845
20/10/38	190,772 C2845
9/5/41	296,613 C3004
28/10/43	385,327 C3004
6/7/46	482,953 C7245
3/6/48	555,236 C2913
21/8/50	644,251 C7226
19/3/53	740,603 C4433
24/8/55	842,393 C6211
2/8/57	935,485 C8265
9/12/59	1,022,347 C9254

Sheds and Works history
9/3/35	Old Oak
15/2/36	Old Oak shops **R**
1/3/37	Swindon Works **I**
20/10/38	Swindon Works **I**
3/6/40	Shrewsbury shops **R**
10/8/40	Old Oak shops **R**
9/5/41	Swindon Works **G**
7/11/41	Old Oak shops **L**
9/1/42	Oxford shops **R**
8/3/43	Weymouth shops **R**
28/10/43	Swindon Works **I**
25/2/44	Old Oak shops **R**
6/7/46	Swindon Works **I**
3/6/48	Swindon Works **G**
30/10/49	Old Oak shed **U**
30/5/50	Newton Abbot shed **U**
21/8/50	Swindon Works **HG**
10/5/51	Old Oak shops **U**
4/9/51	Old Oak shed **U**
21/6/52	Oxford shops **U**
22/8/52	Old Oak shops **U**
19/3/53	Swindon Works **HG**
21/9/54	Swindon Works **U**
9/3/55	Reading shops **U**
12/5/55	Old Oak shops **U**
24/8/55	Swindon Works **HI**
2/8/57	Swindon Works **HG**
5/2/59-13/6/59	Stored at Didcot
11/7/59	Bristol Bath Road
22/7/59	Bristol Bath Road shops **U**
31/10/59	St Philips Marsh
9/12/59	Swindon Works **HI**
26/12/59	Bristol Bath Road
10/9/60	St Philips Marsh
11/5/61	Caerphilly Works **LC**
20/5/61	Shrewsbury shops **U**

Tenders
From new	2427
20/1/37	2610
16/9/38	2734
23/3/41	2438
6/2/43	2713
6/7/46	2880
28/3/48	2896
13/7/50	2437
10/5/51	2692
11/2/53	2705
21/9/54	2573
21/5/55	2391
12/7/55	2904
2/8/57	2446
24/1/59	2754
4/9/59	2563
1/4/59	2688
9/12/59	2571

Mileage 1,112,729

Withdrawn 13/7/62 Cut up 1/12/62

5941 CAMPION HALL ready to depart from Paddington about 1953; crisp, clean lined black. D.K. Jones Collection.

At home at Old Oak, 16 February 1958, now in lined green. Peter Groom.

5942 DOLDOWLOD HALL

Built in 1935 to Lot no.290 at Swindon Works
To traffic 2/1935

Mileages and Boilers
From new	2846
29/6/37	108,566 C2846
19/8/39	199,744 C2846
26/2/41	265,158 C4419
17/11/42	334,143 C4419
15/9/43	353,634 C2942
2/1/46	433,654 C2951
16/8/47	493,037 C2893
6/1/49	551,387 C2893
4/11/49	584,409 C8265
20/3/51	641,033 C9217
10/4/53	718,756 C9221
19/8/55	806,641 C9221
23/4/58	898,636 C4477
6/12/60	991,865 C8253

Sheds and Works history
9/3/35	Old Oak
4/5/35	Reading
4/7/35	Reading shops **R**
24/10/35	Oxford shops **R**
29/7/36	Reading shops **R**
5/11/36	Swindon Works **L**
23/11/36	Swindon Works **L**
29/6/37	Swindon Works **I**
24/7/37	Worcester
13/4/38	Worcester shops **R**
15/10/38	Stafford Road
19/8/39	Swindon Works **I**
26/2/41	Swindon Works **L**
8/11/41	Wolverhampton Works **L**
17/11/42	Swindon Works **I**
15/9/43	Swindon Works **G**
3/4/45	Stafford Road shed **R**
2/1/46	Swindon Works **G**
18/2/47	Stafford Road shed **R**
28/3/47	Stafford Road shed **R**
16/8/47	Swindon Works **L**
6/1/49	Wolverhampton Works **HI**
4/11/49	Swindon Works **HC**
7/10/50	Oxley
20/3/51	Swindon Works **HG**
14/6/52	Reading
17/6/52	Swindon Works **LC**
10/4/53	Swindon Works **HG**
22/10/54	Old Oak shops **U**
19/8/55	Swindon Works **HI**
31/1/56	Bristol Bath Road shops **LC**
5/12/56	Old Oak shops **U**
13/2/57	Old Oak shops **LC**
29/3/57	Reading shops **U**
23/4/58	Swindon Works **HG**
3/10/59	Oxford
26/12/59	Shrewsbury
24/5/60	Shrewsbury shops **U**
6/12/60	Swindon Works **HI**
4/10/62	Wolverhampton Works **LC**
21/12/62	Worcester shops **U**
Transferred to LMR Book Stock 30/12/62	
6/7/63	Tyseley
5/10/63	Shrewsbury

Tenders
From new	2631
17/9/36	2405
9/11/36	2432
25/5/37	2659
3/7/39	2677
13/1/41	2428
17/11/42	2868
19/4/43	2602
12/4/47	2550
16/8/47	2877
30/9/49	4030?
20/2/51	2803
12/5/52	2671
2/3/53	4080
9/10/54	2615
6/11/54	2521
26/4/55	2920
19/8/55	4053
22/4/58	2851
6/12/60	4104

Mileage 1,045,711

Withdrawn 2/12/63 Sold to John Cashmore 28/2/64

5942 DOLDOWLOD HALL with, it is thought, a cross-country service at what might be Hatton. Michael Boakes Collection.

5942 DOLDOWLOD HALL at Crewe South on 19 August 1961; lined green, second emblem, Hawksworth tender. If any faults developed on a Western loco Crewe would repair it as a matter of course unless it was too serious. There were no spares held of course but faults could be corrected with a bit of ingenuity. A Stanier Pacific bogie spring for instance (off one of the later ones with the 'French' bogie) fitted a Castle perfectly, it turned out. David Forsyth, ColourRail

5943 ELMDON HALL

Built in 1935 to Lot no.290 at Swindon Works
To traffic 3/1935

Mileages and Boilers
From new	2847
14/5/37	97,854 C2847
23/3/39	178,459 C2847
25/9/41	268,801 C4436
11/3/44	362,156 C4436
19/1/46	430,251 C4424
18/8/48	527,477 C4913
26/9/50	616,641 C4907
27/3/53	706,747 C2924
1/7/55	805,140 C9220
11/10/57	900,420 C6203
19/1/60	977,670 C2940
10/1/62	1,037,542 C8239

Sheds and Works history
6/4/35	Westbury
25/11/35	Weymouth shops **R**
24/3/36	Weymouth shops **R**
14/5/37	Swindon Works **I**
29/5/37	Weymouth
16/10/37	St Philips Marsh
27/4/38	St Philips Marsh shops **R**
25/8/38	St Philips Marsh shops **R**
23/3/39	Swindon Works **I**
29/4/39	Swindon
27/5/39	Bristol Bath Road
13/5/39	Swindon Works **L**
3/2/40	St Philips Marsh
26/10/40	St Philips Marsh shops **R**
25/9/41	Swindon Works **G**
11/1941	Swindon
11/3/44	Swindon Works **I**
10/1/45	Old Oak shops **R**
19/1/46	Swindon Works **G**
23/9/47	Swindon shed **L**
18/8/48	Swindon Works **I**
26/9/50	Swindon Works **HG**
9/10/50-6/11/50	Stored at Swindon
2/12/50	Worcester
21/2/51	Swindon Works **HC**
6/12/52	Worcester shops **U**
27/3/53	Swindon Works **HG**
1/7/55	Swindon Works **HI**
16/6/56	Laira
3/11/56	Didcot
11/10/57	Swindon Works **HG**
8/8/58	Wolverhampton Works **LC**
19/1/60	Swindon Works **HI**
25/2/61	St Philips Marsh
7/5/61	Westbury shops **U**
7/10/61	Swindon
12/10/61	Swindon shed **U**
10/1/62	Swindon Works **HC**
21/12/62	Carmarthen shops **U**

Tenders
From new	2423
1/4/37	2408
29/7/38	2626
9/1/39	2447
11/7/41	2635
11/3/44	2741
7/12/45	2652
18/8/48	2894
9/10/50	2569
2/1/51	2864
23/2/53	4114
26/5/55	2884
3/11/56	2816
11/10/57	2583
28/12/57	2588
19/1/60	2908
10/1/62	4031

Mileage 1,079,012

Withdrawn 24/6/63 Sold to Messrs Coopers Swindon 31/12/63

A Hall could be put to anything of course; and was. The headlamp code on 5943 ELMDON HALL (carrying a rackety-looking reporting number bracket) at Radipole on 8 July 1946 suggests an ordinary passenger train though the stock, to modern eyes, is anything but ordinary! Weymouth engine shed is beyond the footbridge, on the right. ColourRail

Didcot's 5943 ELMDON HALL draws up alongside Reading General platform 5 with a London bound service on 2 August 1960. Bernard Barlow, a fireman and driver at the shed from the late 1930s until the end of steam, recalls in his *Didcot Engineman* (Wild Swan 1994) that these engines were amongst the best, being free-running and steaming. Didcot retained the services of 5943 until February 1961 when an eight month sojourn at St Philip's March was followed by a move to Swindon where it was withdrawn in June 1963. It was scrapped at Cooper Metals, Sharpness, allegedly one of only twenty-five ex-GWR engines to be cut up there. Others on arrival were resold to Cashmore's of Newport when it became clear the capabilities of the yard had been overestimated and were too limited to deal with the numbers of condemned engines bought in. D.C. Ovenden, ColourRail

5943 ELMDON HALL (lined green, second emblem) on Hemerdon (the straight, steepest part of the eastbound climb) with a Castle on 9 August 1961. This looks like a regular train from the formation of Mark 1s in maroon; not a named train, that is. So it is probably going to the Midlands or North West via Bristol. The Hall was a Swindon engine by this time, a period when Laira was having to replace non-available diesels with Castles. The train could well have started at Penzance, with added coaches at Plymouth. Rail Photoprint.

5944 ICKENHAM HALL

Built in 1935 to Lot no.290 at Swindon Works
To traffic 3/1935

Mileages and Boilers
From new	2849
23/7/37	104,563 C2849
5/9/39	193,946 C4467
13/9/41	280,287 C4467
21/5/43	326,645 C4031
17/2/44	366,612 C4031
24/6/46	443,164 C2827
19/9/49	555,367 C4416
21/11/51	643,620 C8276
13/11/53	724,122 C2869
9/3/56	805,424 C2850
6/6/58	887,169 C4069
21/7/60	960,748 C2839

Sheds and Works history
6/4/35	Oxley
5/12/35	Stafford Road shed **R**
4/2/36	Banbury shops **R**
23/7/37	Swindon Works **I**
4/4/39	Swindon Works **L**
5/9/39	Swindon Works **G**
16/9/39	Stafford Road
13/9/41	Swindon Works **I**
24/8/42	Wolverhampton Works **R**
21/5/43	Swindon Works **L**
17/2/44	Swindon Works **I**
28/11/44	Stafford Road shed **R**
16/2/45	Stafford Road shed **R**
30/8/45	Swindon Works **L**
24/6/46	Swindon Works **G**
24/3/47	Swindon Works **L**
22/12/47	Banbury shops **R**
4/8/48	Wolverhampton Works **L**
25/7/49	Stafford Road shed **U**
19/9/49	Swindon Works **HG**
2/12/50	Oxley
30/3/51	Oxley shops **U**
21/11/51	Swindon Works **HI**
12/7/52	Stafford Road
27/12/52	Oxley
13/11/53	Swindon Works **HG**
23/11/54	Taunton shops **U**
18/1/55	Tyseley shops **LC**
30/8/55	Oxley shops **U**
9/3/56	Swindon Works **HI**
10/5/57	Oxley shops **U**
4/12/57	Stourbridge shops **U**
4/2/58	Oxley shops **U**
6/6/58	Swindon Works **HG**
7/4/60	Oxley shops **U**
21/7/60	Swindon Works **HI**
5/11/60	Stourbridge
28/8/61	Stourbridge shops **U**
7/10/61	Worcester
19/5/62	Gloucester
21/6/62	Worcester shops **U**

Tenders
From new	2533
31/5/37	2629
12/4/39	2397
17/7/39	2791
7/7/41	2537
20/2/43	2672
10/1/44	2783
27/6/45	2593
13/5/46	2576
24/3/47	2857
20/4/48	2384
14/7/49	2857
20/4/48	2384
14/7/49	2857
19/9/49	2664
24/10/51	2557
14/10/53	2778
9/3/56	2534
6/6/58	2853

Mileage 1,043,644

Withdrawn 8/4/63 Sold to J Cashmore Newport 18/9/63

5944 ICKENHAM HALL in the yard at the crumbling old Fratton shed, Portsmouth, in 1961. M.G.H, ColourRail

5946 MARWELL HALL
Built in 1935 to Lot no.290 at Swindon Works
To traffic 3/1935

Mileages and Boilers
From new	4980
26/11/36	88,786 C4478
29/9/38	180,719 C4478
2/7/40	262,102 C4478
20/2/43	369,787 C7206
25/6/46	489,756 C2820
4/2/48	560,218 C4019
15/8/50	663,830 R9287
6/3/53	787,816 C2870
18/4/55	878,367 C2845
25/6/57	969,812 C2845
30/10/59	1,051,428 C4072

Sheds and Works history
6/4/35	Canton
28/7/36	Canton shops R
26/11/36	Swindon Works G
30/10/37	Canton shops R
29/9/38	Swindon Works I
20/7/39	Reading shops R
5/8/39	Swindon Works L
2/7/40	Swindon Works I
27/10/42	Canton shops R
20/2/43	Swindon Works G
14/3/43	Old Oak shops R
30/11/43	Swindon Works L
6/6/44	Swindon Works L
7/9/44	Canton shops R
25/6/46	Swindon Works I
4/2/48	Swindon Works I
5/5/48	Canton shops L
	Tender work only
3/6/48	Canton shops L
15/8/50	Swindon Works HG
8/5/51	Swindon Works LC
6/3/53	Swindon Works HI
15/7/54	Old Oak shops U
11/2/55	Canton shops U
18/4/55	Swindon Works HG
5/7/56	Swindon Works LC
3/9/56	Llanelly shops U
25/6/57	Swindon Works HI
7/8/57	Canton shops U
4/10/57	Caerphilly Works LC
24/1/58	Old Oak shops U
8/5/59	Newport Ebbw Jct shops U
6/8/59	Canton shops U
30/10/59	Swindon Works HG
30/1/60	Taunton
26/3/60	Exeter
7/9/61	Exeter shops U
27/3/62	Newport Ebbw Jct shops U
14/7/62	Fishguard Goodwick

Tenders
From new	2657
26/10/36	2585
29/8/38	2536
21/7/39	2699
2/7/40	2566
27/10/42	2551
13/1/43	2520
5/10/43	2824
28/4/44	2384
11/5/46	2784
12/12/47	2430
26/3/49	2610
17/7/50	2829
1/4/51	2600
15/3/55	2720
5/7/56	2893
25/6/57	2596
8/8/59	4071
30/10/59	2670

Mileage 1,138,917

Withdrawn 10/7/62 Sold to R S Hayes Ltd Bridgend 1/10/62

Exeter's 5946 MARWELL HALL after arrival with the 9.10am ex-Kingswear at Birmingham Moor Street on 3 September 1960. The engine sits partly on the famous traverser which extended under the platform. Michael Mensing.

5946 MARWELL HALL with a train at Pilning in August 1961. A.E. Durrant, Michael Boakes Collection.

119

120

Left. 5947 ST BENET'S HALL at Banbury with the 2.38pm Leamington-Oxford train, 11 September 1937. In late 1934 it was reported running without nameplates; this was doubtless due to the discovery that the apostrophe had been omitted and a few weeks later modified BENET'S plates had been fitted in place of the offending BENETS. H.C. Casserley, courtesy R.M. Casserley.

Below. Lined green 5947 ST BENET'S HALL at Banbury shed, 18 September 1960. It provides an illustration of the limitations of the GWR side fixing lamps. A lamp had brackets either side though strictly speaking there was only one correct way for a given lamp iron. The left-hand one is the wrong side of the iron. The front running plate could do with the attentions of a good stiff broom. B.K.B. Green Collection, Initial Photographics.

5947 SAINT BENET'S HALL

Built in 1935 to Lot no.290 at Swindon Works
To traffic 3/1935

Mileage and Boilers
From new	4981
3/4/37	106,905 C4981
25/8/38	168,721 C2840
27/7/39	206,508 C2840
22/10/41	292,792 C2840
18/8/43	355,378 C2932
15/1/46	439,399 C4916
24/7/47	495,653 C4454
15/9/49	580,739 C4016
28/3/52	681,585 C8274
19/8/54	776,604 C6217
13/12/56	859,833 C6217
30/10/59	948,695 C6223

Sheds and Works history
6/4/35	Oxley
4/5/35	Stafford Road
30/5/36	Oxley
30/10/36	Banbury shops **R**
3/4/37	Swindon Works **I**
10/6/37	Reading shops **R**
25/8/38	Swindon Works **L**
27/7/39	Swindon Works **I**
22/10/41	Swindon Works **I**
18/8/43	Swindon Works **G**
11/11/44	Tyseley shops **R**
15/1/46	Swindon Works **I**
24/7/47	Swindon Works **I**
27/11/48	Old Oak
15/9/49	Swindon Works **HG**
17/3/50	Swindon Works **LC**
27/7/50	Reading shops **U**
28/3/52	Swindon Works **HI**
21/2/53	Banbury
11/8/53	Newton Abbot shed **U**
19/8/54	Swindon Works **HG**
15/2/56	Banbury shops **U**
13/12/56	Wolverhampton Works **HI**
25/1/57	Wolverhampton Works **LC**
16/2/59	Banbury shops **U**
17/4/59	Banbury shops **U**
30/10/59	Swindon Works **HG**
28/11/59	Croes Newydd
23/4/60	Banbury
8/1/62	Banbury shops **U**

Tenders
From new	2565
29/5/37	2601
11/7/39	2646
3/9/41	2565
1/6/43	2391
29/10/46	2898
9/6/47	2747
15/9/49	2417
17/3/50	2920
28/2/52	2561
28/3/53	2575
24/6/54	4031
30/10/59	2596

Mileage 1,042,881

Withdrawn 13/7/62 Cut up 6/10/62

5948 SIDDINGTON HALL with Hawksworth tender at Shrewsbury shed; the period should be post-June 1961 when, according to the Record Card, a Hawksworth tender was first fitted. D.K. Jones Collection.

5948 SIDDINGTON HALL

Built in 1935 to Lot no.290 at Swindon Works
To traffic 3/1935

Mileages and Boilers
From new	4982
16/6/37	112,509 C4982
14/4/39	207,261 C4982
30/5/41	289,608 C4924
4/8/43	365,870 C4924
17/12/45	443,201 C8286
15/4/48	521,233 C2970
19/10/50	603,704 C8232
28/4/53	692,870 R6214
9/12/55	791,149 R6214
17/3/58	872,822 C6209
29/6/61	983,446 C2970

Sheds and Works history
6/4/35	Didcot
4/5/35	Old Oak
8/10/35	Old Oak shops **B**
11/1/36	Old Oak
13/1/36	Swindon Works **L**
4/7/36	Exeter shops R
16/6/37	Swindon Works **I**
14/4/39	Swindon Works **I**
1/1941	Reading
30/5/41	Swindon Works **G**
9/1/42	Reading shops **R**
2/4/42	Canton shops **L**
25/3/43	Reading shops **R**
4/8/43	Swindon Works **I**
24/9/44	Reading shops **R**
17/12/45	Swindon Works **G**
15/4/48	Swindon Works **I**
23/6/48	Swindon Works **L**
19/10/50	Swindon Works **HG**
4/11/50	Gloucester
23/2/52	Severn Tunnel Jct
22/3/52	Worcester
19/4/52	Pontypool Road
28/4/53	Swindon Works **HG**
3/6/53	Severn Tunnel Jct shops **U**
10/12/54	Newport Ebbw Jct shops **U**
9/12/55	Swindon Works **HI**
17/3/58	Swindon Works **HG**
9/2/61	Pontypool Road shops **U**
29/6/61	Swindon Works **HI**
9/7/62	Swindon Works **HC**

Tenders
From new	2617
4/5/37	2533
7/2/39	2438
29/2/41	2812
2/4/42	2414
4/8/43	2821
11/9/45	2796
20/2/48	2520
1/5/48	2537
5/11/49	2799
20/9/50	2606
14/11/51	2886
28/4/53	2799
9/12/55	2882
29/6/61	4372
26/9/62	2712

Mileage 1,051,218

Withdrawn 26/8/63 Sold to R S Hayes Bridgend 1/1/64

Left. 5948 SIDDINGTON HALL on a down relief at Cutmere, a hamlet near St Germans, on 28 June 1952. A. Lathey, transporttreasury

5949 TREMATON HALL
Built in 1935 to Lot no.290 at Swindon Works
To traffic in 4/1935

Mileages and Boilers
From new	4983
10/3/37	105,914 C4983
23/9/38	186,043 C4983
1/3/41	285,836 C4983
15/3/44	393,021 C7211
20/12/46	494,707 C4455
14/2/49	574,483 C7249
15/2/51	651,129 C8235
15/5/53	740,316 C8235
28/10/55	837,925 C4997
14/1/58	936,027 C4955
14/12/59	1,019,655 C4071

Sheds and Works history
4/5/35	Weymouth
30/11/35	Weymouth shops R
13/6/36	Weymouth shops R
13/8/36	Didcot shops R
7/12/36	Weymouth shops R
10/3/37	Swindon Works I
26/3/38	Weymouth shops R
23/9/38	Swindon Works I
15/3/39	Weymouth shops R
9/9/40	Weymouth shops R
1/3/41	Swindon Works I
3/1941	St Philips Marsh
11/9/41	Swindon Works L
15/12/42	Swindon Works L
15/3/44	Swindon Works G
8/11/45	Old Oak shops R
5/10/46	Bristol Bath Road
20/12/46	Swindon Works I
14/2/49	Swindon Works HG
26/2/49	St Philips Marsh
15/2/51	Swindon Works HG
15/5/53	Swindon Works HI
28/11/53	Bristol Bath Road
11/9/54	St Philips Marsh
28/10/55	Swindon Works HG
16/6/56	Bristol Bath Road
30/11/57	St Philips Marsh
14/1/58	Swindon Works HI
22/2/58	Bristol Bath Road
24/7/59	Pontypool Road shops U
14/12/59	Swindon Works HG
8/10/60	Swindon

Tenders
From new	2658
28/1/37	2673
23/8/38	2585
13/1/41	2806
15/12/42	2404
11/1/44	2664
20/12/46	2397
7/1/49	2646
17/1/51	2592
7/4/53	2605
28/10/55	2677
14/12/59	4053

Mileage 1,074,921

Withdrawn 30/5/61   Cut up 7/10/61

Right. 5949 TREMATON HALL on a down Manchester near Whiteball Tunnel, 27 June 1953. A. Lathey, transporttreasury

Hall in heroic mood; 5949 TREMATON HALL with post-1956 second emblem, at an unknown location. ColourRail

5950 WARDLEY HALL
Built in 1935 to Lot no.290 at Swindon Works
To traffic 4/1935

Mileages and Boilers
From new	4984
30/7/37	101,498 C4984
25/5/39	191,807 C4984
27/2/41	259,872 C2549
2/4/42	301,781 C2549
28/7/44	353,902 C2549
25/11/46	471,097 C3004
20/1/49	553,678 C3004
23/2/51	629,428 C8252
8/9/53	716,242 C2946
13/1/56	803,327 C2841
9/1/58	898,435 C2841
12/1/60	964,161 C9273

Sheds and Works history
4/5/35	Old Oak
6/6/35	Danygraig shops **R**
5/11/35	Banbury shops **R**
8/6/36	Exeter shops **R**
30/1/37	Old Oak shops **R**
29/5/37	Oxford
30/7/37	Swindon Works **I**
21/8/37	Old Oak
25/5/39	Swindon Works **I**
9/12/39	Weymouth shops **R**
6/2/40	Swindon Works **L**
27/2/41	Swindon Works **L**
2/4/42	Swindon Works **I**
28/6/43	Old Oak shops **L**
28/7/44	Swindon Works **I**
2/8/45	Swindon Works **L**
28/7/46	Bristol Bath Road shops **R**
25/11/46	Swindon Works **G**
19/6/47	Penzance shops **R**
29/11/47	Tyseley
17/1/48	Tyseley shops **L**
21/2/48	Leamington Spa
20/3/48	Tyseley
20/1/49	Swindon Works **HI**
1/3/50	Tyseley shops **U**
1/8/50	Newton Abbot shed **U**
4/11/50	Banbury
23/2/51	Swindon Works **HG**
6/3/51-15/3/51	Stored at Swindon
8/9/53	Swindon Works **HI**
13/11/53	Banbury shops **LC**
21/5/55	Westbury
18/6/55	Westbury shops **U**
8/10/55	Bristol Bath Road
13/1/56	Swindon Works **HG**
9/1/58	Swindon Works **HI**
13/3/59	Newton Abbot Works **LC**
11/7/59	St Philips Marsh
12/1/60	Swindon Works **HG**
7/2/60	Tyseley shops **U**
29/4/60	Newton Abbot Works **U**
20/5/61	Westbury

Tenders
From new	2659
10/6/37	2581
18/4/39	2639
27/2/41	2530
22/3/42	2578
2/4/42	1560
28/7/44	2660
2/8/45	2387
25/1/46	2852
19/5/47	2592
19/1/51	2585
28/8/55	2934
13/1/56	2707
12/1/60	2687

Mileage 1,032,140

Withdrawn 17/11/61 Cut up 30/12/61

Lined black 5950 WARDLEY HALL (pity about the dislodged boiler casing) in positively dainty pose, at Bristol St Philips Marsh shed; from 5950's 82A Bath Road shed plate, the period is October 1955-July 1959 and as it had a Heavy General at the very beginning of 1956, it would have kept this livery for a while. J. Davenport, Initial Photographics.

5951 CLYFFE HALL

Built in 1935 to Lot no.297 at Swindon Works
To traffic 12/1935

Mileages and Boilers
From new	4019
20/1/38	109,844 C4019
25/5/40	203,803 C4019
25/8/43	293,581 C7233
21/2/46	381,642 C4968
26/10/48	469,861 C4012
1/11/50	554,585 C4433
18/9/52	629,561 C9200
3/8/54	715,083 C7248
5/10/56	801,107 C7248
18/11/58	883,845 C4061
16/10/61	978,042 C2846

Sheds and Works history
14/12/35	Gloucester
19/12/36	Worcester shops L
20/1/38	Swindon Works I
12/4/39	Gloucester shops R
25/5/40	Swindon Works I
11/12/40	Gloucester shops R
14/6/41	Gloucester shops R
18/2/42	Swindon Works L
2/10/42	Swindon Works L
25/8/43	Swindon Works G
28/4/45	Gloucester shops R
21/2/46	Swindon Works I
11/5/47	Oxley shops R
9/8/47	Worcester shops L
20/10/48	Swindon Works I
14/9/49	Worcester shops U
1/11/50	Swindon Works HG
3/11/51	Worcester
18/9/52	Swindon Works HI
27/12/52	Gloucester
3/8/54	Swindon Works HG
25/6/55	Worcester shops LC
5/10/56	Wolverhampton Works HI
18/11/58	Swindon Works HG
16/10/61	Swindon Works HG
26/6/63	Worcester shops U

Tenders
From new	2649
13/12/37	2535
17/4/40	2544
13/2/42	2622
15/6/43	2802
5/12/45	2635
10/9/48	2551
26/4/50	2645
1/10/50	2723
18/9/52	2779
3/8/54	4032
19/4/58	4122
18/11/58	2606
22/11/61	2561
20/6/61	4126
12/8/61	2634
16/10/61	4054

Mileage
1,048,662 as at 28/12/63

Withdrawn 20/4/64 Sold to J Cashmore Great Bridge 27/6/64

5951 CLYFFE HALL in lined black and first emblem, in the period August 1954-April 1958; oil bottle still there by the leading splasher. transporttreasury

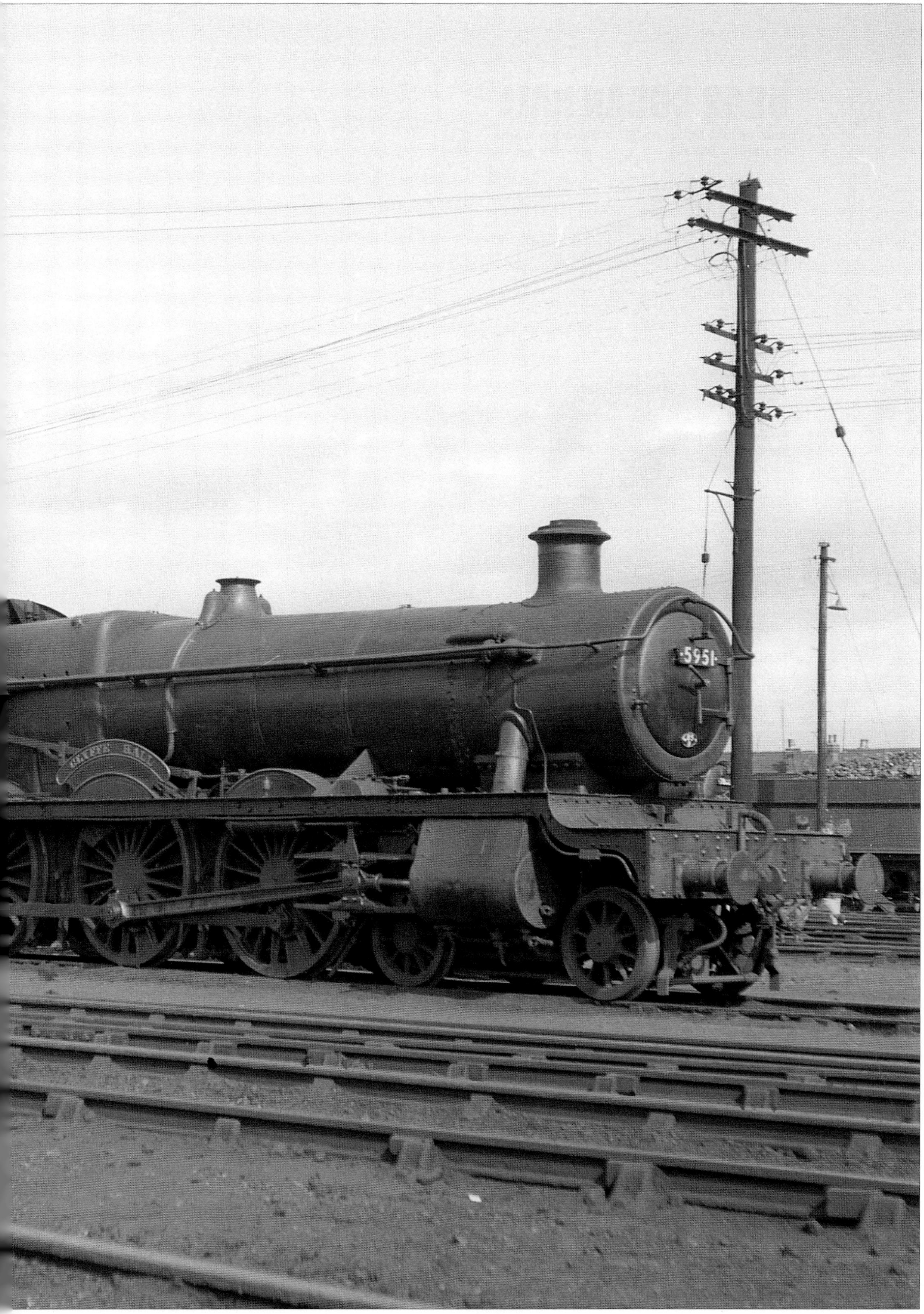
5951

5952 COGAN HALL

Built in 1935 to Lot no.297 at Swindon Works
To traffic 12/1935

Mileages and Boilers
From new	4020
30/3/38	98,849 C4020
4/12/39	173,864 C4486
16/1/41	212,241 C4486
16/8/43	310,146 C4471
1/10/45	397,624 C4471
8/10/47	484,4709 C4471
12/1/50	572,271 C4071
25/3/52	668,443 C2839
21/1/54	734,335 C6202
26/3/56	820,330 C7218
28/4/58	904,918 C2803
26/6/59	946,132 C8244
9/10/61	1,011,439 C9269

Sheds and Works history
14/12/35	Penzance
10/11/36	Newton Abbot shed **L**
27/5/37	Newton Abbot shed **L**
22/12/37	Penzance shops **R**
30/3/38	Swindon Works **I**
23/7/38	Laira
15/10/38	Truro
3/4/39	Truro shops **R**
29/4/39	Penzance
2/8/39	Penzance shops **R**
4/12/39	Swindon Works **L**
23/5/40	Swindon Works **L**
23/8/40	Penzance shops **R**
16/1/41	Swindon Works **I**
15/5/41	Penzance shops **R**
8/1941	St Blazey
12/1941	Canton
2/4/42	Canton shops **R**
25/11/42	Canton shops **R**
16/8/43	Swindon Works **G**
11/1944	Bristol Bath Road
28/1/45	Hereford shops **R**
2/1945	Old Oak
1/10/45	Swindon Works **I**
8/10/47	Wolverhampton Works **I**
23/9/48	Old Oak shops **R**
12/11/48	Old Oak shops **R**
2/12/49	Old oak shed **U**
12/1/50	Swindon Works **HG**
9/9/50	Southall
23/2/51	Southall shops **U**
25/3/52	Swindon Works **HI**
30/6/53	Southall shops **U**
21/1/54	Swindon Works **HI**
4/12/54	Penzance
16/7/55	Laira
13/9/55	Laira shops **U**
8/10/55	Worcester
26/3/56	Swindon Works **HG**
28/4/58	Swindon Works **HI**
26/6/59	Wolverhampton Works **HC**
5/9/59	Hereford
15/6/60	Newton Abbot Works **LC**
9/10/61	Swindon Works **HG**
11/12/61	Hereford shops **U**
31/1/63	Hereford shops **U**
30/11/63	Cardiff East Dock

Tenders
From new	2405
17/10/36	2651
9/2/38	2686
30/10/39	2672
29/3/40	2424
4/12/40	2769
4/6/43	2610
3/9/44	2607
25/7/45	2852
26/7/46	2709
12/1/50	2632
21/1/54	2568
26/3/56	2914
28/4/58	4059
9/10/61	2559

Mileage 1,074,911

Withdrawn 15/6/64
Engine preserved

A scruffy Hall (a phrase much used in these years) 5952
COGAN HALL at Hereford, 13 November 1962. ColourRail

Main photograph. Lined black 5954 FAENDRE HALL at Old Oak Common in August 1956. J. Robertson, transporttreasury

Inset. 7 April 1963 at Westbury shed and Sabbath rest old style on the Western Region with 5954 FAENDRE HALL of St Philips Marsh awaiting a duty to return home to Bristol. 5954 looks lively as the shed crew ensure the water level in the boiler is maintained. Most engines were as dirty as this after the long hard winter of 1963, but in the coming weeks many were cleaned again, even if like 5954 they were not long for this world. Brian Bailey.

5954 FAENDRE HALL

Built in 1935 to Lot no.297 at Swindon Works
To traffic 12/1935

Mileages and Boilers
From new	4022
8/3/38	115,624 C4022
30/1/40	208,648 C4022
8/3/43	328,589 C4488
2/11/45	421,743 C7212
28/7/48	517,188 C4993
24/7/50	538,513 C7221
16/9/52	657,377 C4914
30/3/55	745,022 C8208
7/5/57	821,072 C9288
15/10/58	881,764 C2955
3/2/61	941,141 C2955

Sheds and Works history
14/12/35	Old Oak
6/5/36	Old Oak shops **R**
8/3/38	Swindon Works **I**
30/1/40	Swindon Works **I**
23/10/40	Old Oak shops **L**
22/3/42	Old Oak shops **R**
8/3/43	Swindon Works **G**
16/11/43	Reading shops **R**
31/5/45	Old Oak shops **R**
2/11/45	Swindon Works **I**
23/2/46	Banbury
13/8/46	Swindon Works **L**
25/9/47	Banbury shops **R**
28/7/48	Swindon Works **I**
3/12/49	Leamington Spa
24/7/50	Swindon Works **HG**
29/12/51	Banbury
8/10/51	Leamington Spa shops **U**
16/9/52	Swindon Works **HI**
19/10/53	Banbury shops **U**
30/3/55	Swindon Works **HG**
30/8/55	Banbury shops **LC**
16/6/56	Laira
8/9/56	Old Oak
14/11/56	Caerphilly Works **LC**
7/5/57	Swindon Works **HI**
15/10/58	Swindon Works **HC**
3/11/58-22/12/58	Stored at Old Oak
5/1/59-16/5/59	Stored at Didcot
31/10/59	St Philips Marsh
1/8/60	St Philips Marsh shops **U**
3/2/61	Wolverhampton Works **HI**
3/8/62	Caerphilly Works **LC**
15/9/62	Reading shops **U**
21/8/63	Worcester shops **U**

Tenders
From new	2605
25/1/38	2689
31/3/38	2641
30/1/39	2618
8/3/43	2393
10/8/45	2409
17/6/46	2866
26/5/48	2431
29/5/50	2807
15/8/52	2802
10/2/55	2862
8/9/56	2572
7/5/57	2766
15/10/58	2598

Mileage 1,014,761

Withdrawn 10/10/63 Sold to Messrs Coopers Ltd Swindon 31/12/63

5956 HORSLEY HALL, a visitor to Crewe South shed on 25 June 1960. David Forsyth, ColourRail

5956 HORSLEY HALL

Built in 1935 to Lot no.297 at Swindon Works
To traffic 12/1935

Mileages and Boilers
From new	4025
21/4/38	96,256 C4025
3/11/43	296,094 C4025
30/12/44	332,728 C7215
10/1/47	406,675 C4977
5/1/49	475,564 C2958
6/7/51	564,348 C2811
26/11/52	649,965 C7265
23/4/56	738,922 C4423
23/5/58	820,807 C9290
24/11/60	909,969 C6212

Sheds and Works history
14/12/35	Worcester
19/2/37	Worcester shops R
11/12/37	Oxford shops R
21/4/38	Swindon Works I
19/2/40	Worcester shops R
2/1941	Reading
2/7/43	Reading shops R
3/11/43	Swindon Works I
30/12/44	Swindon Works L
28/9/45	Old Oak shops L
7/9/46	Reading shops L
10/1/47	Swindon Works G
24/1/48	Reading shops R
5/1/49	Swindon Works HG
6/7/51	Swindon Works HI
5/12/52	Old Oak shops U
5/8/53	Exeter shops U
26/11/53	Swindon Works HG
19/4/55	Reading shops U
23/4/56	Swindon Works HI
23/5/58	Swindon Works HG
30/9/59	Reading shops U
24/11/60	Swindon Works HI
6/10/62	Oxford

Tenders
From new	2677
8/3/38	2697
1/11/40	2533
13/8/43	2640
21/10/43	2722
25/10/44	2828
10/1/47	2680
5/1/49	2640
6/6/51	2804
26/10/53	4017
23/4/56	4013
23/5/58	2858
24/11/60	2650

Mileage 979,776

Withdrawn 15/3/63

5957 HUTTON HALL

Built in 1936 to Lot No.297 at Swindon Works
To traffic 20/12/35

Mileages and Boilers
From new	4026	
7/2/38	114,175	C4026
30/7/39	183,261	C4913
2/6/40	218,444	C4913
20/10/43	331,356	C4950
24/4/47	444,377	C7271
11/3/49	514,010	C4058
20/8/51	594,580	C7213
25/3/4	686,698	C7213
16/10/56	769,090	C7207
20/1/59	858,088	C7207
10/8/61	900,055	C2982

Sheds and Works History
4/1/36	Swindon Works Hot box	
18/2/36	Oxley	
7/3/36	Stafford Road	
2/7/37	Wolverhampton Works	L
7/2/38	Swindon Works	L
22/2/38	Swindon Works	L
5/3/38	Oxley	
23/7/38	Stafford Road	
30/7/39	Swindon Works	L
14/10/39	Oxley	
6/1/40	Stafford Road	
2/6/40	Swindon Works	I
25/7/42	Swindon Works	L
20/10/43	Swindon Works	G
25/7/45	Swindon Works	L
14/11/45	Stafford Road shed	R
1/2/46	Tyseley	R
28/6/46	Stafford Road shed	R
15/8/46	Stafford Road shed	R
30/11/46	Oxley	
24/4/47	Swindon Works	I
9/4/48	Oxley	I
	Tender work only	
27/11/48	Reading	
11/3/49	Swindon Works	HG
23/6/50	Reading	U
20/8/51	Swindon Works	HG
25/3/54	Swindon Works	HI
16/4/56	Southall	U
12/5/56	Reading	U
11/6/56	Didcot	U
16/10/56	Swindon Works	HG
8/7/58	Reading	U
20/1/59	Swindon Works	HI
28/11/59	Oxford	
10/8/61	Wolverhampton Works	HG
1/2/62	Wolverhampton Works	U
3/3/62	Oxford	U
26/6/62	Oxford	U
23/12/63	Ebbw Jct	U

Tenders
From new	2678
15/12/37	2384
2/6/40	2673
1/6/42	2654
17/7/43	2686
20/10/43	2533
7/3/47	1513
30/10/48	2683
11/3/49	2850
28/6/51	2586
22/1/54	2548
17/7/54	2901
16/10/56	2672
20/1/59	4087
6/1961	4015
10/1963	2680
?	2724

Mileage as at 28/12/63 1,000,374
Withdrawn 6/7/64 Sold to Birds
Morriston 24/8/64

5957 HUTTON HALL at Stafford Road shed, 31 January 1937; 'shirt button' on the tender. B.K.B. Green Collection, Initial Photographics.

142

5958 KNOLTON HALL leaving Weymouth yard on 18 July 1960. B. Wadey, transporttreasury

Inset. 5958 KNOLTON HALL with a short train leaving Twerton tunnel, 27 June 1962. Rail Photoprint.

5958 KNOLTON HALL

Built in 1936 to Lot no.297 at Swindon Works
To traffic 1/1936

Mileages and Boilers
From new	4027
30/6/38	125,860 C4027
9/5/40	212,786 C4412
4/12/42	315,819 C4412
20/12/44	374,412 C7221
20/12/45	404,496 C7221
25/2/48	483,173 C2833
31/7/50	591,608 C4456
26/9/52	684,605 C8708
26/10/54	771,648 R6222
22/1/57	858,438 C2928
26/3/59	937,871 C4927
31/5/61	1,031,312 C9221

Sheds and Works history
21/1/36	Swindon Works
	Syphon pipe
8/2/36	Taunton
23/5/36	Taunton shops **R**
5/12/36	Taunton shops **R**
13/11/37	Newton Abbot shed **L**
30/6/38	Swindon Works **I**
31/3/39	Taunton shops **R**
9/5/40	Swindon Works **G**
6/1940	Penzance
25/1/41	Penzance shops **R**
6/1941	Severn Tunnel Jct
4/12/42	Swindon Works **I**
2/10/44	Old Oak shops **R**
20/12/44	Swindon Works **L**
20/12/45	Swindon Works **L**
10/8/46	Canton
25/2/48	Swindon Works **G**
31/7/50	Swindon Works **HG**
26/9/52	Swindon Works **HI**
16/5/53	Landore
3/11/53	Neath shops **U**
26/10/54	Swindon Works **HG**
28/3/55	Danygraig shops **U**
19/4/55	Gloucester shops **U**
19/5/56	Carmarthen
6/10/56	Oxley
22/1/57	Swindon Works **HI**
21/9/57	Banbury shops **U**
25/1/58	Shrewsbury
1/11/58	Old Oak
26/3/59	Swindon Works **HG**
31/5/61	Swindon Works **HI**
19/1/62	Old Oak shops **U**
24/2/62	St Philips Marsh
28/4/62	St Philips Marsh shops **U**

Tenders
From new	2679
4/5/38	2437
24/1/40	2820
28/10/42	2840
20/12/44	2546
26/9/45	2835
1/11//48	2779
29/8/52	2768
21/9/54	2565
14/7/55	2449
21/9/57	4051
26/3/59	2904
31/5/61	2863

Mileage 1,116,653 as at 28/12/63

Withdrawn 10/3/64 Sold to R S Hayes Bridgend 23/4/64

143

5959 MAWLEY HALL

Built in 1936 to Lot no.297 at Swindon Works
To traffic 1/1936

Mileages and Boilers
From new	4028
29/10/37	112,143 C4028
1/7/39	185,880 C2884
11/8/41	269,382 C2884
14/3/44	364,641 C4911
6/11/46	450,501 C8238
30/12/48	539,299 C8251
29/3/51	621,975 C4467
23/6/53	713,032 C4908
1/9/55	794,320 C4908
5/2/58	903,319 C4443
4/3/60	986,331 C2845

Sheds and Works history
8/2/36	Reading
29/10/37	Swindon Works I
29/6/38	Swindon Works L
1/7/39	Swindon Works G
11/8/41	Swindon Works I
25/11/41	Swindon Works R
7/4/43	Reading shops R
14/3/44	Swindon Works G
15/8/45	Reading shops R
12/9/45	Reading shops R
6/11/46	Swindon Works I
30/12/48	Swindon Works I
29/3/51	Swindon Works HI
23/6/53	Swindon Works HG
9/10/54	Penzance
1/9/55	Swindon Works HI
8/8/56	Reading
29/12/56	Exeter
23/3/57	Landore
15/6/57	Oxley
13/7/57	Penzance
5/2/58	Swindon Works HG
3/10/59	Tyseley
4/3/60	Swindon Works HG

Tenders
From new	2680
16/5/39	2717
16/6/41	2699
19/1/44	2434
31/10/45	2821
6/11/46	2674
30/12/48	2637
29/3/51	2909
23/6/53	2794
2/9/55	2898
24/1/58	2430
4/3/60	4110
6/10/62	4111

Mileage 1,069,787

Withdrawn 21/9/62 Sold to John Cashmore Great Bridge 17/10/63

In what could be a WR 'Holiday Poster', lined green 5959 MAWLEY HALL departs Dawlish with the 9.10am Kingswear-Birmingham train, on 26 July 1958. A relatively deserted scene for the time of year. B.W.L. Brooksbank, Initial Photographics.

Inset. In very different surrounds, with Hawksworth tender at Birmingham Snow Hill, 10 March 1961. Tony Cooke, ColourRail

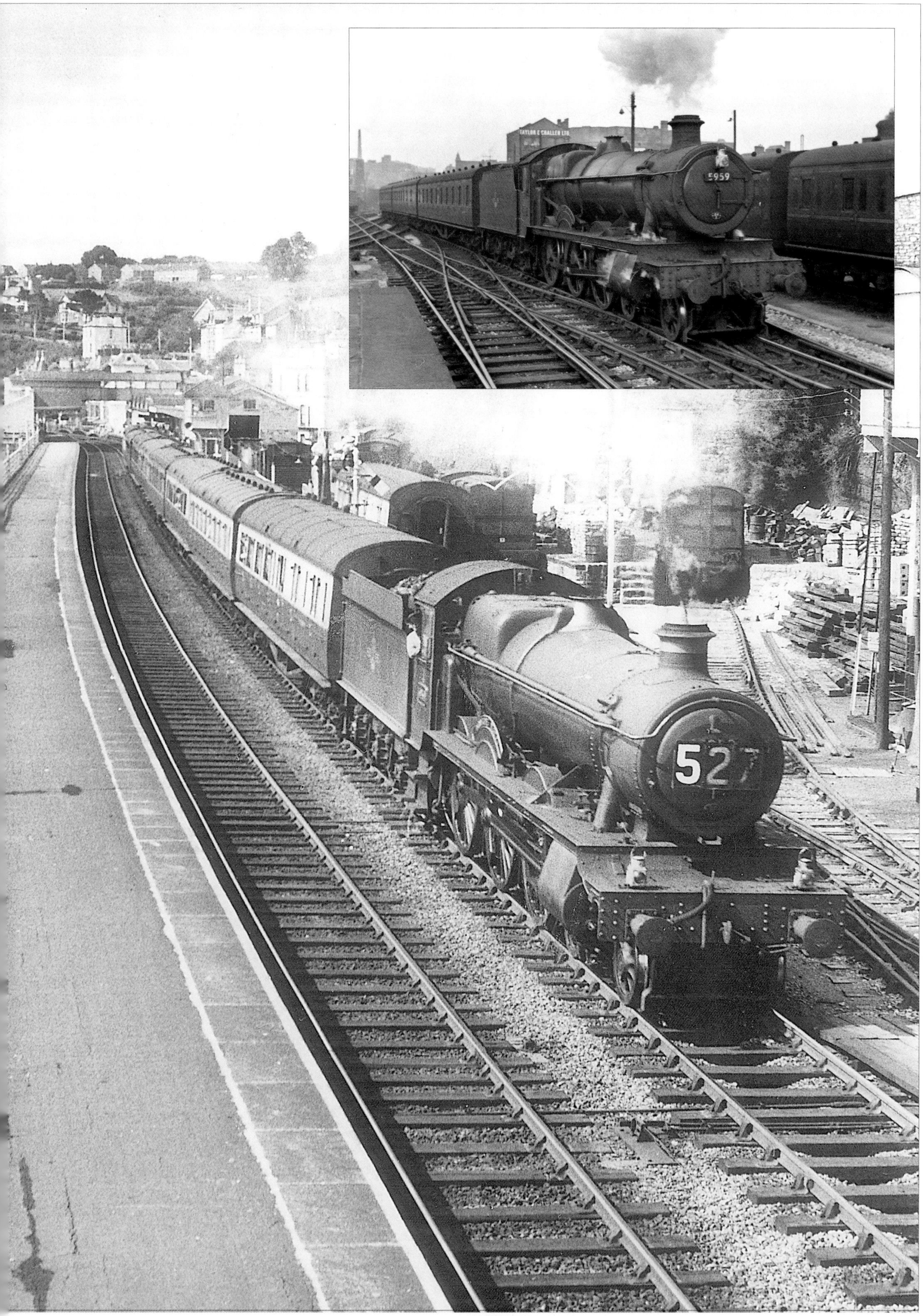
5959
527

146

5960 SAINT EDMUND HALL on the single track at Ashendon Junction with a Paddington-Chester train, 27 August 1955. S. Creer, transporttreasury

Inset. At rest at Shrewsbury shed five years later, in October 1960. Way back in 1937 *The Railway Observer* had asked whether anyone could confirm a suggestion that the engine had originally been turned out as ST. EDMUND HALL. Nearly 80 years later we ask again – can anyone confirm this? D.K. Jones Collection.

5960 SAINT EDMUND HALL

Built in 1936 to Lot no.297 at Swindon Works
To traffic 1/1936

Mileages and Boilers

Date	Mileage
From new	4029
12/1/38	117,793 C4029
24/8/39	207,350 C4029
19/12/41	295,046 C2866
17/7/45	410,540 C8290
28/5/47	486,486 C2850
12/15/48	508,559 C7236
5/7/50	583,639 R9286
13/2/53	683,641 R9286
16/8/55	769,078 C4074
3/2/58	868,760 C4074
10/6/60	957,093 C2968

Sheds and Works history

8/2/36	Oxford
7/10/36	Oxford shops **R**
27/5/37	Oxford shops **R**
12/1/38	Swindon Works **I**
6/2/39	Oxford shops **R**
24/8/39	Swindon Works **I**
9/8/40	Oxford shops **R**
19/12/41	Swindon Works **G**
25/3/43	Oxford shops **R**
22/3/44	Newton Abbot Works **L**
17/7/45	Swindon Works **I**
28/5/47	Swindon Works **I**
12/5/48	Swindon Works **L**
30/8/49	Wolverhampton Works **LC**
22/5/50	Oxford shops **U**
5/7/50	Swindon Works **HG**
21/4/51	St Philips Marsh
1/12/51	Oxford
25/4/52	Old Oak shops **U**
13/2/53	Wolverhampton Works **HI**
8/3/54	Oxford shops U
12/4/54	Old Oak shops **U**
26/1/55	Old Oak shops **U**
16/8/55	Swindon Works **HG**
3/2/58	Swindon Works **HI**
10/6/60	Swindon Works **HG**
1/2/62	Oxford shops **U**

Tenders

From new	2681
2/1936	1834
13/5/37	2253
15/7/37	2381
23/11/37	2422
5/3/38	2266
14/7/39	2601
6/12/39	2173
19/12/41	2856
29/5/45	2400
10/7/46	2540
28/5/47	2535
12/5/48	2769
1/6/50	2413
1/1/53	2563
28/11/53	2683
16/7/55	2794
3/2/58	2933
10/6/60	4000

Mileage 1,037,156

Withdrawn 21/9/62 Sold to A King and sons Hasford Norwich 28/10/63

5962 WANTAGE HALL

Built in 1936 to Lot no.297 at Swindon Works
To traffic 6/1936

Mileages and Boilers
From new	4031
24/3/38	89,416 C4031
28/5/40	192,387 C4031
3/3/43	295,895 C4433
6/10/45	385,469 C2977
4/9/47	465,923 C7264
29/12/49	553,625 C4972
11/6/52	638,525 C2973
6/9/54	731,166 C2834
14/9/56	812,889 C8239
8/1/59	883,292 C7211
2/11/61	981,712 C9293

Sheds and Works history
25/7/36	Old Oak
15/9/36	Swindon Works **L**
24/3/38	Swindon Works **I**
12/9/39	Swindon Works **L**
28/5/40	Swindon Works **I**
7/4/42	Old Oak shops **R**
18/7/42	Old Oak shops **R**
3/3/43	Swindon Works **G**
6/10/45	Swindon Works **I**
15/7/47	Old Oak shops **R**
4/9/47	Swindon Works **I**
20/10/48	Swindon Works **L**
12/10/49	Old Oak shops **U**
29/12/49	Swindon Works **HG**
5/6/50	Old Oak shops **U**
24/7/50	Old Oak shops **U**
5/12/50	Old Oak shops **U**
20/3/51	Laira shops **U**
5/4/51	Old Oak shops **U**
26/9/51	Old Oak shed **U**
4/2/52	Old Oak shops **U**
11/6/52	Swindon Works **HI**
27/7/53	Old Oak shops **U**
8/8/53	Shrewsbury
26/12/53	Chester
6/9/54	Swindon Works **HG**
3/10/55	Tyseley shops **U**
14/9/56	Swindon Works **HI**
11/10/57	Chester shops **U**

Transferred to LMR book stock 23/2/58
27/6/58	Wolverhampton Works **LC**
6/9/58	Canton

Returned to WR book stock 7/9/58
8/1/59	Caerphilly Works **HG**
19/8/60	Caerphilly Works **HC**
30/9/60	Canton shops **U**
23/2/61	Hereford shops **U**
2/11/61	Swindon Works **HI**
11/7/62	Aberdare shops **U**
8/9/62	Cardiff East Dock
3/11/62	Shrewsbury
17/11/62	Cardiff East Dock
30/8/63	Wolverhampton Works **LC**
2/11/63	Pontypool Road
22/6/64	Worcester

Tenders
From new	2698
15/8/39	2701
28/5/40	2774
3/3/43	2706
27/7/45	2590
4/9/47	2424
16/8/48	2597
30/11/49	2401
11/2/51	2561
5/3/52	4004
11/6/52	2809
4/8/54	2697
30/9/55	2811
11/8/56	2891
14/9/56	2437
24/1/59	2418
2/11/61	2759

Mileage 1,042,054 as at 28/12/63

Withdrawn 27/11/64 Sold to J Cashmore Great Bridge 8/1/65

5962 WANTAGE HALL at Chester shed. This is an example of a Hall in *Great Western* lined green with the first BR emblem. The driver is oiling up the big end, close by that knuckle joint *aft* of the crank pin, where it was of course, much easier to get at. The knuckle joint itself called for minimal lubrication. There was no rotation, merely the rise and fall of axles occasioned by track irregularities, especially in shed yards; there was no oil reservoir. ColourRail.

5963 WIMPOLE HALL

Built in 1936 to Lot no.297 at Swindon Works
To traffic 7/1936

Mileages and Boilers
From new	4032
14/6/38	103,145 C4032
29/3/40	200,608 C4032
14/1/43	321,425 R8281
20/2/45	403,282 R8281
5/6/47	486,553 C2995
17/1/50	593,939 C2807
8/2/52	677,652 C9283
8/11/54	777,178 R6223
3/1/57	869,144 R6223
18/3/59	961,484 C2852
2/3/62	1,079,840 C4071

Sheds and Works history
25/7/36	Landore
17/10/36	Carmarthen
14/6/38	Swindon Works I
8/4/39	Carmarthen shops L
29/3/40	Swindon Works I
23/9/41	Carmarthen shops L
5/5/42	Carmarthen shops L
14/1/43	Swindon Works G
19/1/44	Carmarthen shops L
24/8/44	Carmarthen shops L
7/10/44	Bristol Bath Road shops R
20/2/45	Swindon Works I
3/8/46	Carmarthen shops L
5/6/47	Swindon Works I
9/12/48	Carmarthen shops L
	Tender work only
17/1/50	Swindon Works HG
19/10/51	Carmarthen shops U
8/2/52	Swindon Works HI
8/11/54	Swindon Works HG
21/11/55	Carmarthen shops U
25/2/56	Westbury
3/1/57	Wolverhampton Works HI
18/3/59	Swindon Works HG
28/7/61	Westbury shops U
2/3/62	Swindon Works HI
9/2/63	St Philips Marsh

Tenders
From new	2699
20/4/38	2679
16/2/40	2539
14/1/43	2561
1/1/45	2867
5/6/47	2819
3/12/48	2826
7/1/52	2877
11/10/54	2730
4/5/56	2421
18/6/56	2581
3/2/58	2826
18/3/59	2837
2/3/62	2400

Mileage 1,140,896 as at 28/12/63

Withdrawn 8/6/64 Sold to Birds Risca 18/8/64

Above. A comprehensively begrimed 5963 WIMPOLE HALL from St Philips Marsh, at Westbury shed on 7 April 1963. Brian Bailey.

Right. Fully laden 5963 WIMPOLE HALL pressed into service (it was a Westbury engine at the time) at Reading General to convey various stores to the engine shed some time in 1959. The Reading shed weekly wages came down from Paddington in a wooden box and, offloaded from the passenger guard's compartment on arrival at Reading the box was similarly roped in on the front frame of the first available loco going on shed. This practice went for years apparently and suffered no loss either from criminals (unlike at Old Oak Common, famously) or misadventure en route. Michael Boakes Collection.

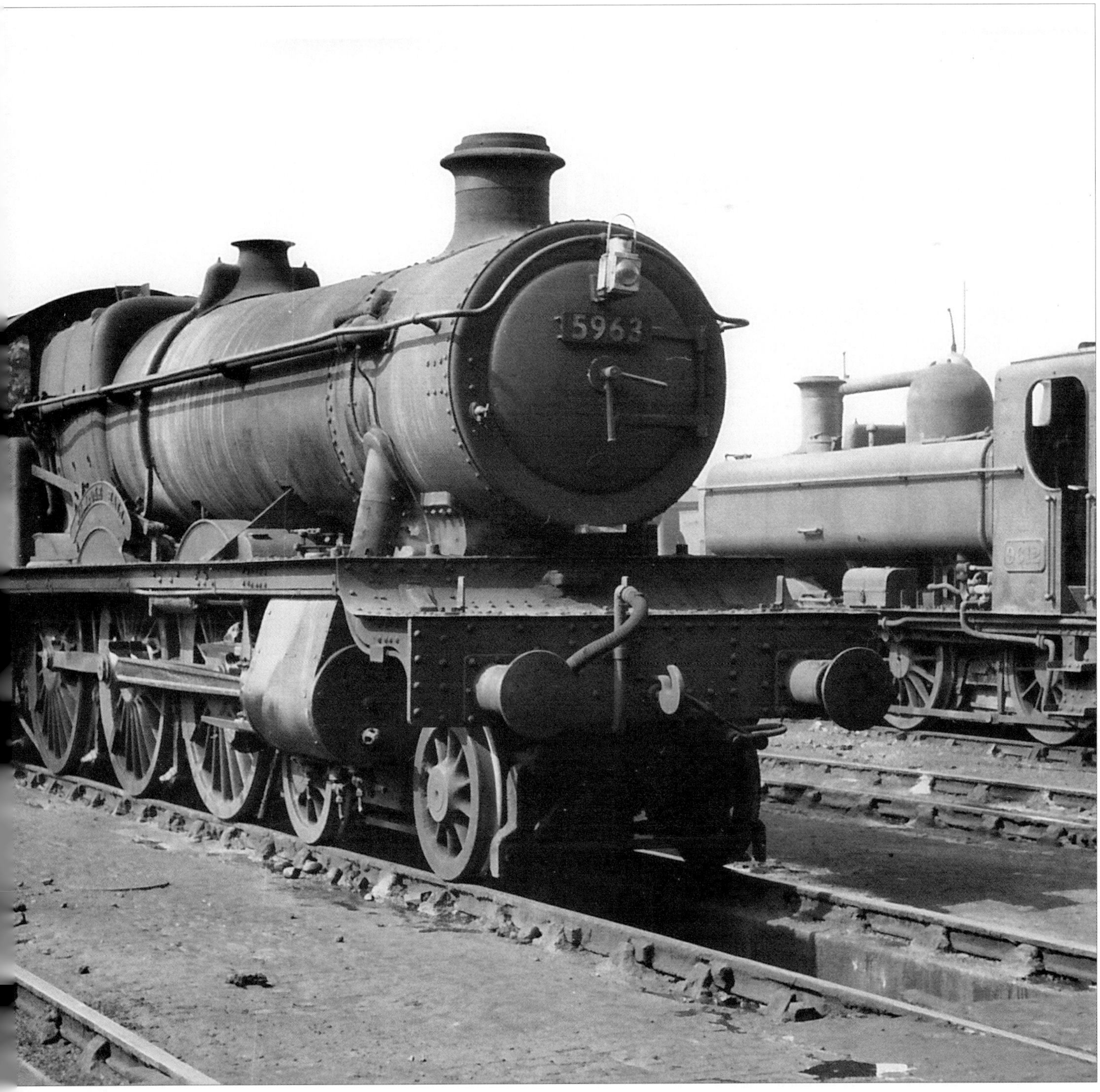
5963

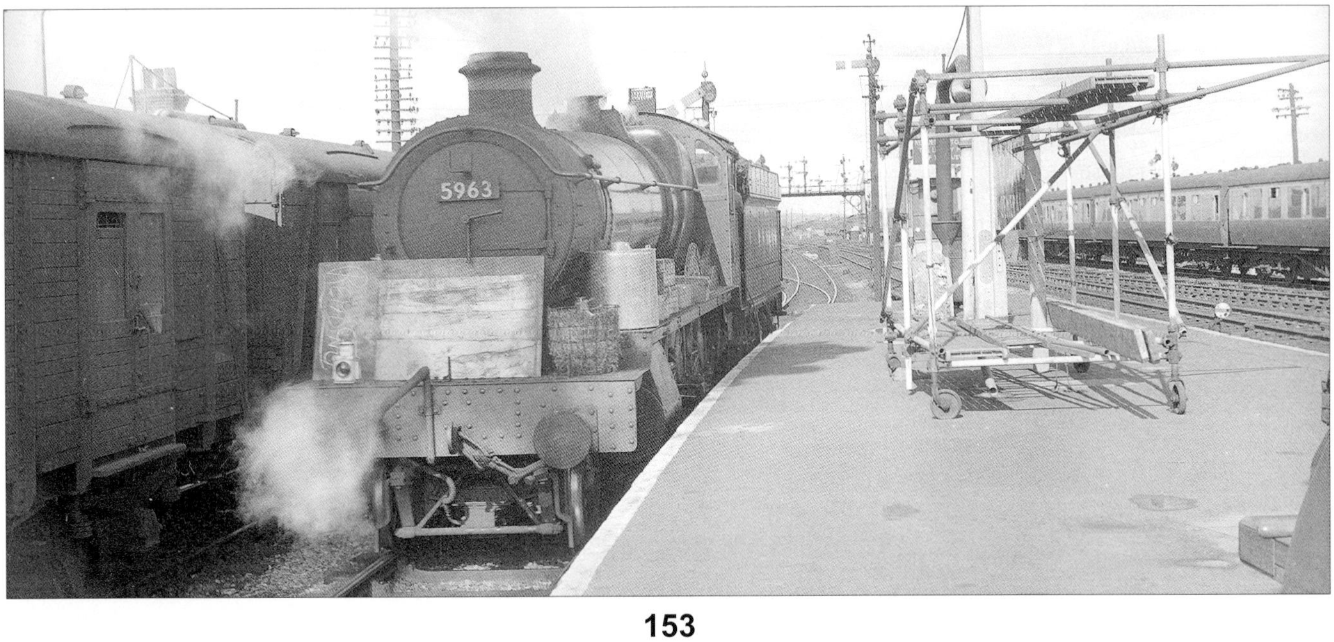
5963

5964 WOLSELEY HALL

Built in 1936 to Lot no.297 at Swindon Works
To traffic 7/1936

Mileages and Boilers
From new	4033
17/5/38	102,910 C4033
7/8/40	199,917 C4033
14/5/43	287,325 C2983
20/11/45	380,177 C4092
16/6/48	460,667 C8259
9/2/51	554,621 C8259
26/8/53	654,803 C8232
24/10/57	844,314 C2940
22/12/59	932,515 C8259

Sheds and Works history
22/8/36	Swindon
17/5/38	Swindon Works I
26/6/38	St Philips Marsh
23/7/38	Weymouth
1/8/39	Weymouth shops R
7/8/40	Swindon Works I
9/1940	St Philips Marsh
22/2/41	St Philips Marsh shops R
11/7/41	Newton Abbot Works R
26/11/41	St Philips Marsh shops R
22/5/42	Swindon Works L
14/5/43	Swindon Works G
20/11/45	Swindon Works I
29/12/45	Swindon
26/1/46	Bristol Bath Road
20/4/46	St Philips Marsh
29/6/46	Old Oak shed R
9/11/46	Tyseley shops L
4/6/47	Reading shops R
6/2/48	St Philips Marsh shops R
16/6/48	Swindon Works I
3/2/49	Laira
13/1/50	Laira shops U
30/1/50	Laira shops U
1/3/50	Laira shops U
27/6/50	Laira shops U
11/10/50	Laira shops U
9/2/51	Swindon Works HI
1/8/52	Laira shops U
30/8/52	Laira shops U
1/5/53	Laira shops U
16/6/53	Laira shops U
26/8/53	Swindon Works HG
15/8/54	Laira shops U
5/1/55	Laira shops U
18/8/55	Newton Abbot Works HI
19/5/56	Bristol Bath Road
14/7/56	Weymouth
24/10/57	Swindon Works HG

Transferred to SR book stock 23/2/58
Returned to WR book stock 7/9/58
6/9/58	Swindon
22/12/59	Swindon Works HI
11/1/61	Swindon Works HC
8/6/61	Caerphilly Works LC
14/7/62	Westbury

Tenders
From new	2700
5/4/38	2540
22/5/42	2626
23/3/43	2407
20/11/45	2608
14/4/48	2785
5/12/50	2646
6/7/53	2853
27/9/57	2909
22/12/59	2818
11/1/61	2928
20/5/61	2932
6/10/62	2594

Mileage 1,013,256

Withdrawn 21/9/62 Cut up 1/12/62

5964 WOLSELEY HALL heading a mogul on the up Cornish Riviera passing Hayle, 19 September 1953. This probably indicates the last of the summer demand, probably with all seats reserved. One of Laira's best Halls would be on the job, with the mogul put inside to give extra power on a known overload, but the top link driver on the Hall would be in charge of controlling the train; in Cornwall the maximum speed would be 60 mph, so the rule about the smaller engine in front would not apply.
A. Lathey, transporttreasury

5964 WOLSELEY HALL heading again, this time a very modest milk train on Hemerdon, bound for Kensington on 12 May 1956. The engine behind this time is 1016 COUNTY OF HANTS. RailOnline

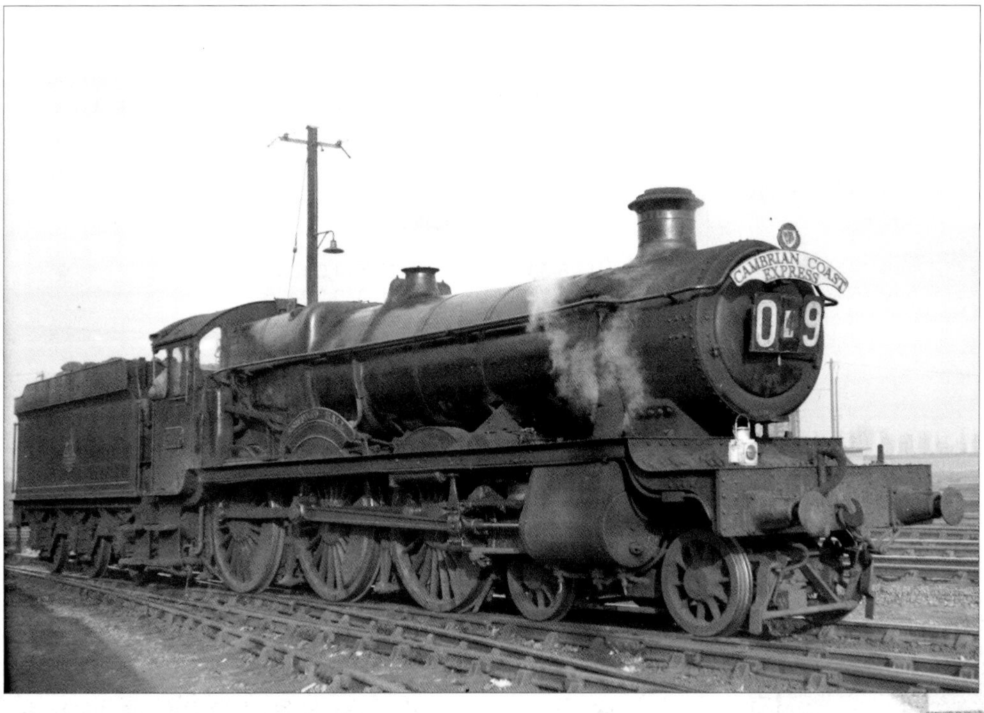
CAMBRIAN COAST EXPRESS
0 4 9

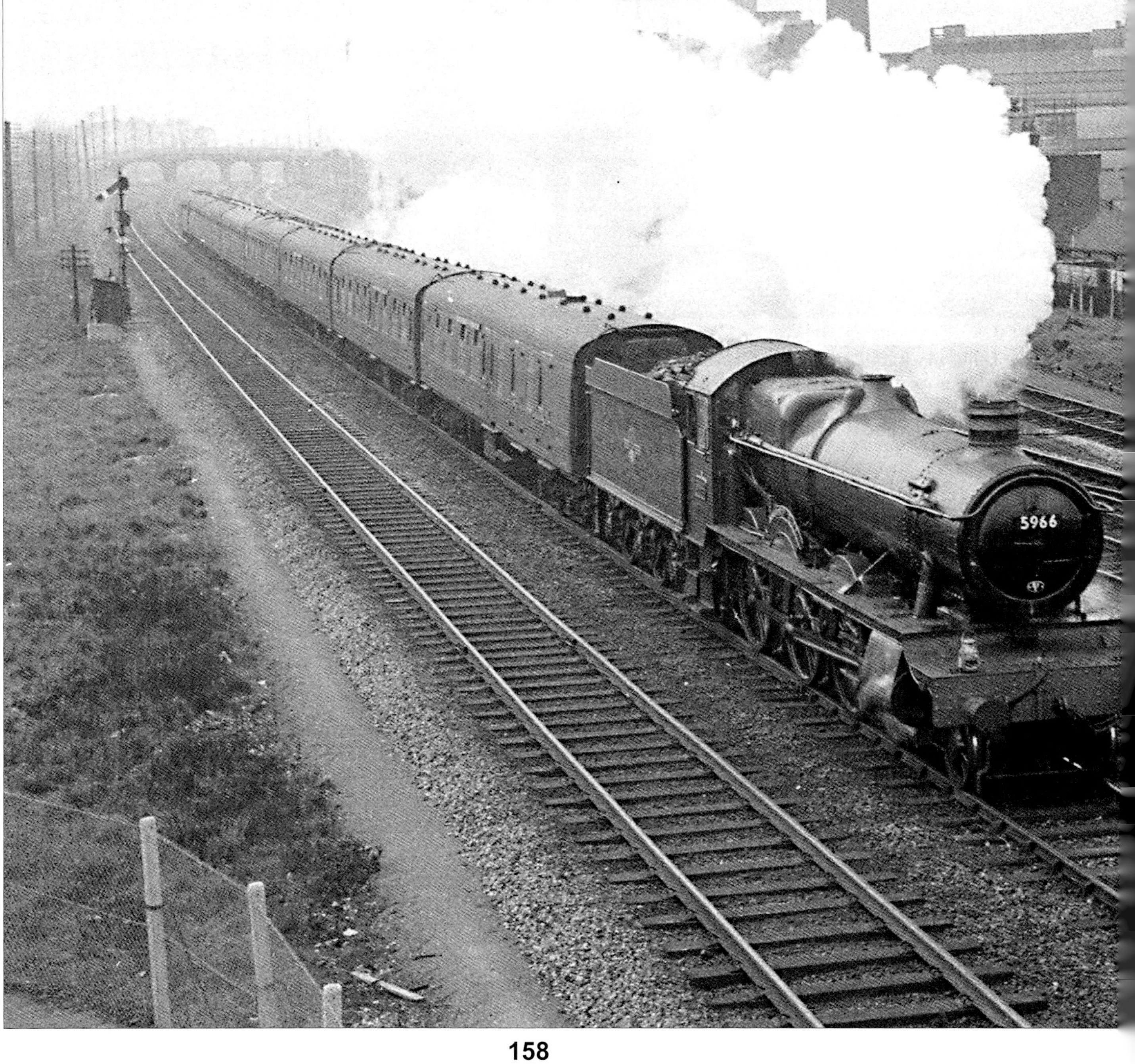
5966

Inset. 5966 ASHFORD HALL at Shrewsbury, about 1958. The engine is in fairly tired lined black and there is no shed plate to suggest what the period might be; ASHFORD HALL was at Leamington, Oxford, then Oxley throughout that part of the 1950s when it carried lined black and none of these sheds had any fixed association with the Cambrian Coast Express. D.K. Jones Collection.

5966 ASHFORD HALL on the 8.50am Cheltenham-Paddington, approaching Hayes & Harlington on 13 March 1960, a Sunday. B. Wadey, transporttreasury

5966 ASHFORD HALL

Built in 1937 to Lot no.304 at Swindon Works
To traffic 3/1937

Mileages and Boilers

From new	4035
27/3/39	102,143 C4035
3/4/41	186,777 C4020
23/8/43	266,950 C4020
2/9/44	302,602 C4480
3/9/46	366,189 C4050
29/1/48	405,308 C8277
3/8/49	446,369 C2982
10/8/51	517,014 C8247
17/7/53	578,046 C8247
24/6/55	640,525 C2968
13/11/57	736,191 C2965
10/3/60	820,049 C4984

Sheds and Works history

3/4/37	Oxley
27/3/39	Swindon Works I
29/4/39	Chester
3/4/41	Swindon Works G
19/3/42	Birkenhead shops L
23/8/43	Swindon Works I
2/9/44	Swindon Works L
2/6/45	Tyseley shops R
3/9/46	Swindon Works I
24/2/47	Chester shops R
9/4/47	Chester shops R
15/9/47	Chester shops R
29/1/48	Swindon Works L
12/4/48	Chester shops L
	Tender Work only
31/12/48	Chester shops R
13/4/49	Taunton shops U
3/8/49	Swindon Works HG
21/3/50	Chester shops U
4/11/50	Leamington Spa
15/11/50	Chester shops
10/8/51	Swindon Works HG
3/11/52	Oxley
19/11/52	Oxley shops U
21/5/53	Tyseley shops U
17/7/53	Wolverhampton Works HI
18/10/54	Oxley shops U
21/5/55	Oxford
24/6/55	Swindon Works HG
28/3/56	Didcot shops U
13/11/57	Wolverhampton Works HI
10/3/60	Swindon Works HG
19/5/60	Oxford shops U
30/3/61	Leamington Spa shops U
8/1/62	Old Oak shops U
9/2/62	Oxford shops U

Tenders

From new	2705
16/2/39	2651
12/2/41	2751
23/8/43	2818
15/6/44	2541
22/7/46	2565
29/1/48	2739
3/8/49	2639
26/2/55	2069
24/6/55	2797
30/12/61	2647

Mileage 893,114

Withdrawn 21/9/62 Sold to A King and Sons Harford Norwich 28/10/63

5968 CORY HALL

Built in 1937 to Lot no.304 at Swindon Works
To traffic 3/1937

Mileages and Boilers
From new	4037
29/4/39	98,590 C4037
12/11/41	202,242 C4037
24/5/44	285,128 C4985
4/11/46	377,070 C4411
5/1/50	474,240 R9288
18/1/52	556,652 C4034
8/9/54	648,923 C4034
16/1/57	732,991 C7203
11/4/60	827,270 C4473

Sheds and Works history
3/4/37	Westbury
18/11/37	Westbury shops **R**
14/3/38	Westbury shops **R**
23/12/38	Swindon Works **L**
29/4/39	Swindon Works **I**
27/5/39	Weymouth
30/3/40	Westbury
24/10/40	Westbury shops **R**
26/2/41	Westbury shops **R**
12/11/41	Swindon Works **I**
12/1941	St Philips Marsh
24/5/44	Swindon Works **G**
16/12/44	Reading shops **R**
24/3/45	St Blazey shops **R**
4/11/46	Swindon Works **I**
2/3/47	Bristol Bath Road shops **R**
23/1/48	Weymouth shops **R**
21/7/48	Swindon Works **L**
24/6/49	Weymouth shops **U**
5/1/50	Swindon Works **HG**
27/1/51	Laira
6/10/51	Chester
11/10/51	Chester shops **U**
18/1/52	Swindon Works **HG**
20/2/53	Tyseley shops **U**
27/7/53	Chester shops **U**
23/5/54	Chester shops **U**
8/9/54	Swindon Works **HI**
12/1/56	Tyseley shops **U**
24/3/56	Shrewsbury
22/5/56	Shrewsbury shops **U**
10/10/56	Stafford Road shed **U**
16/1/57	Swindon Works **HG**
15/9/58-13/6/59	Stored at Shrewsbury
5/9/59	Leamington Spa shops **U**
11/4/60	Swindon Works **HI**
26/10/61	Wolverhampton Works **LC**
4/11/61	Gloucester

Tenders
From new	2707
23/12/38	2407
13/9/41	1515
20/4/44	2587
10/1/45	2745
24/5/44	2817
18/9/46	2628
9/7/48	2661
11/12/51	2401
20/7/54	2792
29/9/56	2417
16/1/57	4057
11/4/60	2531

Mileage 908,492

Withdrawn 27/9/62 Sold to J Cashmore Ltd 16/9/63

Above. Shrewsbury's pristine 5968 CORY HALL reverses out of Platform 3 (one of the three 'Western' bays) at Chester General on 24 April 1960. The engine is waiting to proceed to shed after bringing in a train from Shrewsbury, maybe an ex-Paddington. Alec Swain, transporttreasury.co.uk

Right. 5968 CORY HALL at Teignmouth with the 7.40am St Austell-Birmingham train, 30 July 1960. J. Davenport, Initial Photographics.

163

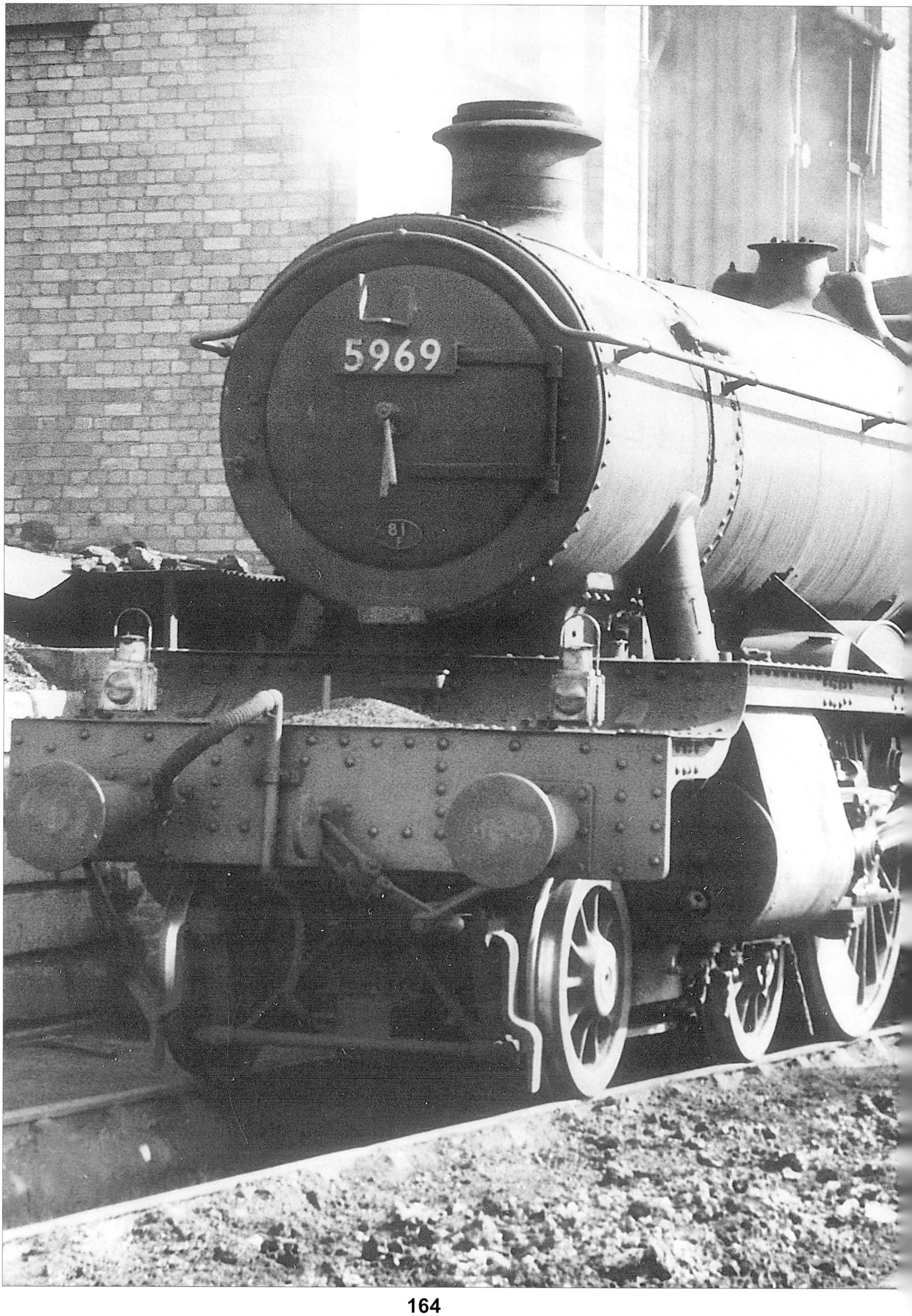
5969

5969 HONINGTON HALL at the coal stage, Oxford in the 1950s. The Oxford 81F plate relates to the three weeks or so it was there in April-May 1956 but the tender has the second emblem (it's just visible on the original print) so this view is later. Didcot presumably did not change the plate. J. Davenport, Initial Photographics.

5969 HONINGTON HALL

Built in 1937 to Lot no.304 at Swindon Works
To traffic 4/1937

Mileages and Boilers
Date	Mileage
From new	4039
17/2/39	108,182 C4039
13/10/41	216,706 C4039
23/3/44	306,903 C4441
31/1/47	404,286 C7215
1/10/48	452,901 C7251
28/7/50	523,950 C8254
3/2/53	640,073 C9284
26/4/55	746,616 C4035
6/5/57	829,093 C4035
17/11/59	930,128 C6226

Sheds and Works history
29/5/37	Bristol Bath Road
22/9/37	Bristol Bath Road shops **R**
17/2/39	Swindon Works **I**
1/4/39	St Philips Marsh
4/9/40	Swindon Works **L**
13/10/41	Swindon Works **I**
23/3/44	Swindon Works **G**
8/9/44	St Philips Marsh shops **R**
7/5/45	Bristol Bath Road shops **L**
22/9/45	Bristol Bath Road shops **L**
18/3/46	St Philips Marsh shops R
31/1/47	Swindon Works **I**
22/3/47	Weymouth
22/1/48	Weymouth shops **R**
3/3/48	Weymouth shops **L**
15/5/48	St Philips Marsh
1/10/48	Swindon Works **I**
21/7/49	Newton Abbot shed **U**
3/12/49	Laira
20/5/50	Penzance
28/7/50	Swindon Works **HG**
3/2/53	Swindon Works **HI**
30/4/54	Newton Abbot Works **LC**
26/4/55	Swindon Works **HG**
24/3/56	Canton
21/4/56	Oxford
19/5/56	Didcot
6/5/57	Swindon Works **HI**
17/5/58	St Philips Marsh
9/7/58	Old Oak shops **U**
17/11/59	Swindon Works **HG**
26/12/59	Fishguard Goodwick
1/3/60	Swindon Works **LC**
15/7/61	Carmarthen
23/11/61	Newport Ebbw Jct shops **U**

Tenders
From new	2708
16/1/39	2626
4/9/40	2635
26/7/41	2576
15/2/44	2890
23/3/44	2604
6/10/45	2909
31/1/47	2413
31/12/47	2614
7/7/48	2914
16/6/50	2431
30/12/52	2832
21/3/55	2400
6/5/57	2816
17/11/59	2803
8/10/60	2747
25/3/61	2886

Mileage 1,019,388

Withdrawn 29/8/62 Cut up 3/11/62

5970 HENGRAVE HALL

Built in 1937 to Lot no.304 at Swindon Works.
No repaint for the tender!
To traffic 4/1937

Mileage and Boilers
From new	4040
5/5/39	106,316 C4040
24/1/42	212,539 C4040
23/11/44	314,142 C4917
19/8/47	405,007 C2944
11/5/49	468,724 C4483
19/11/51	572,296 R6202
18/12/53	667,658 C7254
16/3/56	761,957 C7254
24/2/58	850,481 C2849
16/6/61	966,891 C4997

Sheds and Works history
29/5/37	Canton
5/5/39	Swindon Works I
23/6/41	Landore shops L
24/1/42	Swindon Works I
9/7/42	Gloucester shops R
7/8/42	Canton shops R
26/6/44	Canton shops R
23/11/44	Swindon Works G
7/8/45	Laira shops R
23/3/46	Swindon Works L
28/11/46	Old Oak shops R
19/8/47	Swindon Works I
11/5/49	Swindon Works HG
15/12/50	Hereford shops U
18/8/51	Banbury shops U
19/11/51	Swindon Works HG
18/12/53	Swindon Works HG
10/9/55	Shrewsbury shops U
16/3/56	Caerphilly Works HI
24/2/58	Swindon Works HG
25/9/58	Gloucester shops U
30/12/58	Newport Ebbw Jct shops U
11/7/59	Pontypool Road
3/5/60	Newport Ebbw Jct shops U
21/10/60	Pontypool Road shops U
16/6/61	Swindon Works HG
22/3/62	Pontypool Road shops U
14/7/62	Hereford

Tenders
From new	2709
24/3/39	2748
3/4/41	2403
18/12/41	2870
23/11/44	2702
6/12/45	2604
23/3/46	2667
7/4/49	2932
19/10/51	2436
14/11/53	2929
24/2/58	2812
25/3/61	2440
16/6/61	4116
14/5/63	2697

Mileage 1,043,315

Withdrawn 11/11/63 Sold to John Cashmore Newport 3/1/64

5970 HENGRAVE HALL hurries along with vans at Cholsey on 22 June 1961. A Pontypool Road engine and sparkling in new lined green, it is probably running in after its very recent Heavy General at Swindon. No repaint for the tender though! That blemish on the lower part of the boiler above the leading splasher was from a driver's flare lamp carelessly positioned when oiling up or after dark; sadly a common occurrence. J. Davenport, Initial Photographics.

5971 MEREVALE HALL

Built in 1937 to Lot no.304 at Swindon Works
To traffic 4/1937

Boilers and Mileages
Date	Mileage	Boiler
From new	2957	
17/12/38	106,102	C2957
2/4/41	197,581	C2957
18/11/43	288,780	C2840
11/3/46	364,096	C4924
2/9/48	445,849	C4424
19/9/50	516,661	C8262
8/5/52	570,629	C2813
1/9/53	624,873	C2952
17/1/56	718,552	C8249
4/3/58	802,005	C2924
11/11/60	892,557	C4964
4/10/63	950,571	C7237

Sheds and Works history
29/5/37	Weymouth
19/5/38	Weymouth shops R
17/12/38	Swindon Works I
7/1/39	St Philips Marsh
19/7/39	St Philips Marsh shops R
28/2/40	St Philips Marsh shops R
19/8/40	Bristol Bath Road shops L
2/4/41	Swindon Works I
4/1941	Weymouth
24/1/42	Weymouth shops L
24/4/42	Westbury shops R
5/1942	Westbury
19/7/42	Westbury shops L
17/12/42	Westbury shops R
18/11/43	Swindon Works G
11/3/46	Swindon Works I
10/8/46	Westbury shops R
3/4/47	Reading shops R
19/1/48	Westbury Shops L
24/3/48	Westbury shops R
2/9/48	Swindon Works I
7/9/49	Westbury shops U
25/11/49	Bristol Bath Road shops U
19/9/50	Swindon Works HG
10/10/50-6/11/50	Stored at Swindon
4/11/50	Worcester
2/7/51	Oxford shops U
8/5/52	Swindon Works HC
29/12/52	Tyseley
21/2/53	Gloucester
1/9/53	Swindon Works HI
10/3/55	Hereford shops U
17/1/56	Swindon Works HI
15/3/57	Wolverhampton Works LC
4/3/58	Swindon Works HG
9/7/59	Wolverhampton Works LC
8/8/59	Shrewsbury
17/12/59	Chester shops U
11/11/60	Swindon Works HI
15/12/62	Southall
6/4/63	Old Oak
4/10/63	Swindon Works HG
7/2/64	Newport Ebbw Jct shops U
22/6/64	Southall
5/10/64	Reading
26/12/64	Oxford
9/1/65	Worcester
7/8/65	Bristol Barrow Road

Tenders
From new	2711
17/12/38	2658
4/2/41	2647
17/3/42	2722
18/11/43	2893
21/12/45	2865
29/7/48	2927
19/9/50	2634
29/3/52	2885
29/7/53	2424
19/2/54	2721
28/11/54	2688
17/1/56	2927
4/3/58	4002
11/11/60	2554
4/10/63	2655

Mileage 956,920 as at 28/12/63

Withdrawn 31/12/65 Sold to J Cashmore Newport 11/2/66

Old Oak's 5971 MEREVALE HALL, a bit tired-looking, stands in Oxford shed yard. There is no date but the period is between April 1963 when the Hall went to Old Oak from Southall and June 1964, when it went back there. J. Davenport, Initial Photographics.

5972 OLTON HALL
Built in 1937 to Lot no.304 at Swindon Works
To traffic 4/1937

Mileages and Boilers
From new	2961
21/2/39	102,124 C2961
21/2/41	200,358 C2961
15/2/44	323,636 C2962
22/2/46	402,609 C8223
12/8/48	496,762 C2957
25/1/51	595,845 C4989
2/10/53	697,324 C4445
17/4/56	798,467 C4425
1/7/58	904,027 C7204
15/3/61	1,013,325 C6240

Sheds and Works history
29/5/37	Neath
26/6/37	Carmarthen
7/2/38	Carmarthen shops **L**
21/2/39	Swindon Works **I**
21/2/41	Swindon Works **I**
29/7/42	Carmarthen shops **L**
1/3/43	Carmarthen shops **L**
15/2/44	Swindon Works **I**
29/9/45	Carmarthen Shops **L**
22/2/46	Swindon Works **G**
16/3/46	Old Oak shops **R**
23/5/46	Carmarthen shops **R**
12/8/48	Swindon Works **I**
24/2/50	Carmarthen shops **U**
25/1/51	Swindon Works **HI**
27/1/51	Laira
14/7/51	Newport Ebbw Jct
11/8/51	Stafford Road
1/11/52	Oxley
15/1/53	Oxley shops **U**
2/10/53	Swindon Works **HG**
19/6/54	Truro
8/10/55	Penzance
17/4/56	Swindon Works **HI**
26/8/57	Penzance shops **U**
1/7/58	Swindon Works **HG**
29/11/58	Laira
8/8/59	Severn Tunnel Jct
18/6/60	Neath
15/3/61	Swindon Works **HI**
15/12/62	Fishguard Goodwick
29/6/63	Cardiff East Dock

Tenders
From new	2712
13/1/39	2653
21/9/41	2585
15/2/44	2672
15/1/46	2802
21/6/48	2821
29/12/50	2573
7/8/52	2628
31/8/53	2861
17/4/56	2750
1/7/58	2603
15/3/61	4100

Mileage 1,074,579

Withdrawn 28/12/63 Sold to Woodham Bros 30/4/64

5972 OLTON HALL (Swansea High Street box in the background) just about to enter the terminus of the same name on 7 November 1961. J.A.C. Kirke, transporttreasury

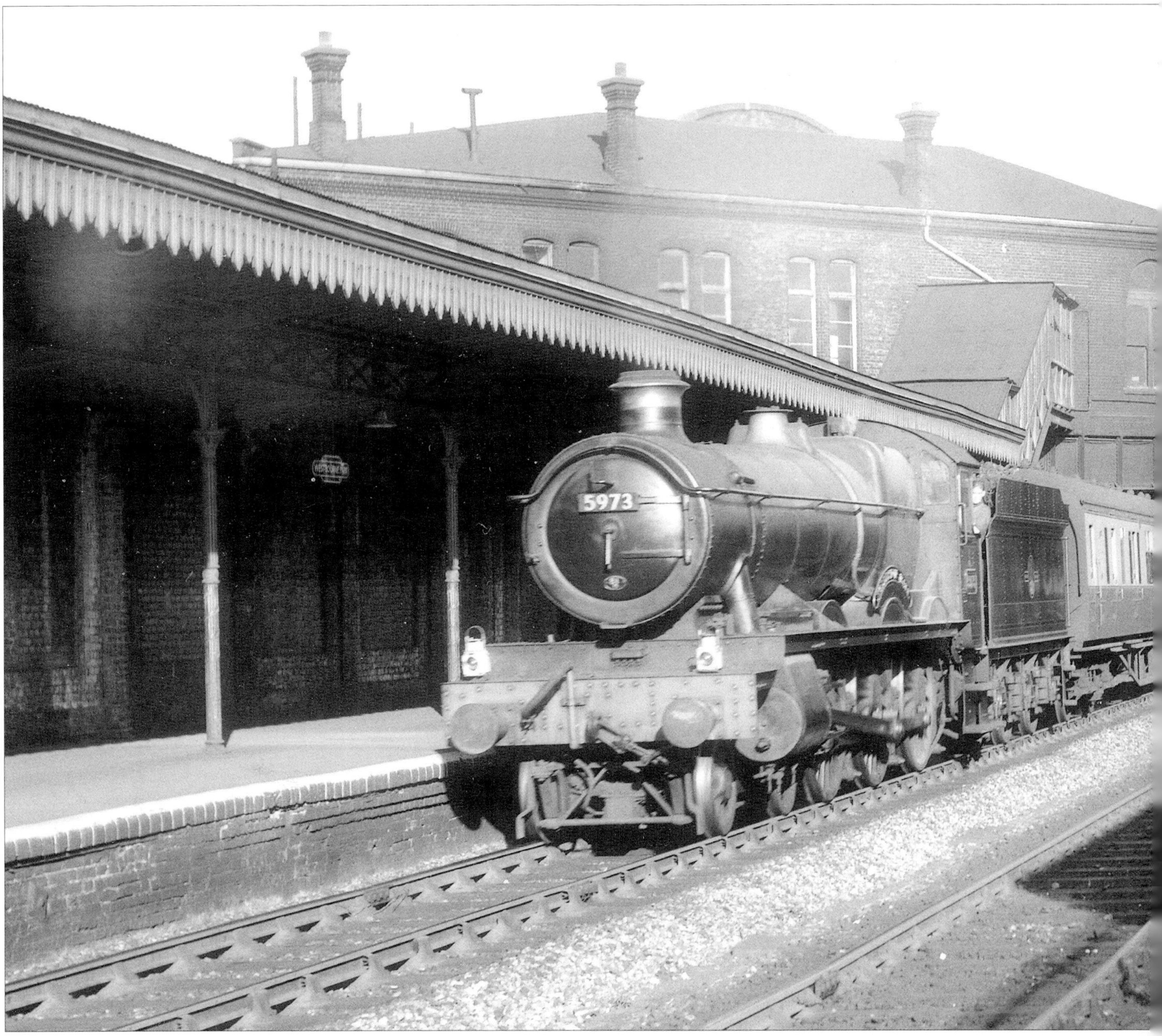
5973

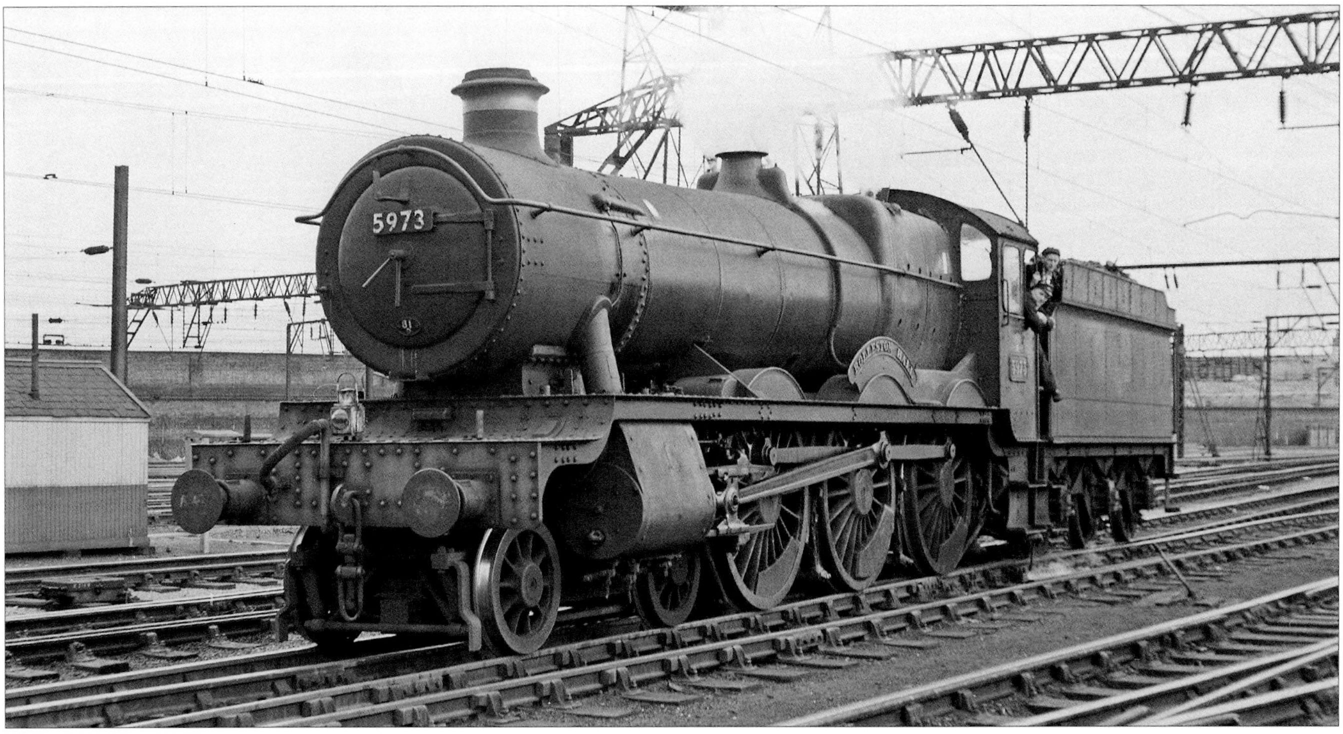
5973

Above. 5973 ROLLESTON HALL runs through Westbourne Park on 11 August 1958. L. Nicolson, transporttreasury

Left. 5973 ROLLESTON HALL has found its way to Crewe (it has electrification flashes but not the 'safety bracket' on the tender – see Part One) on 18 August 1962; it was a Reading 'homer' almost from the first through to withdrawal which, perhaps surprisingly given its relatively smart condition here, was only a few weeks away. Rail Photoprint.

5973 ROLLESTON HALL

Built in 1937 to Lot no.304 at Swindon Works
To traffic 6/1937

Boilers and Mileages
From new	2966
9/2/39	103,313 C2966
1/8/41	187,848 C2966
1/1/44	271,113 C4411
23/10/46	366,017 C4051
10/5/49	440,441 C2984
25/9/51	515,817 C2814
17/9/53	578,148 C4991
31/1/56	658,721 C4063
14/2/58	735,796 C4063
20/10/60	822,932 C6208

Sheds and Works history
26/6/37	Old Oak
24/7/37	Reading
12/4/38	Swindon Works **L**
9/2/39	Swindon Works **I**
1/8/41	Swindon Works **I**
17/6/42	Reading shops **R**
19/7/43	Bristol Bath Road shops **R**
9/10/43	Newton Abbot Works **R**
1/1/44	Swindon Works **G**
8/1/45	Reading shops **R**
9/2/45	Reading shops **R**
18/5/45	Reading shops **R**
9/2/46	Reading shops **R**
23/10/46	Swindon Works **I**
20/2/47	Bristol Bath Road shops **R**
3/6/47	Bristol Bath Road shops **R**
27/12/47	Reading shops **R**
23/9/48	Newton Abbot shed **R**
10/5/49	Swindon Works **HG**
7/11/49	Old Oak shops **U**
25/9/51	Swindon Works **HI**
29/5/52	Old Oak shops **U**
17/9/53	Swindon Works **HI**
1/8/55	Exeter shops **U**
31/1/56	Swindon Works **HG**
14/2/58	Swindon Works **HI**
13/3/59	Newton Abbot Works **LC**
23/8/60	Southall shops **U**
20/10/60	Swindon Works **HI**

Tenders
From new	2713
30/1/39	2720
2/6/41	2560
2/11/43	2689
23/10/46	2395
7/4/49	2430
30/8/51	2871
24/6/53	2719
31/1/56	2801
14/2/58	2924
20/10/60	2915

Mileage 888,710

Withdrawn 21/9/62 Cut up 1/12/62

5974 WALLSWORTH HALL

Built in 1937 to Lot no.304 at Swindon Works
To traffic 4/1937

Mileages and Boilers
From new	2967
24/7/39	107,810 C2967
7/4/42	222,517 C2967
27/9/43	260,127 C4052
11/2/46	326,450 C8234
24/1/47	358,016 C2963
1/12/48	411,740 C4968
9/2/50	449,820 C4095
6/6/51	499,612 C4983
1/5/53	584,323 R6215
25/4/55	689,254 C4473
26/3/57	785,986 C4031
13/3/59	894,806 C4031
27/11/61	1,007,373 C9228

Sheds and Works history
29/5/37	Westbury
20/3/38	Westbury shops R
14/12/38	Westbury shops L
24/7/39	Swindon Works I
12/4/40	Westbury shops R
1/5/41	Westbury shops R
10/1941	Old Oak
7/4/42	Swindon Works I
7/9/42	Bristol Bath Road shops I
2/2/43	Old Oak shops R
27/9/43	Swindon Works L
7/1944	Weymouth
16/1/45	Weymouth shops R
1/1945	Westbury
22/9/45	Westbury shops R
11/2/46	Swindon Works G
21/3/46	Westbury shops L
24/1/47	Swindon Works L
25/4/47	Westbury shops R
1/12/48	Swindon Works I
2/11/49	Westbury shops U
9/2/50	Swindon Works HC
21/11/50	Westbury shops U
6/6/51	Swindon Works HG
1/5/53	Swindon Works HG
25/4/55	Swindon Works HI
26/10/55	Westbury shops U
17/4/56	Westbury shops U
23/8/56	Westbury shops U
26/3/57	Swindon Works HG
13/3/59	Swindon Works HI
27/11/61	Swindon Works HI
4/3/63	Reading shops U
15/11/63	Westbury shops U
24/8/64	Severn Tunnel Jct

Tenders
From new	2715
4/11/38	2576
25/5/39	2680
7/4/42	2400
12/7/42	2415
2/4/43	2756
30/11/45	2841
24/1/47	2621
12/2/47	2672
16/11/48	2784
9/2/50	2831
25/3/53	2917
12/3/55	2615
26/3/57	2661
13/3/59	2643
27/11/61	2811

Mileage 1,070,686 as at 28/12/63

Withdrawn 4/1/65

5974 WALLSWORTH HALL in Westbury shed yard, 18 March 1962. M. Dart, transporttreasury

Inset. 5974 WALLSWORTH HALL at Reading West, 7 July 1952. D.K. Jones Collection.

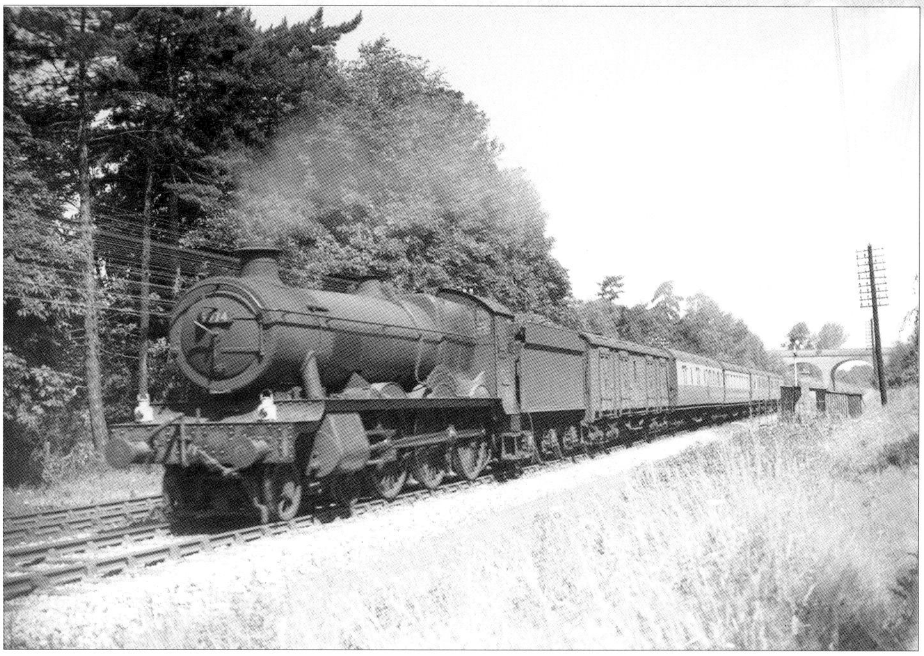

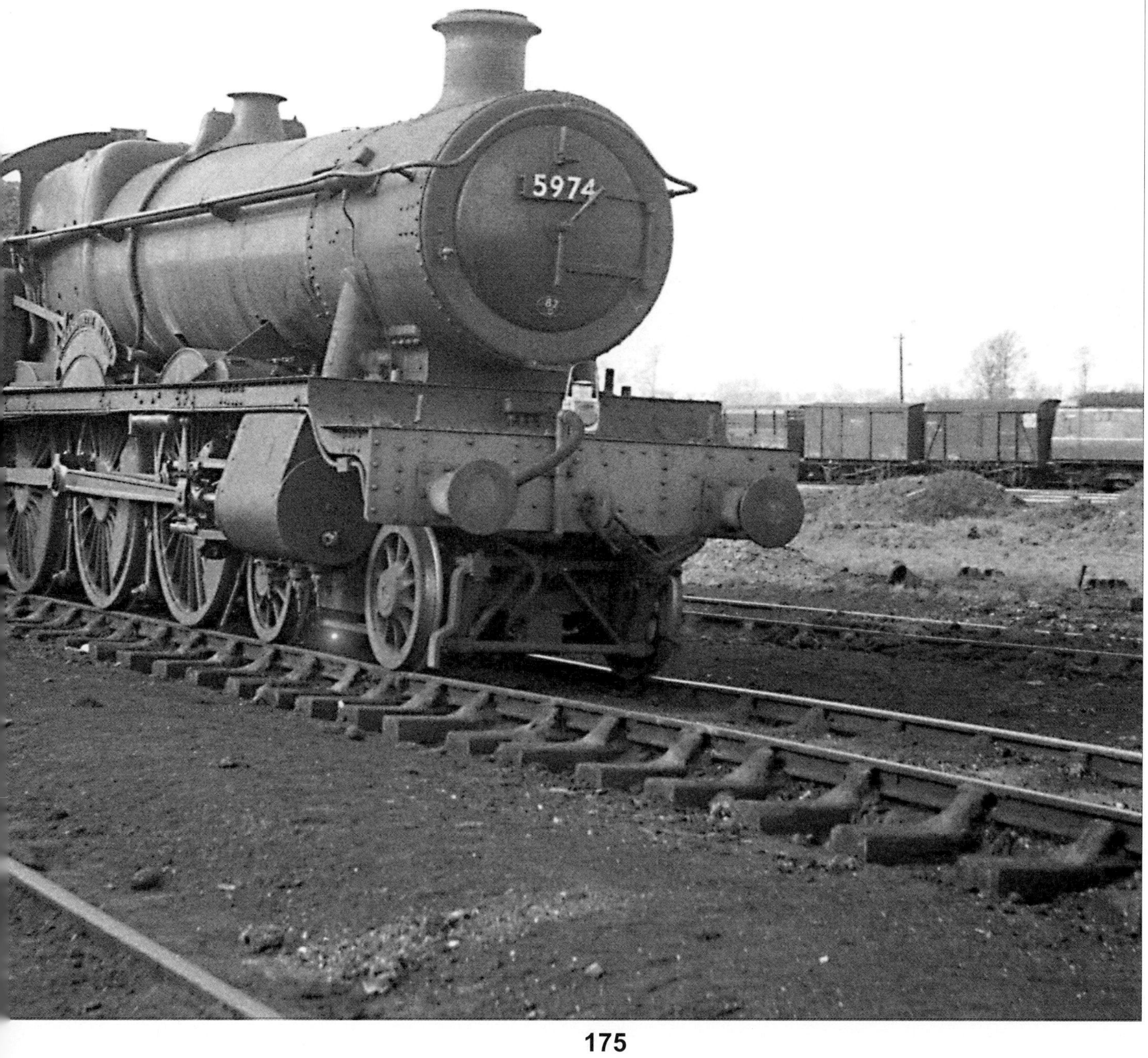
5974

5975 WINSLOW HALL heads for Swindon with ballast at Kemble, 28 March 1958. D.K. Jones Collection.

5975 WINSLOW HALL with a freight at Savernake Low Level, 6 July 1959. H.C. Casserley, courtesy R.M. Casserley.

5975 WINSLOW HALL

Built in 1937 to Lot no.304 at Swindon Works
To traffic 5/1937

Mileages and Boilers

From new	2970
18/3/39	106,585 C2970
25/6/42	219,922 C2970
2/4/44	277,484 C4482
25/3/47	383,668 C4985
9/6/49	466,266 C2946
26/1/51	549,612 C4052
11/12/52	636,358 C8240
13/5/55	748,801 C6215
9/4/57	824,038 c7273
29/4/59	930,085 C7273
3/11/61	1,023,517 C7223

Sheds and Works history

26/6/37	Westbury
16/10/37	Newton Abbot
18/3/39	Swindon Works I
29/4/39	Gloucester
29/7/41	Gloucester shops R
25/6/42	Swindon Works I
7/1942	Pontypool Road
14/7/43	Bristol Bath Road shops R
2/4/44	Swindon Works G
1/1/47	Pontypool Road shops L
25/3/47	Swindon Works I
24/1/49	Old Oak shops U
26/4/49	Pontypool Road shops U
9/6/49	Swindon Works HG
12/9/50	Oxley shops U
7/10/50	St Philips Marsh
4/11/50	Westbury
26/1/51	Swindon Works HI
14/7/51	Westbury shops U
11/12/52	Swindon Works HG
5/9/53	Swindon
13/5/55	Swindon Works HI
1/12/56	Old Oak
29/12/56	St Philips Marsh
23/3/57	Westbury
9/4/57	Swindon Works HG
29/4/59	Swindon Works HI
13/8/60	Bristol Bath Road
10/9/60	St Philips Marsh
3/11/61	Swindon Works HG
21/6/63	Wolverhampton Works LC
14/7/62	Llanelly
22/6/64	Bristol Barrow Road

Tenders

From new	2720
16/2/39	2706
17/8/40	2681
27/1/44	2564
25/3/47	2655
6/4/49	2611
8/12/50	2660
6/11/52	2416
14/4/55	2751
9/4/57	2594
29/4/59	2767
3/11/61	2801

Mileage 1,088,421 as at 28/12/63

Withdrawn 24/7/64 Sold to J Cashmore Newport 4/9/64

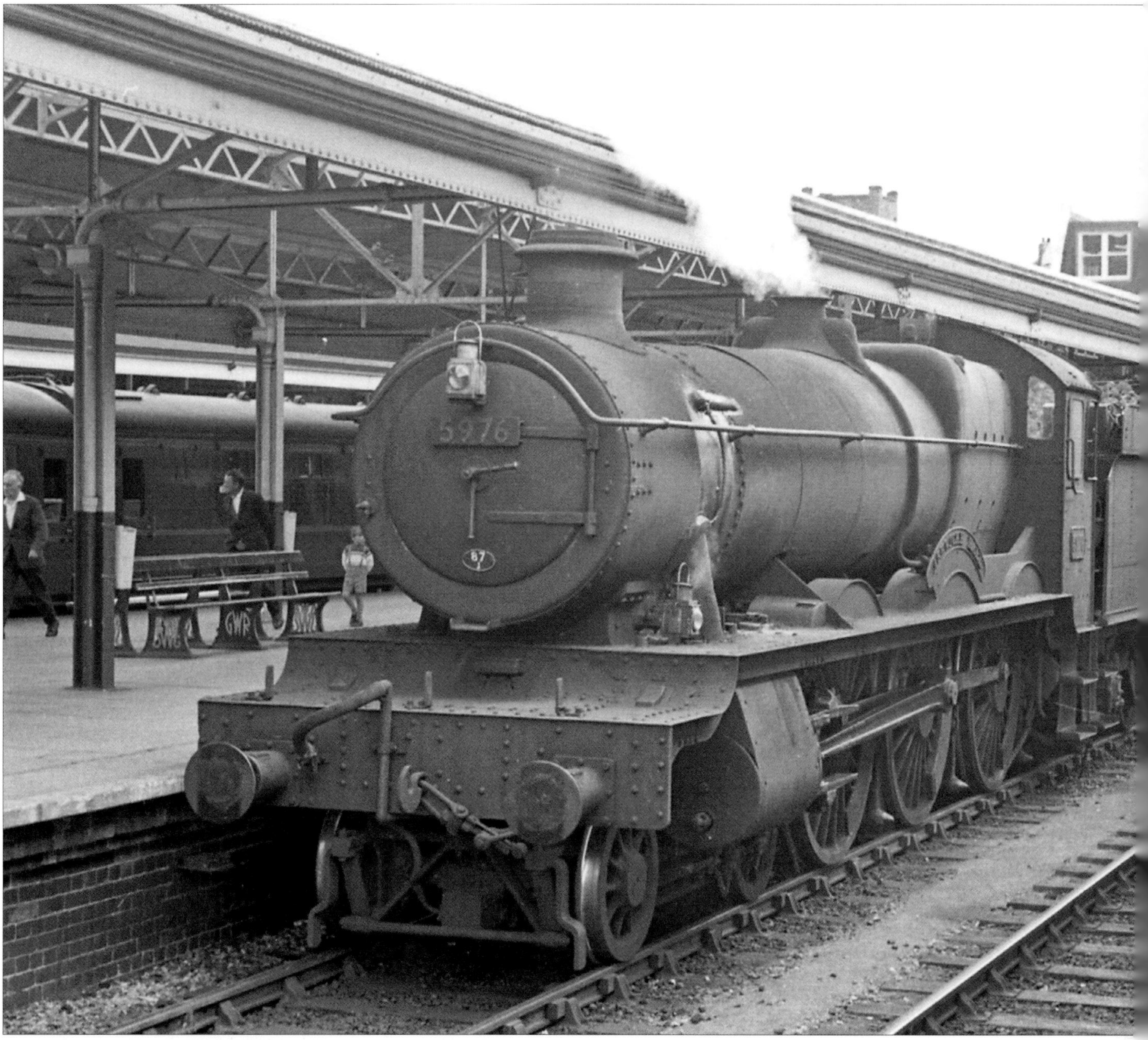
5976
GWR

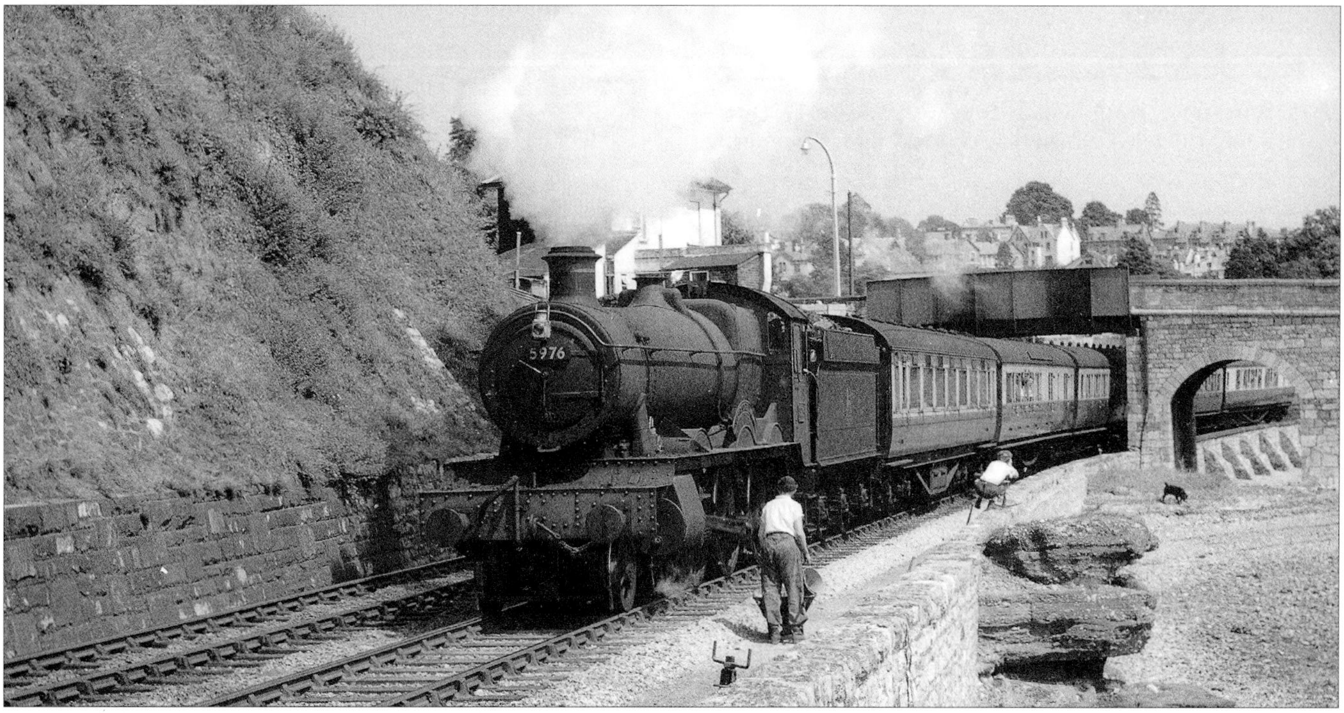
5976

5976 ASHWICKE HALL

Built in 1938 to Lot no.311 at Swindon Works
To traffic 9/1938

Mileages and Boilers
From new	4046
20/2/40	87,184 C4046
18/6/42	171,183 C4046
3/11/43	212,352 C4422
11/12/44	246,331 C4422
18/4/47	329,674 C7218
23/11/48	356,507 C2743
14/12/49	399,532 C8234
30/4/52	494,729 C4400
15/10/54	585,742 C4483
19/11/56	679,796 C7242
8/10/58	758,666 C7266
20/12/61	848,350 C4981

Sheds and Works history
17/9/38	Tyseley
19/8/39	Tyseley shops **L**
20/2/40	Swindon Works **I**
30/3/40	Stafford Road
4/1940	Oxley
18/6/42	Swindon Works **I**
3/11/43	Swindon Works **L**
18/2/44	Oxley shops **R**
11/12/44	Swindon Works **I**
10/12/46	Oxley shops **R**
23/1/47	Tyseley shops **R**
18/4/47	**Swindon Works G**
	Oil burner renumbered 3951
29/11/47	St Philips Marsh
29/2/48	St Philips Marsh shops **R**
5/5/48	St Philips Marsh shops **R**
23/11/48	**Swindon Works L**
	Coal burner renumbered 5976
23/4/49	Exeter
14/12/49	Swindon Works **HG**
30/4/52	Swindon Works **HI**
17/1/53	Exeter shops **U**
24/7/53	Exeter shops **U**
15/10/54	Swindon Works **HG**
19/11/56	Swindon Works **HG**
8/10/58	Swindon Works **HG**
3/11/58-28/12/58	Stored at Exeter
11/1/59-13/6/59	Stored at Exeter
15/8/60	Exeter shops **U**
20/1/61	Exeter shops **U**
20/12/61	Swindon Works **HI**
29/6/63	Fishguard Goodwick
29/9/63	Pontypool Road
14/12/63	Newport Ebbw Jct shops **U**
11/3/64	Newport Ebbw Jct shops **U**

Tenders
From new	2752
20/2/40	2736
2/5/42	2844
3/1/43	2729
3/11/43	2693
15/10/44	2840
11/3/47	2877
6/9/48	2581
14/12/49	2626
21/3/52	2911
15/9/54	2767
19/11/56	2726
8/10/58	2728
7/1/61	4121
20/12/61	2833

Mileage 911,848

Withdrawn 24/7/64 Sold to J Cashmore Newport 4/9/64

A useful comparison of chimneys on 5976 ASHWICKE HALL, with a down train (left) on the sea wall at Teignmouth (the later one which was narrower) and at Swansea High Street (above) with the original, more squat version. With this loco, the two grab irons by the window gave way to one curved all in one piece, though it is not all that obvious here – see 5979 for a clearer illustration. The revised 'L' hand rail by the cab window was introduced with Lot 311; namely from 5976. Michael Boakes Collection and ColourRail

5978 BODINNICK HALL

Built in 1938 to Lot no.311 at Swindon Works
To traffic 5/9/38

Mileages and Boilers
From new	4048
20/8/40	96,049 C4048
11/2/43	196,098 C4048
27/7/45	276,240 C4429
3/10/47	353,317 C2903
24/2/50	436,142 C4429
1/8/52	525,697 C4457
16/2/55	628,592 C2817
9/4/57	716,915 C4023
17/4/59	800,989 C4023
26/4/62	897,378 C9261

Sheds and Works history
15/10/38	Old Oak
20/8/40	Swindon Works **I**
4/1942	Swindon
11/2/43	Swindon Works **I**
18/2/44	Swindon Works **R**
25/1/45	Swindon Works **L**
27/7/45	Swindon Works **G**
29/12/45	St Philips Marsh
26/1/46	Swindon
2/4/47	Banbury shops **R**
31/7/47	Swindon shed **L**
3/10/47	Swindon Works **I**
15/5/48	Weymouth
2/8/49	Weymouth shops **U**
24/2/50	Swindon Works **HG**
3/12/51	Weymouth shops **U**
21/2/52	Weymouth shops **U**
1/8/52	Swindon Works **HG**
10/6/54	Newton Abbot Works **LC**
16/2/55	Swindon Works **HI**
9/4/57	Swindon Works **HG**

Transferred to SR book stock 23/2/58
Returned to WR book stock 7/9/58

6/9/58	Swindon
17/4/59	Swindon Works **HI**
27/7/59	Old Oak shops **U**
15/9/60	Reading shops **U**
26/4/62	Swindon Works **HI**
9/3/63	St Philips Marsh

Tenders
From new	2754
6/7/40	2649
11/2/43	2807
25/1/45	2685
11/6/45	2691
3/10/47	2712
24/1/50	2535
24/2/50	2912
16/6/52	2607
18/1/55	2417
3/10/55	2548
9/4/57	2669
26/4/62	2690

Mileage 945,406

Withdrawn 21/10/63 Sold to Messrs Coopers Ltd Swindon 31/12/63

Above. 5978 BODINNICK HALL in wartime black and very scruffy, at Oxford on 12 October 1949; tender bare of lettering/badge, taper buffers. H.C. Casserley, courtesy R.M. Casserley.

Right. 5978 BODINNICK HALL, scarcely any cleaner, at Bristol Temple Meads in 1955. D.K. Jones Collection.

182

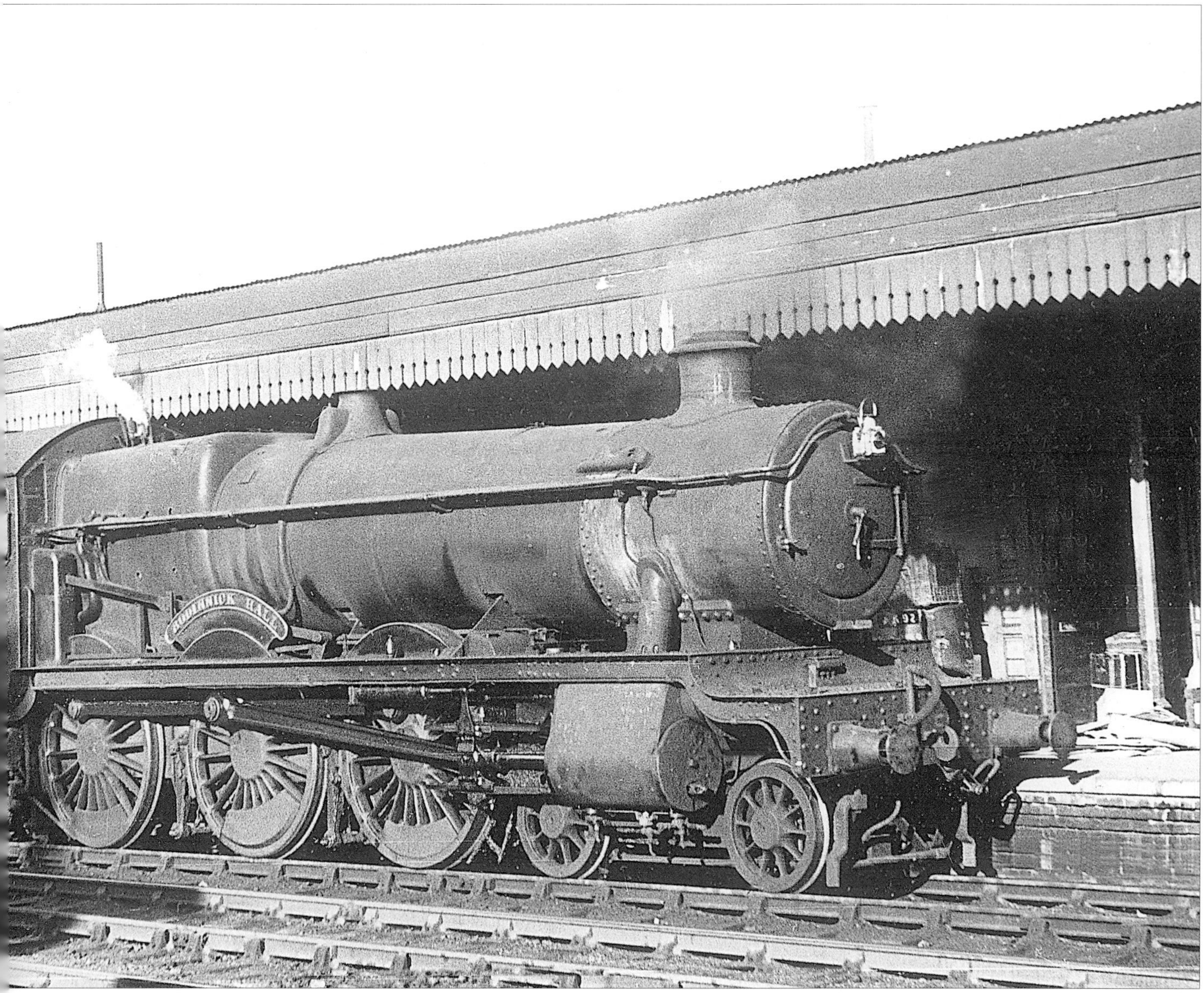
BODINNICK HALL

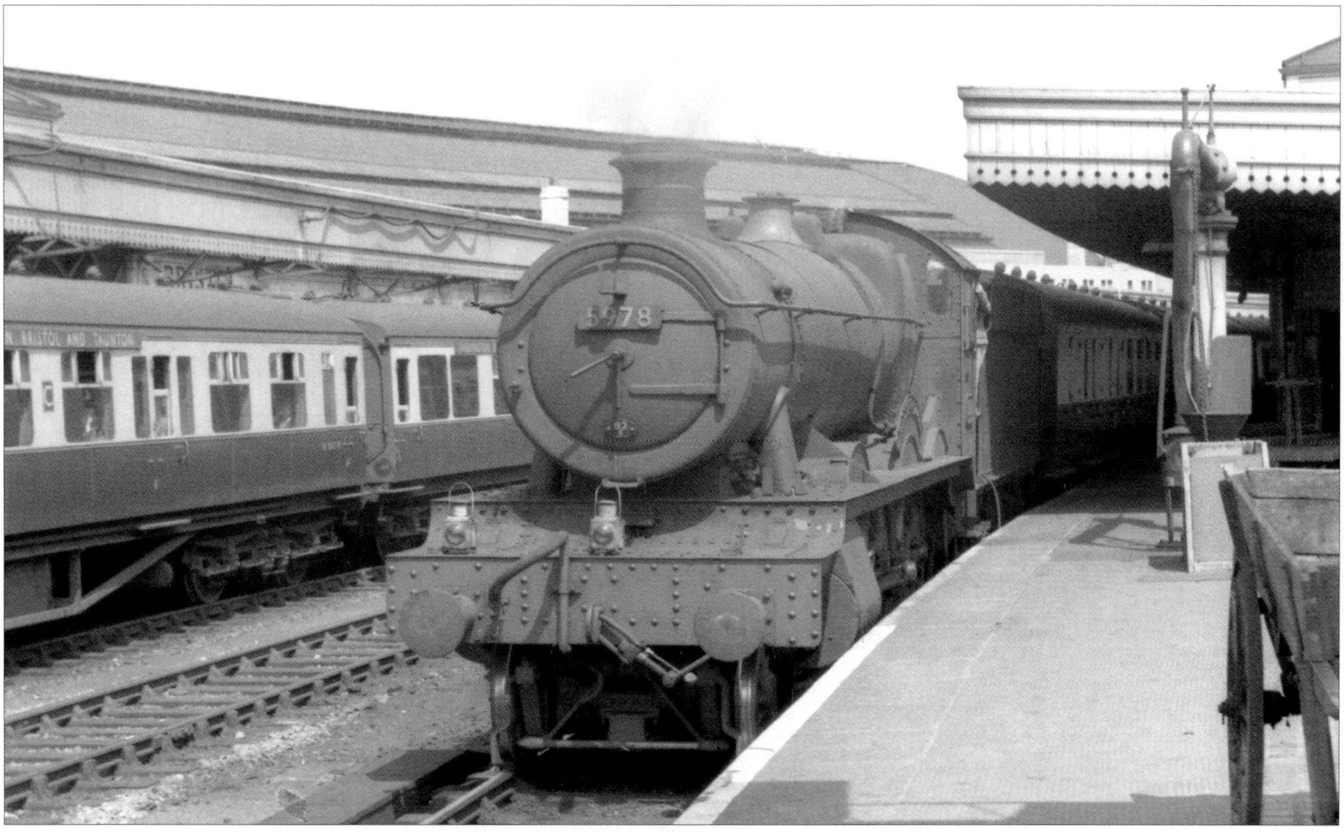
BRISTOL AND TAUNTON
5978

5979 CRUCKTON HALL

Built in 1938 to Lot no.311 at Swindon Works
To traffic 9/1938

Mileages and Boilers
From new		4049
16/1/41	103,329	C4049
30/9/43	200,356	C4049
2/5/45	243,641	C8206
16/4/47	303,702	C4482
19/4/49	374,801	C4426
4/12/51	479,306	C7223
6/8/54	567,472	C7223
28/11/56	651,057	C7277
28/4/59	735,279	C7277
8/2/62	835,012	C7279

Sheds and Works history
17/9/38	Bristol Bath Road
7/9/39	Bristol Bath Road shops **R**
30/3/40	St Philips Marsh
16/1/41	Swindon Works **I**
30/9/43	Swindon Works **I**
19/6/44	St Philips Marsh shops **R**
2/5/45	Swindon Works **G**
18/3/46	Old Oak shops **R**
6/2/47	Reading shops **R**
16/4/47	Swindon Works **I**
9/8/47	Oxley
27/11/48	Reading
19/4/49	Swindon Works **HG**
18/8/50	Taunton shops **U**
4/12/51	Swindon Works **HG**
30/9/53	Old Oak shops **U**
6/8/54	Swindon Works **HI**
12/10/55	Southall shops **U**
28/11/56	Swindon Works **HG**
18/1/57	Old Oak shops **LC**
6/3/59	Banbury shops **U**
28/4/59	Swindon Works **HI**
8/2/62	Swindon Works **HI**
6/4/63	Gloucester
24/2/64	Gloucester shops **U**
21/3/64	Worcester shops **U**
5/10/64	Worcester

Tenders
From new	2756
28/11/40	2753
20/7/43	2768
30/9/43	2844
22/2/45	2538
16/4/47	2406
19/4/49	2676
5/11/51	2735
2/6/54	2532
4/12/54	2548
24/3/56	2920
28/11/56	4111
28/4/59	2788
28/1/61	2402
8/2/62	4056

Mileage 893,201 as at 28/12/63

Withdrawn 6/11/64 Sold to R S Hayes Bridgend 12/1/65

Above. 5979 CRUCKTON HALL, another long-term Reading Hall, at Cardiff General in the early 1960s. The two grab irons by the window are now one curved piece, it can be noted; this modification first appeared with 5976. This illustrates the 'reversed L' of the hand rail on this (the driver's) side of the cab. J. Davenport, Initial Photographics.

Right. 5979 CRUCKTON HALL undergoing attention in the roundhouse at Bristol St Philips Marsh, 12 June 1963. Michael Boakes Collection.

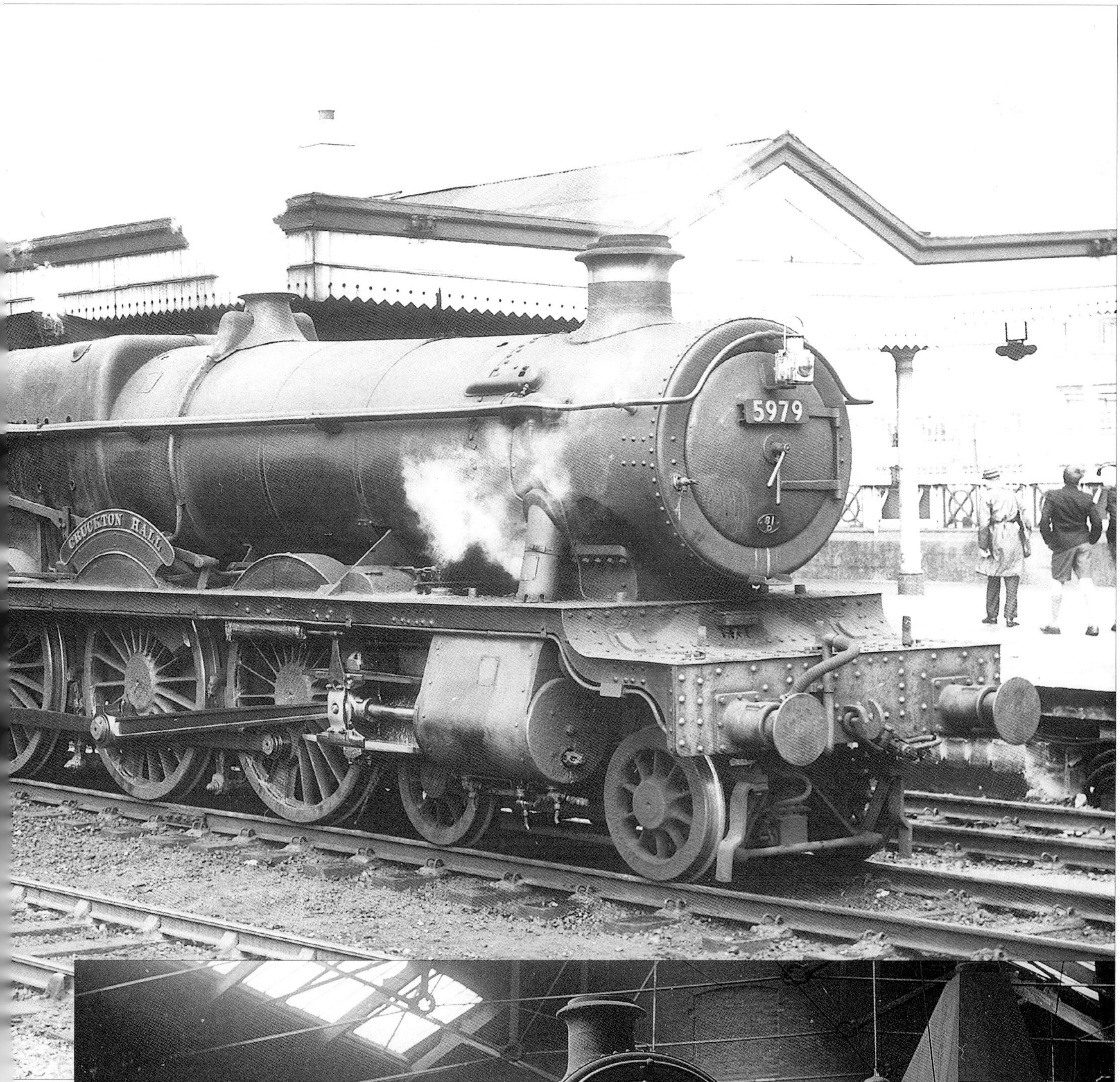
5979
CRUCKTON HALL

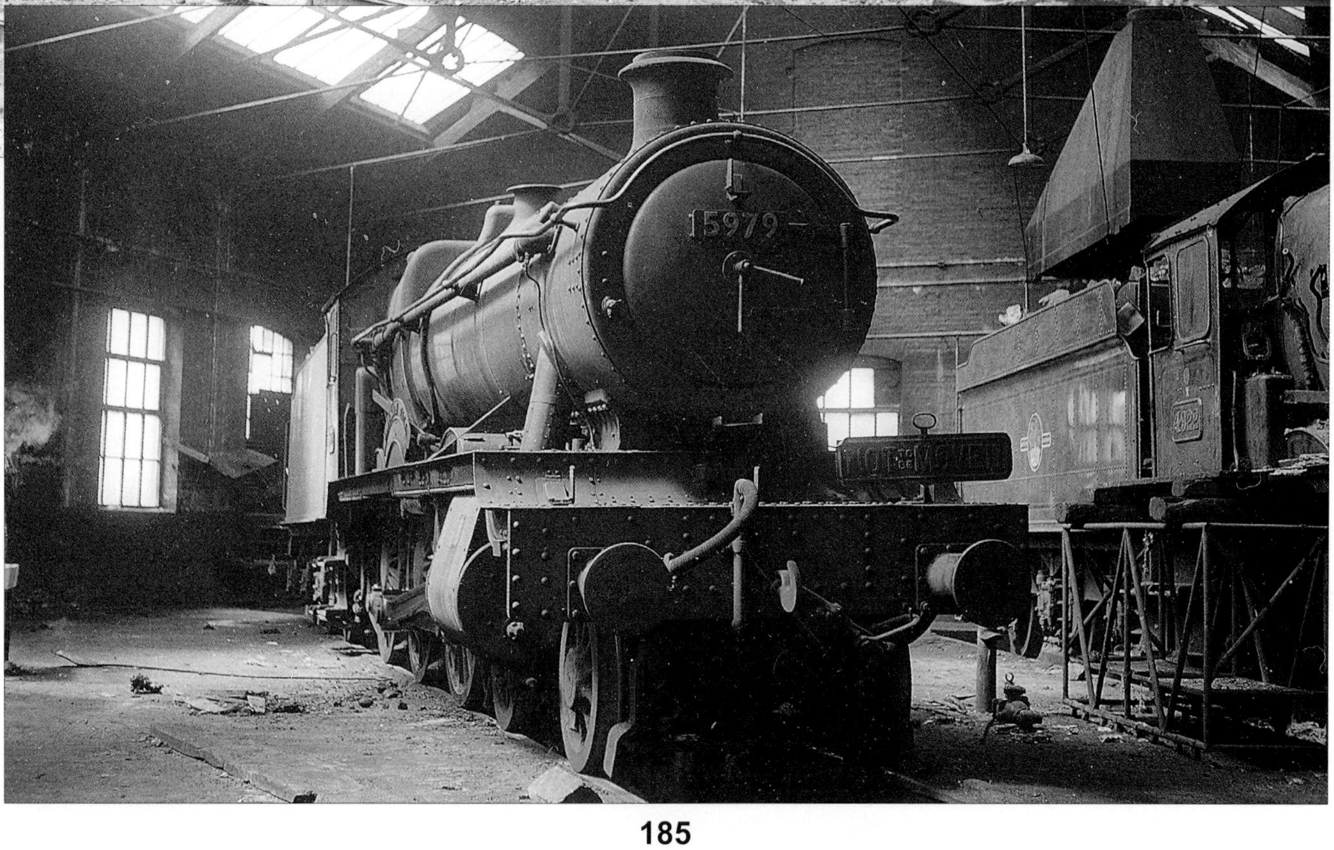

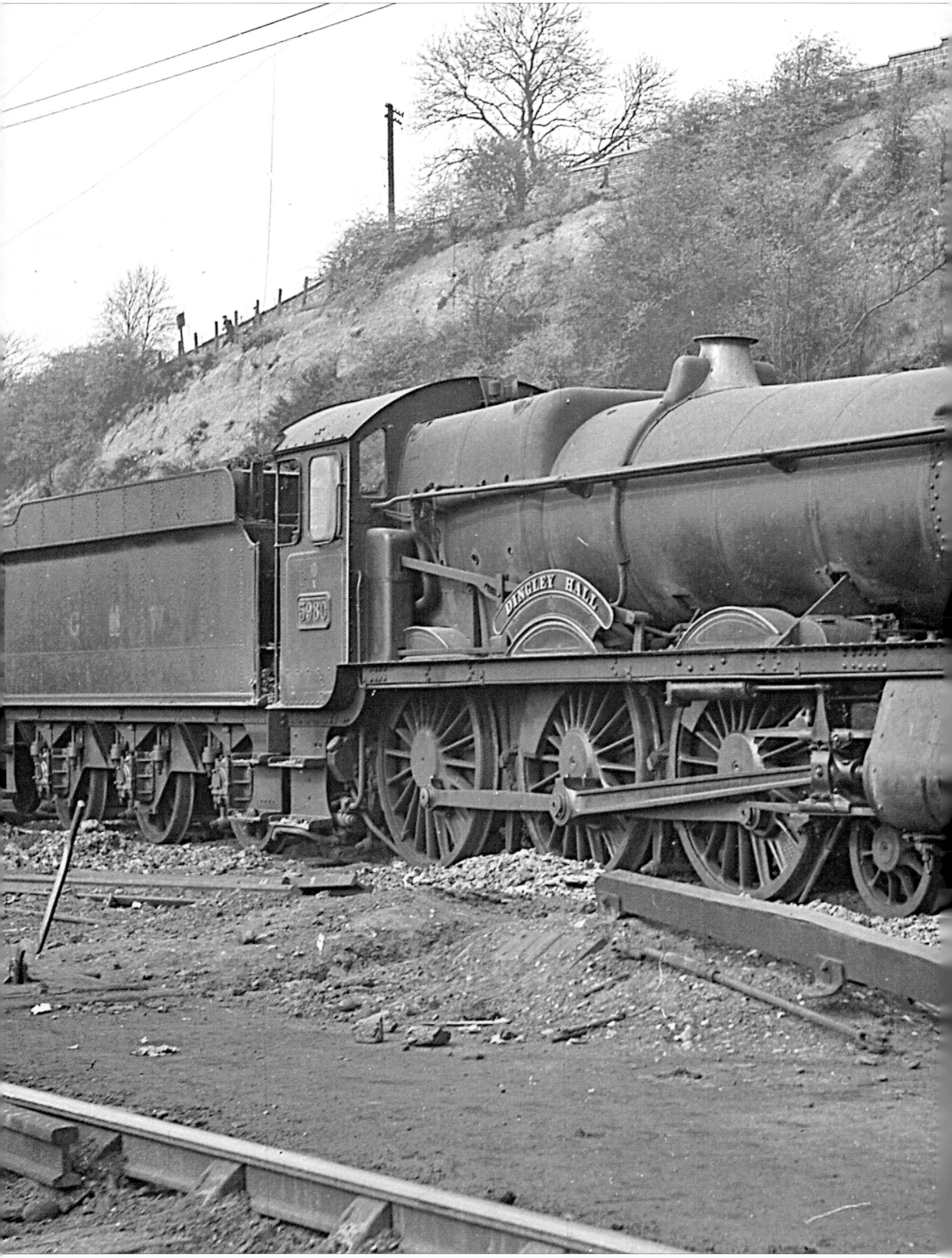
5980
DINGLEY HALL
G W

5980 DINGLEY HALL

Built in 1938 to Lot no.311 at Swindon Works
To traffic 10/1938

Mileages and Boilers
From new	4050
5/7/41	94,695 C4050
28/6/44	185,947 C4464
30/5/46	256,725 C2958
17/9/48	341,804 C4951
29/1/51	430,418 C2840
31/8/53	532,126 C2840
3/11/55	627,794 C2865
2/10/57	707,418 C2865
5/4/60	792,694 C4035

Sheds and Works history
15/10/38	Gloucester
5/7/41	Swindon Works I
21/5/42	Gloucester shops R
28/6/44	Swindon Works G
13/9/45	Gloucester shops R
30/5/46	Swindon Works I
5/5/47	Worcester shops L
26/1/48	Gloucester shops R
17/9/48	Swindon Works I
29/1/51	Swindon Works HG
31/8/53	Swindon Works HI
3/11/55	Swindon Works HG
21/7/57	Gloucester shops U
2/10/57	Swindon Works HI
25/11/58	Worcester shops U
29/11/58	Worcester
11/7/59	Llanelly
23/7/59	Llanelly shops U
8/8/59	Severn Tunnel Jct
5/4/60	Swindon Works HG
18/6/60	Neath
20/5/61	Westbury
4/11/61	Worcester
13/1/62	Worcester shops U
24/3/62	Gloucester

Tenders
From new	2765
30/4/41	2422
28/6/44	2914
12/9/48	2660
20/12/50	2594
15/6/52	2606
23/2/53	2569
31/8/53	2619
28/3/55	2757
3/11/55	4099
5/4/60	2844

Mileage 873,786

Withdrawn 21/9/62 Sold to J Cashmore Ltd 16/9/6

A hybrid 5980 DINGLEY HALL, date unrecorded. The location is Worcester, with the Rainbow Hill-Tunnel Junction loop behind the loco. At the top of the embankment is Railway Walk, that favourite view point for spotters; in fact the tiny outline of one can just be seen by the fence, looking down on the shed yard. The loco is in BR lined black, the tender plain black with GW and the badge. Tender swaps could produce endless unexpected livery combinations! Later on it got a black lined Hawksworth tender which looked better and for a period in late 1958 had a white cab roof, applied for some special working. ColourRail

5981 FRENSHAM HALL

Built in 1938 to Lot no.311 at Swindon Works
To traffic 3/10/38

Mileages and Boilers

From new	4990
26/9/40	98,190 C4990
18/12/43	195,168 C4916
3/1/46	202,896 C7222
31/5/48	339,412 C2911
10/11/50	422,464 C2911
30/2/53	490,591 C4988
3/11/55	578,341 C4988
24/2/58	665,642 C8279
28/4/60	744,322 C4047

Sheds and Works history

12/11/38	Stafford Road
17/1/39	Stafford Road shed **L**
26/9/40	Wolverhampton Works **R**
11/1940	Shrewsbury
26/6/41	Shrewsbury shops **R**
21/4/42	Shrewsbury shops **R**
18/6/42	Stafford Road shed **L**
18/12/43	Swindon Works **G**
3/1/46	Swindon Works **I**
18/1/47	Shrewsbury shops **R**
21/6/47	Tyseley shops **R**
7/1/48	Shrewsbury shops **R**
2/3/48	Banbury shops **R**
31/5/48	Swindon Works **I**
9/9/48	Shrewsbury shops **R**
7/2/49	Stourbridge shops **U**
30/9/49	Shrewsbury shops **U**
10/11/50	Wolverhampton Works **HI**
14/6/51	Hereford shops **U**
3/4/52	Shrewsbury shops **U**
15/1/53	Shrewsbury shops **U**
30/2/53	Swindon Works **HG**
13/12/54	Shrewsbury shops **U**
23/9/55	Shrewsbury shops **U**
3/11/55	Swindon Works **HI**
16/10/56	Shrewsbury shops **U**
29/12/56	St Philips Marsh
23/3/57	Worcester
15/6/57	Weymouth
2/10/57	Weymouth shops **U**

Transferred to SR book stock 23/2/58

24/2/58	Swindon Works **HG**

Returned to WR book stock 7/9/58

6/9/58	Swindon
21/11/58	Swindon shed **LC**
28/4/60	Swindon Works **HI**
17/6/61	Newton Abbot
6/11/61	Newton Abbot shed **U**
14/7/62	Neath

Tenders

From new	2766
7/8/40	2614
27/10/43	2560
25/3/48	2605
15/7/50	2651
17/4/53	2855
31/8/55	2871
3/11/55	2417
29/9/56	2792
24/2/58	2926
28/4/60	2424

Mileage 808,362

Withdrawn 21/9/62 Sold to R S Hayes Bridgend 26/8/63

5981 FRENSHAM HALL out on the road; it is in lined black with the first emblem (all faintly visible on the original print) and a Shrewsbury engine, in the period up to 1956. The upper quadrant signal indicates that it is not GWR territory. ColourRail

5981 FRENSHAM HALL at Shrewsbury, alongside the 'boundary wall' between the GWR and LMS premises, 1952. D.K. Jones Collection.

5982 HARRINGTON HALL
Built in 1938 to Lot no.311 at Swindon Works
To traffic 1938

Mileages and Boilers
From new	4991
29/11/40	105,699 C4991
5/6/43	198,323 C4991
22/5/45	256,684 C4025
17/3/48	341,751 C2870
6/3/50	410,604 C9208
12/12/52	504,214 C8273
17/6/55	605,341 C8273
2/1/58	699,896 C7202
8/7/60	819,720 C7202

Sheds and Works history
12/11/38	Carmarthen
29/11/40	Swindon Works I
1/1941	Taunton
7/11/41	Taunton shops R
15/1/42	Taunton shops R
3/1942	Penzance
17/9/42	Penzance shops R
12/11/42	Penzance shops R
5/6/43	Swindon Works I
7/1943	Taunton
25/8/43	Taunton shops R
4/12/43	Taunton shops R
12/3/44	Taunton shops R
8/9/44	Taunton shops R
25/11/44	Taunton shops R
14/2/45	Taunton shops R
25/5/45	Swindon Works G
10/7/45	Taunton shops R
24/11/45	Taunton shops L
20/4/46	Exeter
31/7/46	Newton Abbot Works L
5/10/46	Taunton
27/11/46	Taunton shops R
6/2/47	Newton Abbot Works R
28/8/47	Taunton shops R
22/1/48	Taunton shops R
17/3/48	Swindon Works I
22/4/49	Taunton shops U
24/5/49	Swindon Works LC
23/9/49	Taunton shops U
6/3/50	Swindon Works HG
23/3/50-11/6/50	Stored at Swindon
17/6/50	St Philips Marsh
2/11/50	Newport Ebbw Jct shops U
26/9/51	Old Oak shops U
1/3/52	Bristol Bath Road shops
12/12/52	Swindon Works HG
17/6/55	Swindon Works HI
5/1/57	Newton Abbot Works LC
23/3/57	Westbury
2/1/58	Swindon Works HG
27/12/58	Reading
11/5/60	Old oak shops U
8/7/60	Swindon Works HI

Tenders
From new	2767
29/11/40	2612
5/6/43	2814
29/3/45	2417
10/8/46	2791
28/1/48	2578
24/5/49	2654
6/3/50	2789
10/11/52	2604
12/12/52	2408
2/1/58	2639
7/10/61	2845
4/11/61	2684
16/6/62	2763

Mileage 891,615

Withdrawn 1/9/62 Sold to A King Norwich 8/11/63

5982 HARRINGTON HALL takes a Birkenhead-Paddington express through the wide cutting between the Dee crossing and Saltney Junction as it leaves Chester, in 1949. The loco will have come on at Chester General and the train will have reversed direction, having been brought in by a tank of some description from the Wirral. The splendid rake still appears to be in its GWR finery, though carmine and cream was beginning to appear by then. The set is magnificent, and a far cry from the short trains formed of polychromatic units which now ply their trade on this once great main line. It appears to be made up principally of 1930s-built Collett express stock. What the roof-mounted destination boards proclaim will be known by students of the GWR, but by the time BR Mk1s formed these services, the boards read 'Paddington Birmingham, Shrewsbury Chester & Birkenhead'. Wolverhampton, despite its importance for loco-changing, was omitted. At this point, the train is on LMR metals, but shortly after passing beneath the occupation bridge on which the photographer is standing, it'll turn south at Saltney Junction and be on the WR, complete with control by GWR lower-quadrant signals. Rail Photoprint.

5982 HARRINGTON HALL, in lined black, by the coal stage at Shrewsbury shed, 28 February 1956. D.K. Jones Collection.

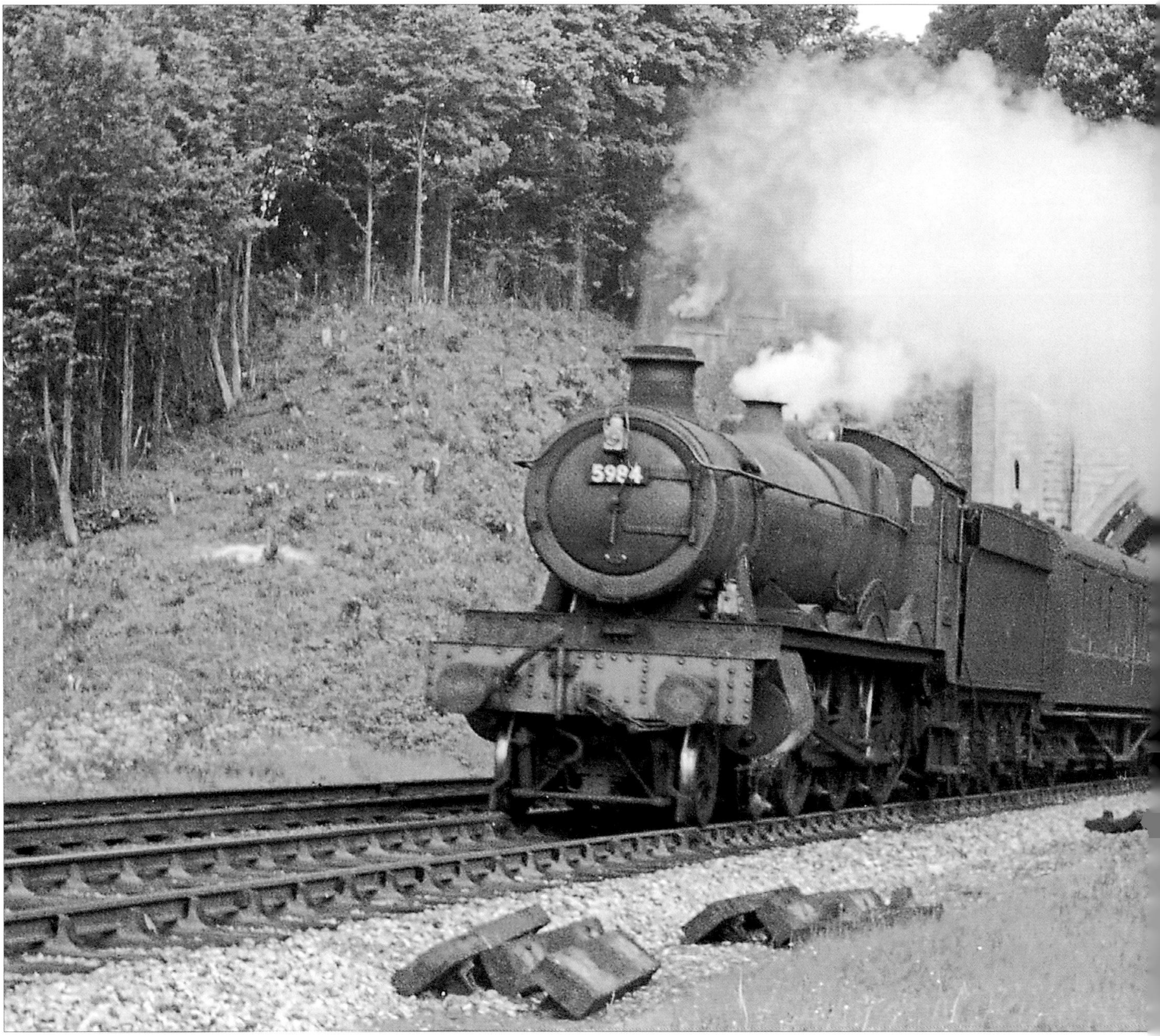
5984

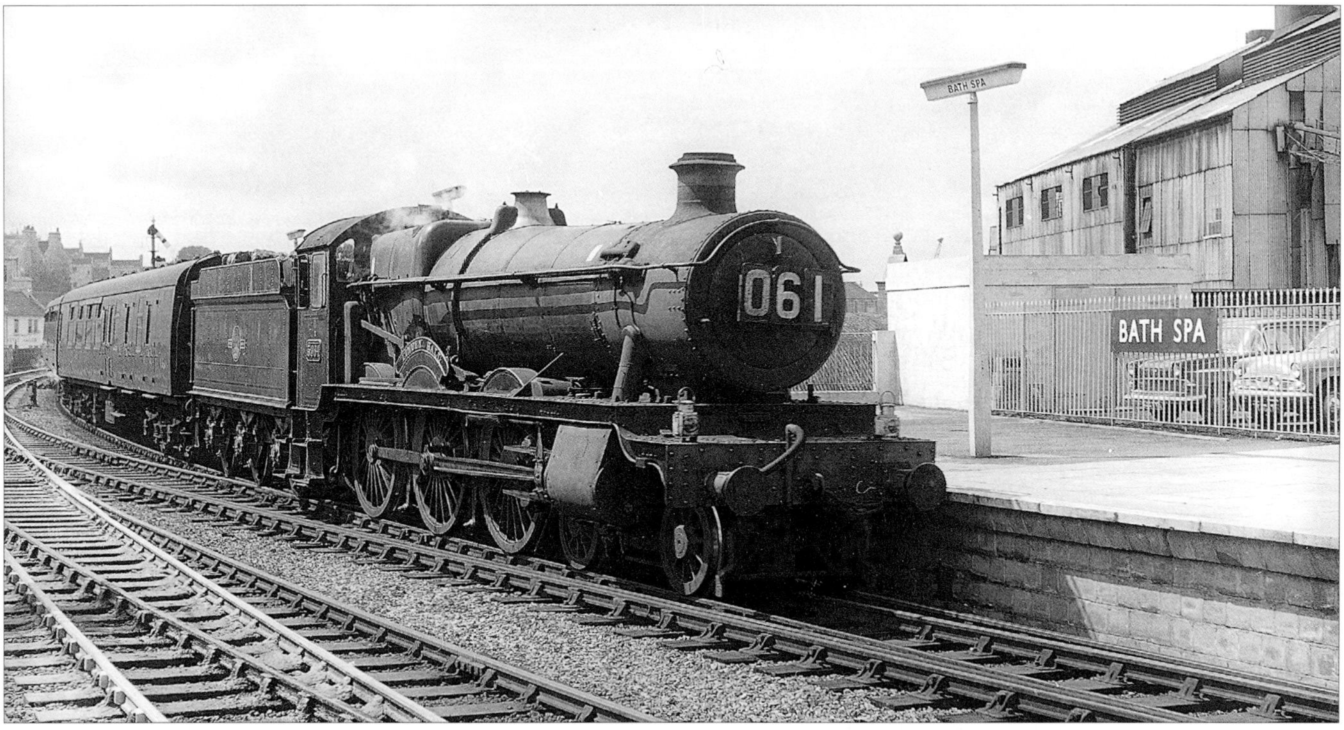
BATH SPA
061
BATH SPA

Above. 5984 LINDEN HALL emerging from Twerton tunnel on 30 May 1963. Rail Photoprint.

Left. 5984 LINDEN HALL in lined green runs into Bath Spa with an up express, 10 May 1962. Michael Boakes Collection.

5984 LINDEN HALL
Built in 1938 to Lot no.311 at Swindon Works
To traffic 10/1938

Mileages and Boilers
From new	4993
18/11/40	104,949 C4993
10/12/43	211,716 C7244
3/7/46	302,525 C7206
13/10/48	378,099 C4092
14/11/50	450,207 C2978
23/9/53	552,543 C4990
4/5/56	647,424 C4990
4/11/58	742,379 C2850
3/2/61	826,639 C4029

Sheds and Works history
12/11/38	Weymouth
23/2/39	Weymouth shops **R**
4/4/40	Weymouth shops **R**
18/11/40	Swindon Works **I**
24/12/40	Weymouth shops **L**
1/1941	St Philips Marsh
29/7/42	St Philips Marsh shops **R**
8/8/43	St Philips Marsh **R**
10/12/43	Swindon Works **G**
26/6/44	Shrewsbury shops **R**
3/7/46	Swindon Works **I**
1/7/47	Bristol Bath Road shops **R**
5/11/47	Penzance shops **R**
7/3/48	St Philips Marsh shops **R**
13/10/48	Swindon Works **I**
21/5/49	Bristol Bath Road
3/12/49	Carmarthen
4/4/50	Swindon Works **LC**
14/11/50	Swindon Works **HG**
1/1/51	Caerphilly Works **U**
23/9/53	Swindon Works **HG**
4/12/54	Neyland
8/10/55	Swindon
4/5/56	Swindon Works **HI**
1/12/56	Westbury
23/2/57	Tyseley
26/9/57	Southall shops **U**
5/10/57	Worcester
4/11/58	Swindon Works **HG**
11/7/59	Llanelly
18/6/60	Carmarthen
8/10/60	Canton
3/2/61	Swindon Works **HI**
2/3/62	Swindon Works **HC**
6/10/62	Neath
9/10/62	Canton shops **U**
3/11/62	Old Oak
18/1/63	Old Oak shops **U**
4/5/63	Cardiff East Dock

Tenders
From new	2769
10/10/40	2666
12/10/43	2589
3/7/46	2420
4/9/48	2696
4/4/50	2748
24/11/50	2844
15/12/50	2565
29/12/51	2884
23/9/53	2413
4/5/56	2679
4/11/58	2656
3/2/61	4058
2/3/62	2792

Mileage 917,443 as at 28/12/63

Withdrawn 15/1/65 Sold to J Buttigieg Newport 2/11/65

5986 ARBURY HALL

Built in 1939 to Lot no.327 at Swindon Works
To traffic 11/1939

Mileages and Boilers
From new	8200
5/8/42	97,857 C8200
21/10/44	168,747 R2995
13/5/47	250,870 C2851
1/2/50	297,792 C2928
8/1/52	353,471 C4073
12/2/54	451,821 C4964
5/7/56	544,493 C4964
22/10/58	622,280 C4073
2/3/61	708,072 C8291

Sheds and Works history
6/1/40	Reading
5/8/42	Swindon Works I
7/12/43	Reading shops L
21/4/44	Reading shops R
21/10/44	Swindon Works G
28/2/45	Westbury shops R
13/5/47	Swindon Works I
	Oil fired-renumbered 3954
13/5/47	Old Oak
24/9/47	Old Oak shops R
27/2/48	Old Oak shops R
14/5/48	Old Oak shed R
8/8/48	Old Oak shops R
12/10/48-5/1/50	Stored at Swindon
1/2/50	Swindon Works HC
	Coal fired-renumbered 5986
16/2/50-15/7/50	Stored at Swindon
20/2/51	Bristol Bath Road shops U
22/6/51	Old Oak shops HC
8/1/52	Swindon Works HI
12/5/53	Old Oak shops U
12/2/54	Swindon Works HG
6/11/54	Shrewsbury
2/3/55	Wolverhampton Works U
6/6/55	Tyseley
18/6/55	Shrewsbury shops U
8/9/55	Shrewsbury
5/7/56	Swindon Works HI
7/9/57	Swindon
22/10/58	Swindon Works HG
6/9/60	Old Oak shops U
2/3/61	Swindon Works HG
7/10/61	Reading
6/10/62	Westbury

Tenders
From new	2804
5/8/42	2600
21/10/44	2883
26/3/47	2721
12/10/48	2641
3/12/51	2624
11/1/54	2580
30/11/57	2567
20/6/58	2598
22/10/58	2679
26/5/60	2881
2/3/61	4010

Mileage 796,306

Withdrawn 10/9/63 Sold to Messrs Coopers Ltd Swindon 31/12/63

Above. 5986 ARBURY HALL in lined black at Oxley shed, 27 February 1955. D.K. Jones Collection.

Right. No place or date, but the circumstances look unusual, *writes Michael Back:* 'There are two parallel goods running loops; this we know because the signals have rings on them. 5986 ARBURY HALL is carrying class B headlamps, unless it is a class H with the bottom lamp removed. This would not appear to be 'Rule 55' in action because the loco isn't attached to the ballast wagons behind and the exit signal is already off. The driver looks to be on the footplate and the fireman is at the phone box, watched by either the guard or the shunter. Are they asking about the working, or have they just set this lot back into the loop, detached off the train in the next road, or is all this connected with the loose sleepers and piles of chairs lying about? And note the signal arm – it hasn't come off sufficiently for the lamp to show through the spectacle.' ColourRail

199

202

5988 BOSTOCK HALL

Built in 1939 to Lot no.327 at Swindon Works
To traffic 11/1939
Only ERCs available

Sheds and Works history
6/1/40	Hereford
4/7/42	Not listed **I**
8/1942	Gloucester
25/3/44	Swindon Works **L**
28/10/44	Swindon Works **G** 67,463 167,702
14/9/46	Worcester shops **L**
26/10/46	Gloucester shops **L**
5/7/47	Swindon Works **I** 69,005
4/9/48	Worcester shops **L**
9/4/49	Swindon Works **HG** 64,418 133,423
10/2/51	Swindon Works **HI** 80,474
22/3/52	Worcester
31/1/53	Swindon Works **HG** 79,178 159,652
10/4/53	Worcester shops **LC**
16/5/53	Landore
21/9/55	Swindon Works **HI**
13/1/58	Swindon Works **HG** boiler 8270
26/3/60	Banbury
18/10/60	Swindon Works **HG** 78529 boiler 2995
11/8/62	Stourbridge
3/11/62	Old Oak
6/7/63	Tyseley
18/9/64	Swindon Works **HC**

Tenders
BR no dates
4035
2571
2430
2601
2705
4123

Mileage 782,729

Withdrawn 10/65

5988 BOSTOCK HALL crosses the River Dee at Chester on its way towards Shrewsbury hauling a summer extra comprised entirely of LMS-built carriages on 29 July 1962. It looks as if a previous job had been a special, judging by '1Z27' chalked on the smokebox door, but '1X92' carried on the wooden board attached to the top lamp bracket is the designation of this train. The train is on the up WR line (as far as Saltney Junction) which also served as the down LMR slow. Its adjacent road is the down WR line and up LMR slow from the North Wales coast. The two other tracks are the down and up LMR fasts to the coast. The photographer is standing on the occupation bridge linking Curzon Park with Chester's rather exclusive Golf Club. B. Wadey, transporttreasury

Inset. At home at Banbury shed about 1960-61.
J. Davenport, Initial Photographics.

5990 DORFORD HALL

Built in 1939 to Lot no.327 at Swindon Works
To traffic 12/1939
Only ERCs available

Sheds and Works history
3/2/40	Gloucester		
7/11/42	No location I		
21/7/45	Swindon Works **G**	86,144	184,821
20/9/47	Swindon Works **I**	73,348	
12/11/49	Swindon Works **HG**	84,736	158,084
8/3/52	Swindon Works **HG**	94,287	
11/10/54	Swindon Works **HI**		
24/3/56	Southall		
21/4/56	Penzance		
16/6/56	Landore		
26/3/60	Banbury		
24/10/60	Wolverhampton Works **LI**		
10/8/61	Wolverhampton Works **LI**		
2/4/62	Swindon Works **LI**		
21/3/62	Swindon Works **HG**	180,748	boiler 6207
2/4/62	Swindon Works **U**		

Mileage 867,836

Withdrawn 1/65 Sold to J Firswell & Son Banbury

Right. 5990 DORFORD HALL with an inter-regional train of SR stock at Basingstoke; its near-shimmering condition and the Banbury shed plate indicates the period to be very shortly after its final Heavy General of March 1962. ColourRail.

Below. 5990 DORFORD HALL in lined green with Hawksworth tender at Gloucester, 23 November 1957. R.J. Buckley, Initial Photographics.

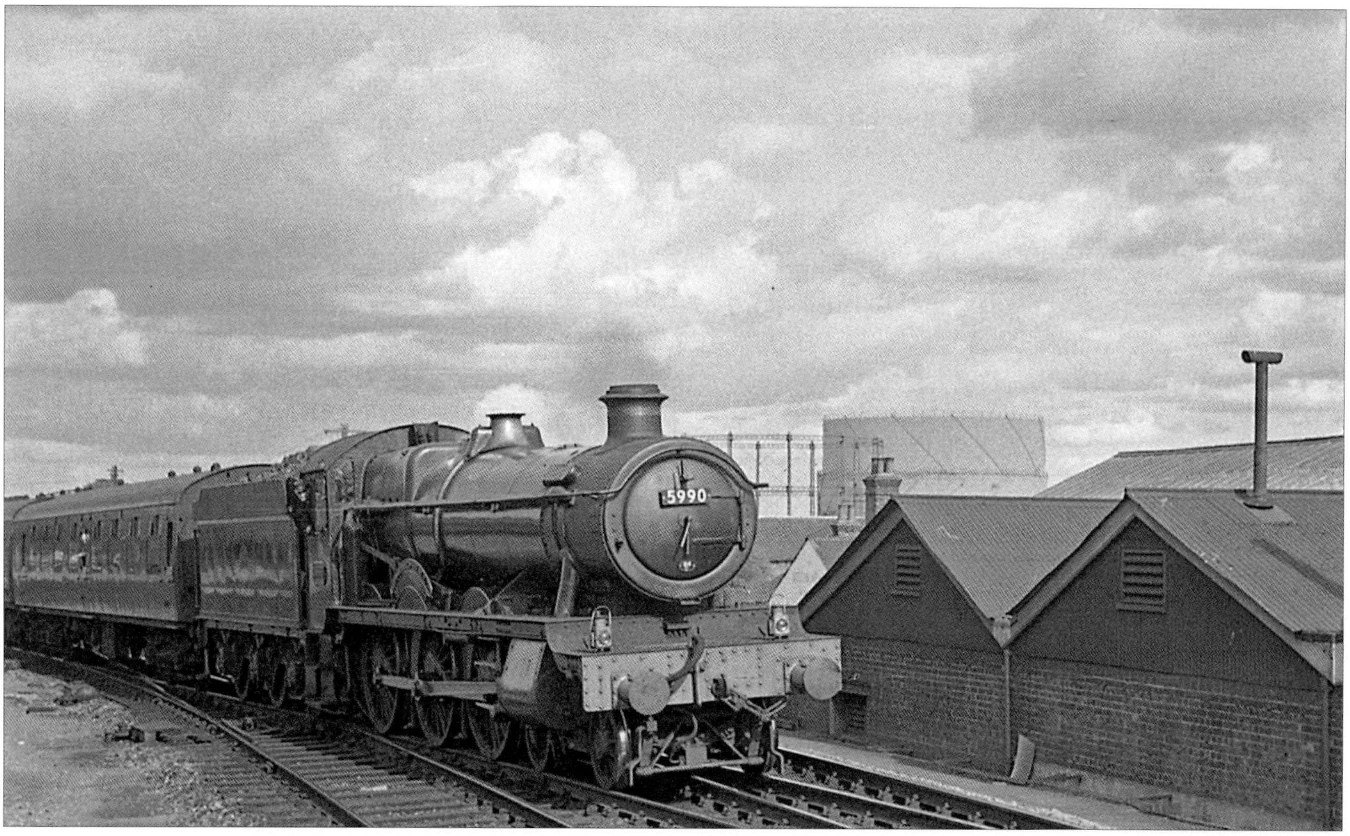
5990

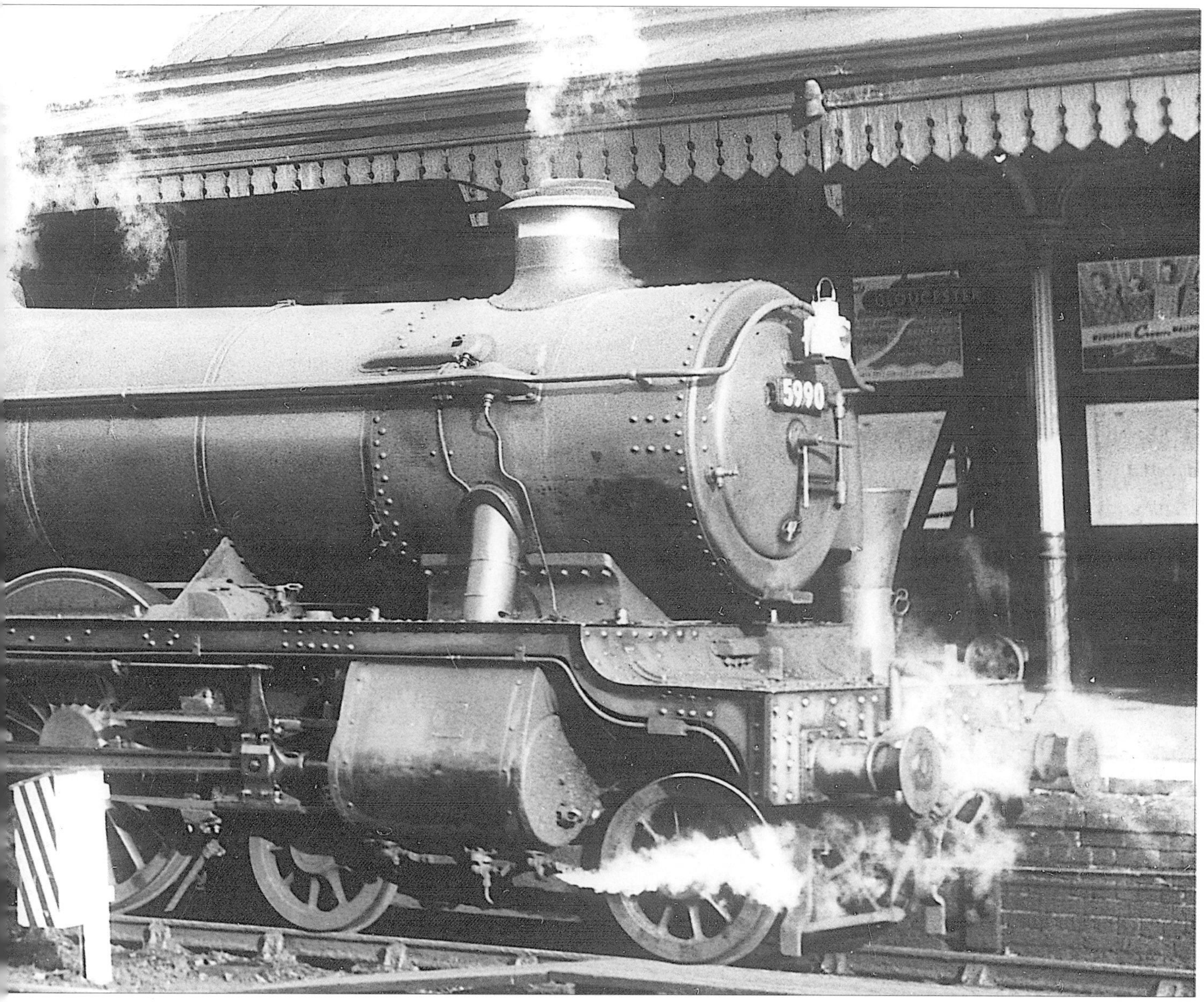
5990

5991 GRESHAM HALL

Built in 1939 to Lot no.327 at Swindon Works
To traffic 12/1939
Only ERCs available

Sheds and Works history
3/2/40	Banbury		
20/2/43	Swindon Works	109,525	
3/6/44	Swindon Works **L**		
3/3/45	Swindon Works **HG** 57,240	166,815	
22/11/47	Swindon Works **HI** 90,455		
23/4/49	Oxley		
27/5/50	Swindon Works **HG** 87,475	177,930	
8/3/52	Swindon Works **HI** 67,386		
16/10/53	Swindon Works **HI** 66,451		
6/9/55	Swindon Works **HG**		
12/10/59	Wolverhampton Works **LI**		
25/1/60	Swindon Works **HG** 152,921	boiler 7216	
20/6/60	Wolverhampton Works **U**		
6/4/62	Swindon Works **HI** 66,147	boiler 4020	
22/4/61	Shrewsbury		

Mileage 803,940

Withdrawn 7/64

5991 GRESHAM HALL at Shrewsbury at an unrecorded date. It is irredeemably in 'BR grey' but there are one or two fragments of black lining struggling to be seen and there is the faintest ghost of the first emblem on the tender. These are its days as an Oxley engine; it was still in black with the first emblem in 1958 and would have 'gone green' with its Heavy General of 1960. ColourRail

5992 HORTON HALL

Built in 1939 to Lot no.327 at Swindon Works
To traffic 12/1939

Mileages and Boilers
From new	8206
26/2/43	103,722 C8206
15/12/44	162,088 C7217
8/10/46	222,803 C8280
12/11/48	298,051 C2800
23/11/50	370,123 C4952
23/12/52	454,876 C7270
1/4/55	549,834 C4457
15/5/57	636,445 C4483
13/5/59	721,815 C4483
10/8/62	826,795 C6221

Sheds and Works history
3/2/40	Banbury
2/5/42	Stafford Road shed L
26/2/43	Swindon Works I
28/2/44	Banbury shops R
15/12/44	Swindon Works L
19/9/45	Tyseley shops R
26/1/46	Banbury shops R
29/5/46	Banbury shops R
8/10/46	Swindon Works I
13/9/47	Shrewsbury shops R
12/11/48	Swindon Works G
14/6/49	Neyland
16/7/49	St Philips Marsh
23/11/50	Swindon Works HG
23/12/52	Swindon Works HG
28/11/53	Taunton
19/6/54	Exeter
11/9/54	Taunton
26/10/54	Taunton shops U
1/4/55	Swindon Works HI
15/5/57	Swindon Works HG
13/5/59	Swindon Works HI
13/1/60	Newton Abbot Works LC
18/2/60	Taunton shops U
7/5/62	Banbury shops U
10/8/62	Swindon Works HI
7/11/63	Newport Ebbw Jct shops LC
5/10/64	Westbury
9/1/65	Gloucester
10/7/65	Newport Ebbw Jct

Tenders
From new	2808
26/2/43	2546
15/12/44	2720
8/10/46	2807
29/9/48	2672
25/10/50	2662
20/11/52	2801
7/3/55	2556
7/4/55	2253
15/5/57	2385
26/3/60	2604
10/8/62	2633

Mileage 864,867 as at 18/12/63

Withdrawn 9/8/65 Sold to Birds Bynea 6/9/65

Right. Hall on the Wall. 5992 HORTON HALL at Dawlish on 14 August 1960 and the crowd in the background indicates a fine day. A picture that the GWR Publicity Department might well have converted to a poster, an image of the 'Riviera'. Val Doonican strolls by with his lady and favourite jumper. L.W. Rowe, Colourail.

Below. 5992 HORTON HALL at Swindon on 3 June 1962, accompanied by Modified Hall 7900 SAINT PETER'S HALL. Both locos are awaiting a move into 'AE' Shop, for Classified Repair. Their first move will be on to the Stripping Gang, just inside the Shop, east side of traverser. RailOnline

211

5993 KIRBY HALL

Built in 1939 to Lot no.327 at Swindon Works
To traffic 12/1939

Mileages and Boilers
From new	8207
29/10/42	110,744 C8207
30/9/44	175,661 C4050
30/8/46	238,735 C7274
27/9/48	312,128 C4989
9/1/51	406,531 C7232
17/3/53	489,986 R6262
29/11/55	594,665 R6262
3/3/58	683,560 C4903
4/11/60	781,930 C4903

Sheds and Works history
3/2/40	Tyseley
26/11/41	Tyseley shops **R**
7/3/42	Tyseley shops **R**
5/1942	Leamington Spa
7/1942	Tyseley
29/10/42	Swindon Works **I**
26/6/44	Tyseley shed **R**
30/9/44	Swindon Works **G**
6/12/44	Tyseley shops **R**
27/12/44	Tyseley shops **R**
21/4/46	Tyseley shed **R**
30/8/46	Swindon Works **I**
30/11/46	Leamington Spa
10/3/47	Swindon Works **L**
14/6/47	Tyseley
27/9/48	Swindon Works **I**
9/1/51	Swindon Works **HI**
27/1/51	Laira
26/5/51	Laira shops **U**
19/7/51	Laira shops **U**
11/8/51	Tyseley
19/4/52	Oxley
14/6/52	Reading
17/3/53	Swindon Works **HG**
29/11/55	Swindon Works **HI**
3/3/58	Swindon Works **HG**
21/10/59	Old Oak shops **U**
11/6/60	Reading shops **U**
4/11/60	Swindon Works **HI**
10/4/62	Gloucester shops **U**
20/4/63	Reading shops **U**

Tenders
From new	2809
14/9/42	2577
1/8/44	2402
30/8/46	2692
10/3/47	2714
21/8/48	2614
29/11/50	4010
6/9/52	2560
17/3/53	4081
29/11/55	2661
22/2/57	2871
23/2/57	2555
3/3/58	2442

Mileage 854,055

Withdrawn 13/5/63 Cut up 7/9/63

Above. 5993 KIRBY HALL gets under way with vans at Banbury, 24 May 1962. Ken Fairey, ColourRail.

Right. KIRBY HALL, its lining on green livery particularly apparent for once. Note difference in weathering/angle of light below the horizontal rivet line of the tender. 5993 has charge of an up freight at Acton in April 1961. A.E. Durrant, Michael Boakes Collection.

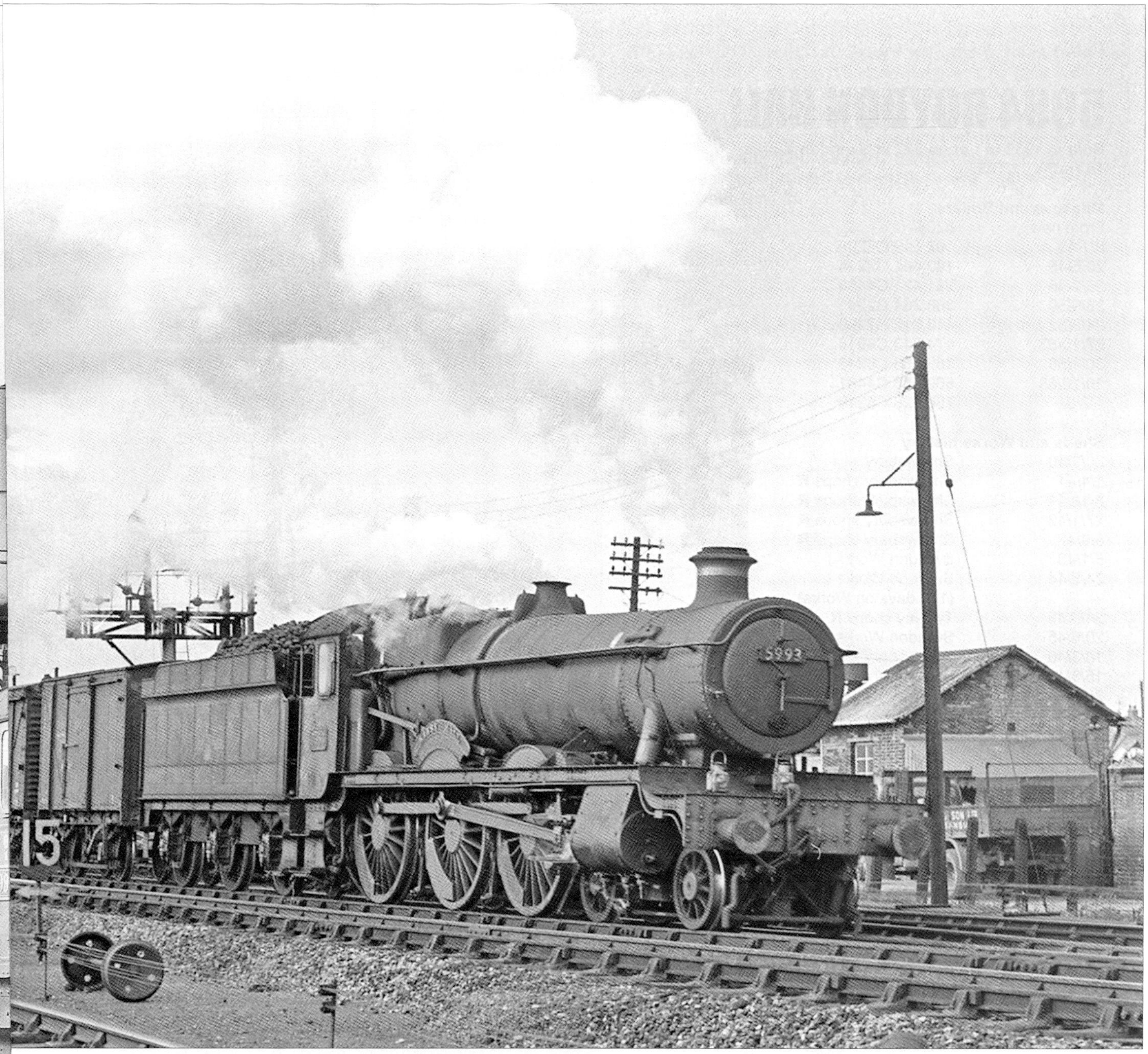
5993
15

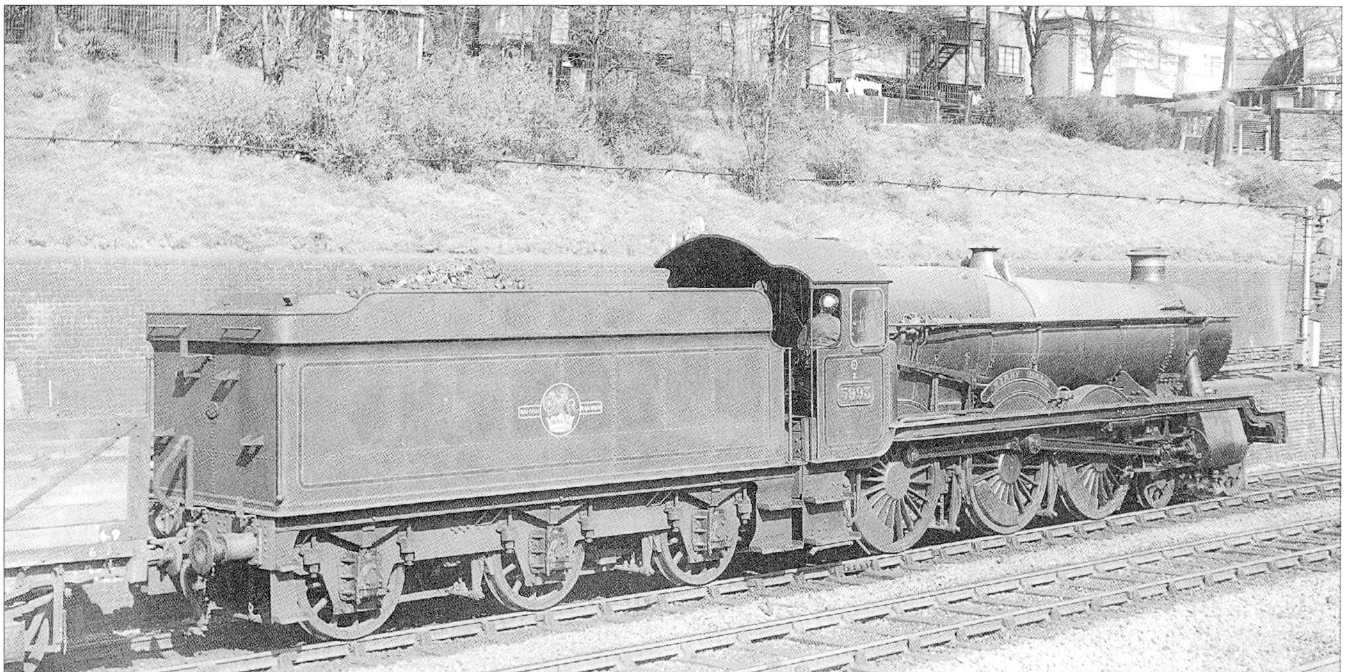

5995 WICK HALL

Built in 1940 to Lot no.327 at Swindon Works
To traffic 1/1940

Mileages and Boilers
From new	8209
23/7/42	103,795 C8209
7/5/43	129,526 C4044
24/4/45	200,526 C4044
14/10/46	259,130 C2962
4/1/49	344,002 C7217
3/2/51	427,930 C7217
7/10/52	480,873 C7221
25/11/53	525,776 C2949
31/12/54	565,032 C7246
28/6/56	612,523 C8244
16/10/58	696,161 C2945
6/2/61	772,285 C4477

Sheds and Works history
30/3/40	Stafford Road
23/7/42	Swindon Works **I**
7/5/43	Swindon Works **L**
10/11/44	Stafford Road shed **R**
23/12/44	Reading shops **R**
24/4/45	Swindon Works **I**
14/10/46	Swindon Works **G**
9/1/47	Banbury shops **R**
21/2/48	Didcot shops **R**
4/1/49	Swindon Works **HG**
7/10/50	Oxley
23/2/51	Swindon Works **HI**
7/10/52	Swindon Works **HC**
5/12/52	Oxley shops **U**
25/11/53	Swindon Works **HI**
31/12/54	Swindon Works **HC**
28/6/56	Swindon Works **HG**
19/12/57	Croes Newydd shops **U**
11/4/58	Banbury shops **U**
16/10/58	Swindon Works **HG**
16/7/60	Oxley shops **U**
28/10/60	Oxley shops **U**
6/2/61	Swindon Works **HI**
14/9/61	Oxley shops **U**
20/9/62	Oswestry shops **U**

Transferred to LMR book stock 30/12/62

Tenders
From new	2811
8/6/42	2828
7/5/43	2419
1/3/45	2637
4/1/49	2432
13/8/49	2792
7/10/52	2584
23/10/53	2622
10/11/54	2572
26/5/56	2865
28/6/56	2439
15/5/57	2703
14/10/58	2808
6/2/61	2659

Mileage 835,560

Withdrawn 25/4/63 Cut up 13/7/63

5995 WICK HALL at Shrewsbury on 13 May 1950; tender bare, as were many in this period. transporttreasury

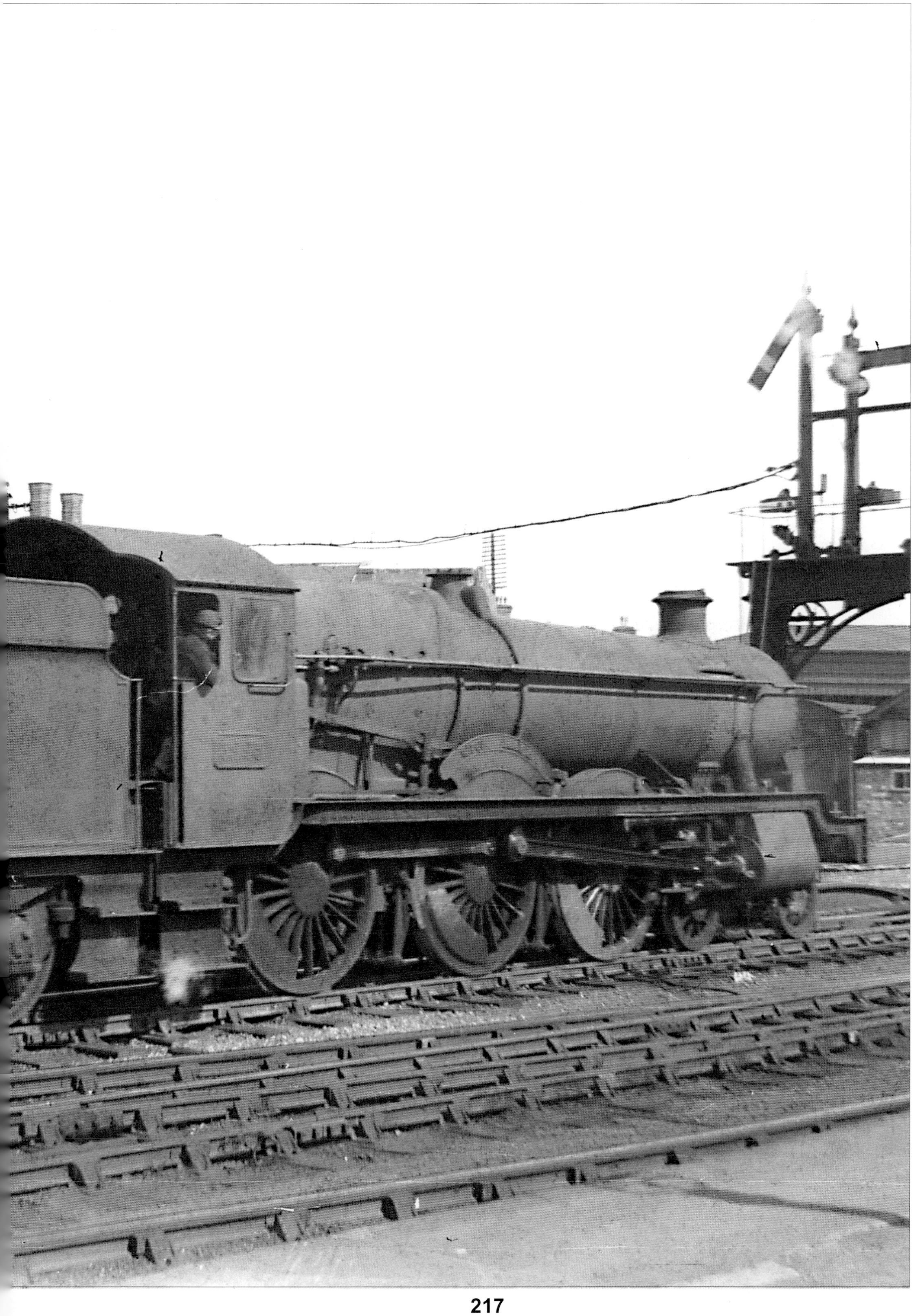

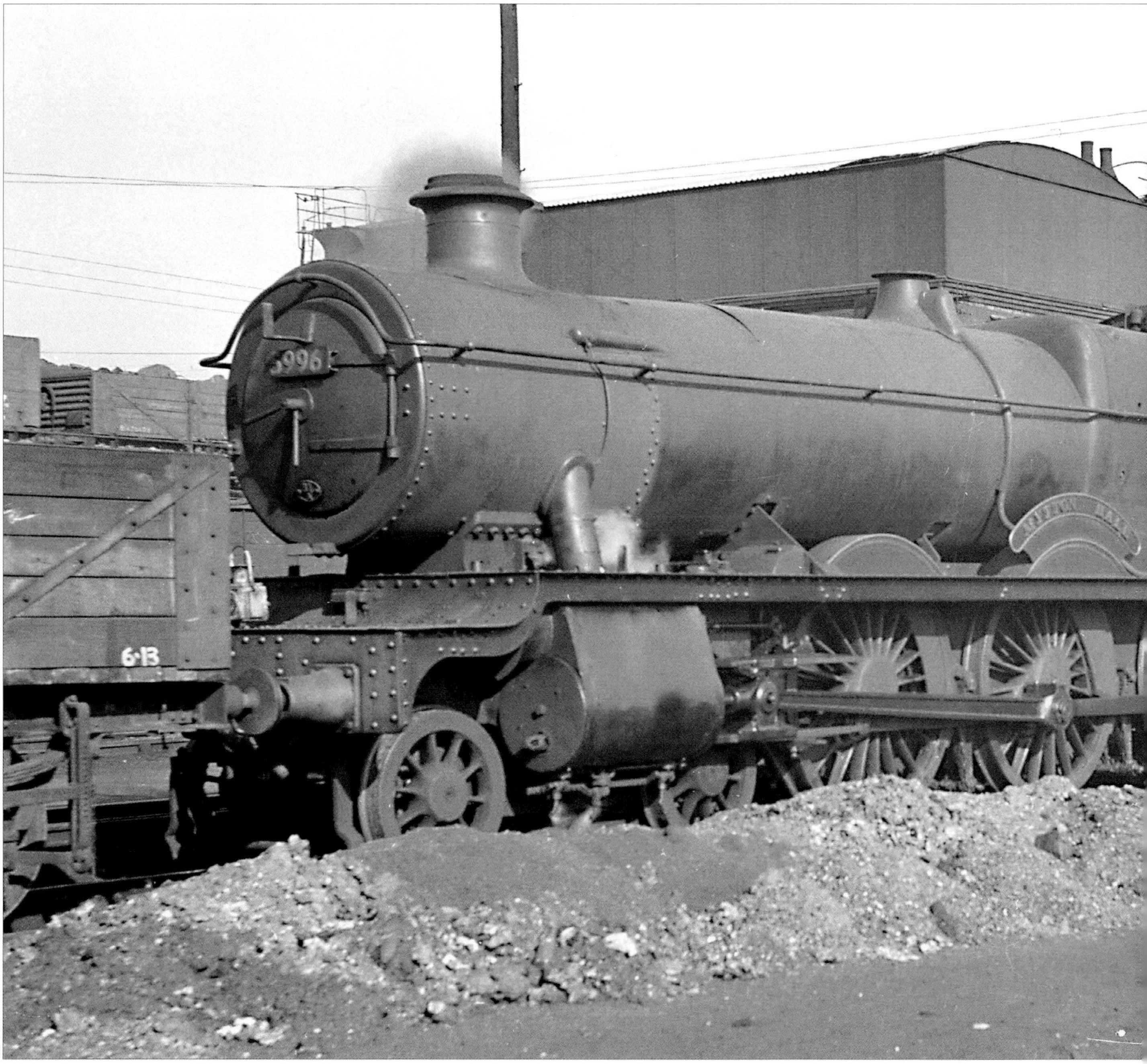
5996
6-13

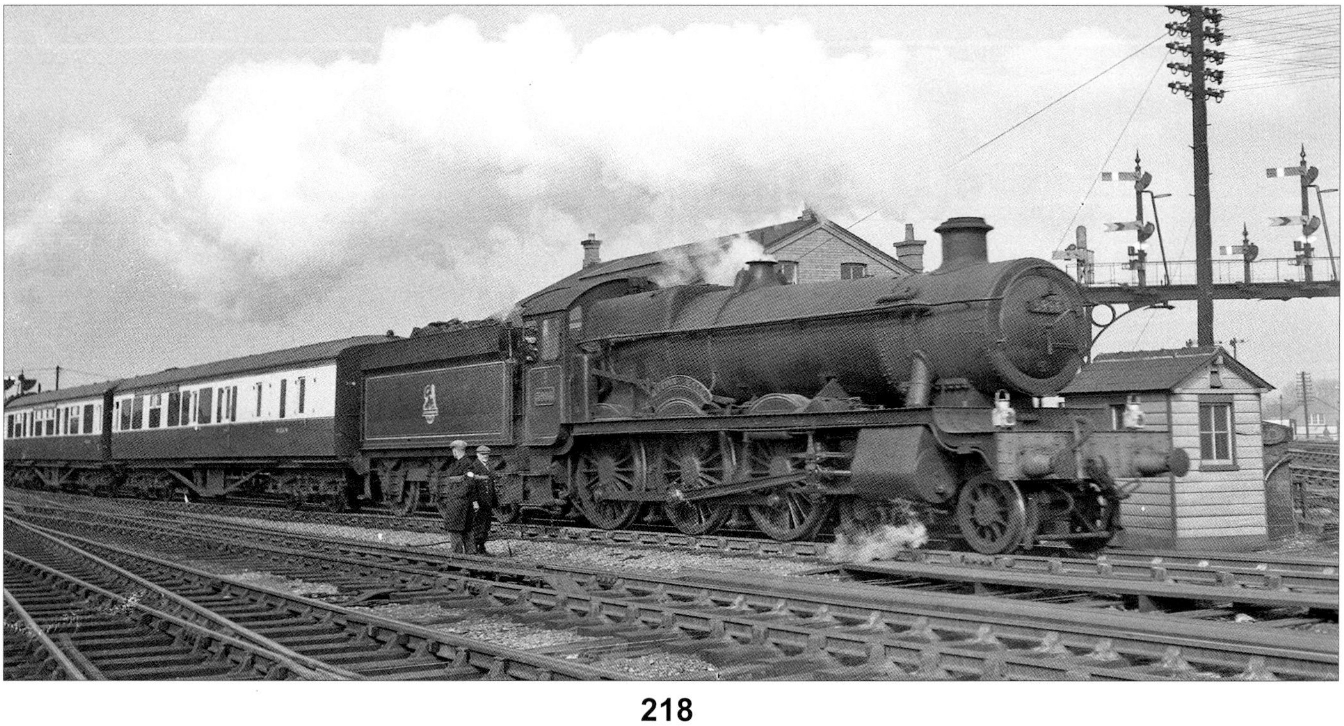

Above. 5996 MYTTON HALL at what looks like Old Oak Common; GW and the badge still on tender (unlined, in another mixed pairing) while lining on loco is post-February 1952. transporttreasury

Left. Now with matching lined tender; location unknown. ColourRail

5996 MYTTON HALL

Built in 1940 to Lot no.333 at Swindon Works
To traffic 6/1940

Mileages and Boilers
From new	4071
24/10/42	92,863 C4071
21/12/44	173,279 C4071
15/2/47	251,135 C4417
21/2/52	448,088 C2984
17/9/54	557,540 C2984
4/9/56	647,031 C8213
7/8/58	723,636 C8213
18/1/61	806,721 C9220

Sheds and Works history
9/1940	Old Oak
26/9/40	Didcot shops **R**
24/10/42	Swindon Works **I**
6/3/43	Old Oak shops **L**
24/4/44	Old Oak shed **R**
21/12/44	Swindon Works **I**
8/9/45	Southall
15/6/46	Old Oak
15/2/47	Swindon Works **G**
9/12/47	Old Oak shed **R**
27/10/48	Old Oak shops **R**
27/5/49	Taunton shops **U**
21/2/52	Swindon Works **HG**
14/9/53	Old Oak shops **U**
11/2/54	Old Oak shops **U**
17/9/54	Swindon Works **HI**
4/9/56	Swindon Works **HG**
23/3/57	Southall
4/6/58	Southall shops **U**
7/8/58	Swindon Works **HI**
19/9/58	Old Oak shops **U**
28/11/59	Worcester
18/1/61	Swindon Works **HI**
15/7/61	Oxley
4/11/61	Worcester
2/12/61	Oxley
1/2/62	Swindon Works **HC**

Tenders
From new	2873
24/10/42	2445
21/12/44	2886
15/2/47	2925
24/6/49	2739
17/1/52	2711
11/8/54	2401
23/4/55	2391
21/5/55	2573
8/10/55	2405
4/9/56	2796
8/11/60	2702
18/1/61	2616

Mileage 865,093

Withdrawn 27/8/62 Cut up 3/11/62

5997 SPARKFORD HALL

Built in 1940 to Lot no.333 at Swindon Works
To traffic 7/6/40

Mileages and Boilers
From new	4072
10/5/43	107,187 C4072
17/12/46	210,753 C4489
24/1/49	288,131 C4977
9/3/51	383,860 C2921
22/4/53	476,743 R6213
4/5/55	566,755 R6213
30/5/57	656,412 C2847
27/10/59	758,221 C2842

Sheds and Works history
8/1940	Tyseley
15/11/40	Tyseley shops **R**
29/1/42	Tyseley shops **R**
4/7/42	Tyseley shops **L**
10/5/43	Swindon Works **I**
7/10/43	Tyseley shops **R**
21/7/44	Tyseley shed **R**
6/12/44	Wolverhampton Works **L**
30/12/44	Tyseley shops **R**
17/1/45	Tyseley shops **R**
2/8/45	Gloucester shops **R**
19/1/46	Old Oak shops **R**
30/3/46	Tyseley shops **R**
17/12/46	Swindon Works **I**
7/5/48	Old Oak shops **L**
	Tender work only
24/1/49	Swindon Works **HG**
5/8/49	Newport Ebbw Jct shops **U**
8/3/50	Gloucester shops **U**
9/3/51	Swindon Works **HG**
12/1/52	Exeter shops **U**
19/4/52	Oxley
14/6/52	Laira
17/12/52	Laira shops **U**
28/12/52	Exeter shops **U**
22/4/53	Swindon Works **HG**
3/10/53	Swindon
19/6/54	Weymouth
4/5/55	Swindon Works **HI**
30/5/57	Swindon Works **HG**

Transferred to SR book stock 23/2/58
Returned to WR book stock 7/9/58

6/9/58	Swindon
27/10/59	Swindon Works **HI**
16/7/60	Bristol Bath Road
8/10/60	Swindon
9/5/61	Swindon shed **U**

Tenders
From new	2824
5/4/43	2782
14/12/46	2836
30/12/48	4070
25/3/50	2721
1/2/51	2426
20/3/53	2606
23/3/55	2560
6/10/55	2653
30/5/57	2905
27/10/59	2720

Mileage 842,719

Withdrawn 24/7/62 Sold to John Cashmore Ltd Newport 18/9/62

Right. 5997 SPARKFORD HALL early in BR ownership with serif lettered tender, at Shrewsbury shed about 1950. This is GWR hybridisation if ever there was; a loco in BR lined black and a tender in lined GW dark green lettered BRITISH RAILWAYS! Keith Jones Collection.

Below. 5997 SPARKFORD HALL in lined black, at Oxford. M. Robertson, transporttreasury

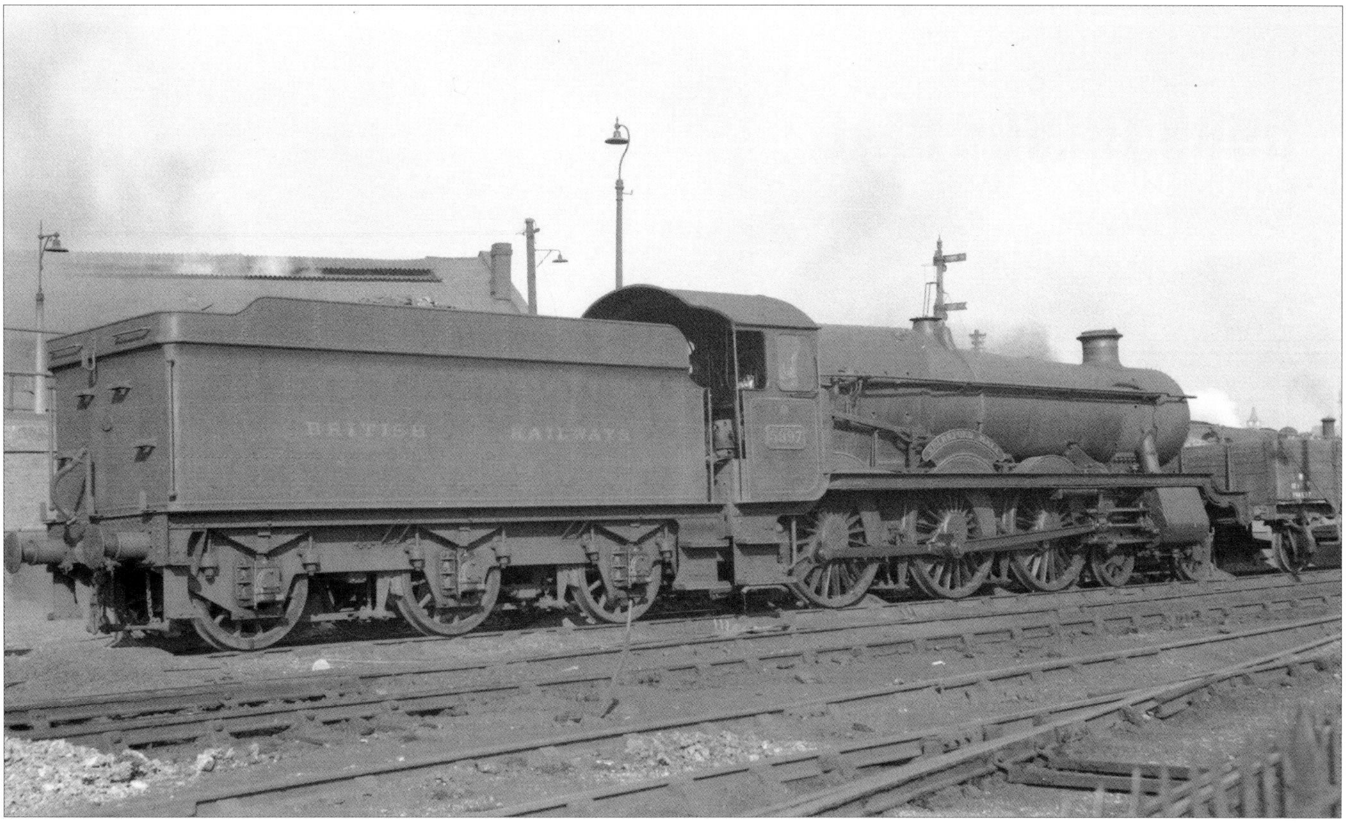
BRITISH RAILWAYS

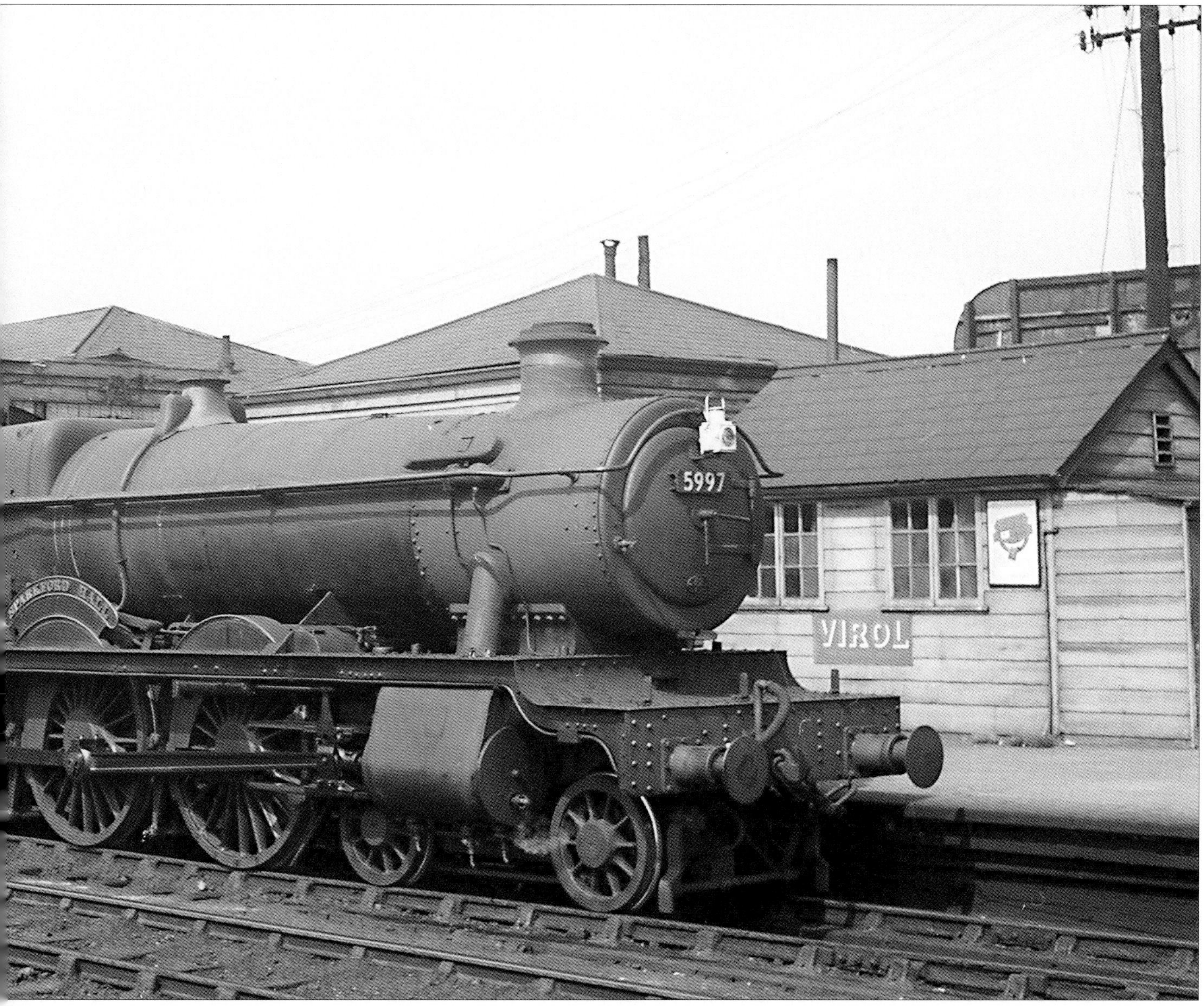
5997
SPARKFORD HALL
VIROL

5998 TREVOR HALL

Built in 1940 to Lot no.333 at Swindon Works
To traffic 6/1940

Mileages and Boilers
From new	4073
26/6/42	85,250 C4073
19/12/44	187,134 C2846
20/10/47	308,094 C4024
17/3/50	393,891 C8201
15/2/52	485,449 C8244
12/3/54	584,458 C8244
8/3/56	679,438 C2803
7/3/58	765,760 C4455
20/4/61	861,727 C4058

Sheds and Works history
8/1940	Laira
2/1941	Oxford
3/1941	Laira
2/5/42	Penzance shops **R**
26/6/42	Swindon Works **I**
6/8/43	Laira shops **R**
25/2/44	Newton Abbot shed **L**
19/12/44	Swindon Works **G**
6/3/46	Laira shops **R**
27/4/46	Newton Abbot Works **L**
21/1/47	Laira shops **R**
20/10/47	Swindon Works **I**
29/7/49	Laira shops **U**
15/12/49	Laira shops **U**
17/3/50	Swindon Works **HG**
3/7/51	Laira shops **U**
15/2/52	Swindon Works **HG**
23/12/52	Laira shops **U**
26/3/53	Laira shops **U**
16/5/53	Penzance
31/10/53	Laira
12/3/54	Swindon Works **HI**
8/10/55	Hereford
8/3/56	Swindon Works **HG**
7/3/58	Swindon Works **HI**
29/4/58	Hereford shops **U**
14/6/58	Shrewsbury
12/7/58	Hereford
24/9/58	Caerphilly Works **LC**
26/4/60	Newton Abbot Works **LC**
26/5/60	Taunton shops **U**
20/4/61	Swindon Works **HG**
30/11/63	Pontypool Road

Tenders
From new	2825
26/6/42	2745
30/6/42	2605
19/12/44	2722
20/10/47	2904
16/2/50	2820
17/1/52	2709
27/1/54	4077
8/3/56	2899
7/3/58	2896
20/4/61	2809
6/2/62	4058

Mileage 927,489 as at 28/12/63

Withdrawn 17/3/64 Sold to J Cashmore Great Bridge 30/4/64

Right. 5998 TREVOR HALL with Hawksworth tender at Hereford on the 9.40am to Shrewsbury, 17 March 1963. H.C. Casserley, courtesy R.M. Casserley.

Below. 5998 TREVOR HALL at Winson Green, Birmingham in March 1956; repainted that month, it is in lined black with first emblem. D. Preston, ColourRail.

223

5999 WOLLATON HALL

Built in 1940 to Lot no.333 at Swindon Works
To traffic 6/1940

Mileages and Boilers

From new	4074
28/3/43	102,900 C4074
9/1/45	162,474 C7255
6/4/46	203,924 C8273
28/7/48	281,342 C7272
18/10/50	370,190 C7240
11/6/53	477,475 C4019
9/8/55	569,350 C4474
5/11/57	658,873 C7270
23/9/60	776,146 C9210

Sheds and Works history

8/1940	Newton Abbot
12/1940	Oxford
3/1941	Penzance
9/8/41	Penzance shops **R**
3/1942	Taunton
11/6/42	Newton Abbot Works **L**
28/3/43	Swindon Works **I**
10/10/43	Taunton shops **R**
30/1/44	Taunton shops **R**
21/7/44	Taunton shops **R**
9/1/45	Swindon Works **L**
4/10/45	Taunton shops **R**
8/12/45	Taunton shops **R**
6/4/46	Swindon Works **I**
26/2/47	Taunton shops **R**
8/11/47	Taunton shops **R**
12/1/48	Taunton shops **R**
28/7/48	Swindon Works **G**
30/1/49	Taunton shops **U**
3/6/50	Taunton shops **U**
18/10/50	Swindon Works **HG**
20/6/51	Taunton shops **U**
31/10/52	Taunton shops **U**
11/6/53	Swindon Works **HG**
21/6/54	Taunton shops **U**
2/1/55	Taunton shops **U**
9/8/55	Swindon Works **HI**
29/3/56	Newton Abbot Works **LC**
24/5/56	Taunton shops **U**
5/11/57	Swindon Works **HG**
4/5/60	Taunton shops **U**
23/9/60	Swindon Works **HI**
2/6/61	Taunton shops **U**
7/10/61	Westbury
27/6/62	Caerphilly Works **U**

Tenders

From new	2826
16/2/43	2403
26/1/44	2886
10/11/44	2804
5/2/46	2594
12/6/46	2423
25/3/48	2849
25/9/50	2893
6/5/53	2694
5/9/53	2542
22/5/54	2795
2/1/55	2881
9/8/55	2391
5/11/57	2416
23/9/60	2397
30/12/61	2387

Mileage 838,329

Withdrawn 21/9/62 Cut up 1/12/62

5999 WOLLATON HALL is lined black at Swindon 14 June 1953. R.J. Buckley, Initial Photographics.